The Complete Travellers' France

Arthur Eperon is one of the most experienced and best-known travel writers in Europe. Since leaving the RAF in 1945 he has worked as a journalist in various capacities, often involving travel. He has concentrated on travel writing for the past twenty-five years and contributed to many publications including *The Times, Daily Telegraph, New York Times, Woman's Own, Popular Motoring* and the *TV Times*. He has also appeared on radio and television and for five years was closely involved in Thames Television's programme *Wish You Were Here*. He has been wine writer to the RAC publications and a number of magazines.

He has an intimate and extensive knowledge of France and its food and wine, as a result of innumerable visits there over the last forty years. In 1974 he won the Prix des Provinces de France, the annual French award for travel writing.

The Complete Travellers'

Arthur Eperon

FRANCE

Maps and drawings by Ken Smith

Pan Original
Pan Books London, Sydney and Auckland

Also by Arthur Eperon in Pan Books

Le Weekend
The French Selection
The British Selection
Eperon's French Wine Tour
Eperon's Guide To The Greek Islands

How to use this book

Each page is divided into three columns.

The left-hand column gives you the road numbers to follow along the route, the places you will go through and towns or villages which are worth stopping at. The distances are given in parentheses.

The middle column recommends places to eat and stay at.

The right-hand column mentions points of historic, architectural or scenic interest about the area.

First published 1988 by Pan Books Ltd,
Cavaye Place, London SW10 9PG
9 8 7 6 5 4 3 2 1

Routes 1, 2, 3, 4, 5 and 6 in this book were originally published in *Travellers' France* © Arthur Eperon 1979, 1982, 1984, 1986
Routes 7, 8, and 9 in this book were originally published in *Encore Travellers' France* © Arthur Eperon 1982

ISBN 0 330 30232 9

Phototypeset by Input Typesetting Ltd, London

Printed and bound in Great Britain by Richard Clay Ltd, Bungay, Suffolk

Acknowledgements

My sincere thanks to everybody in Britain and France who has helped me with *Travellers' France* since the first edition in 1979, especially to Tom Savage, founder-producer of the BBC's *Holiday Programme*, who saw its TV potential, Frank and Nesta Bough who road-tested a route so sympathetically for that programme, and to my wife, travel writer Barbara Eperon, who does so much driving, eating, drinking and talking for me around France but still keeps her figure. Thanks also to the ferry companies who have carried me to France.

Above all, thanks to readers for their comments on hotels and restaurants. They may contradict each other sometimes but every comment, opinion and recommendation is extremely useful. I am truly sorry that travel prevents me from answering most of these hundreds of letters each year.

Arthur Eperon

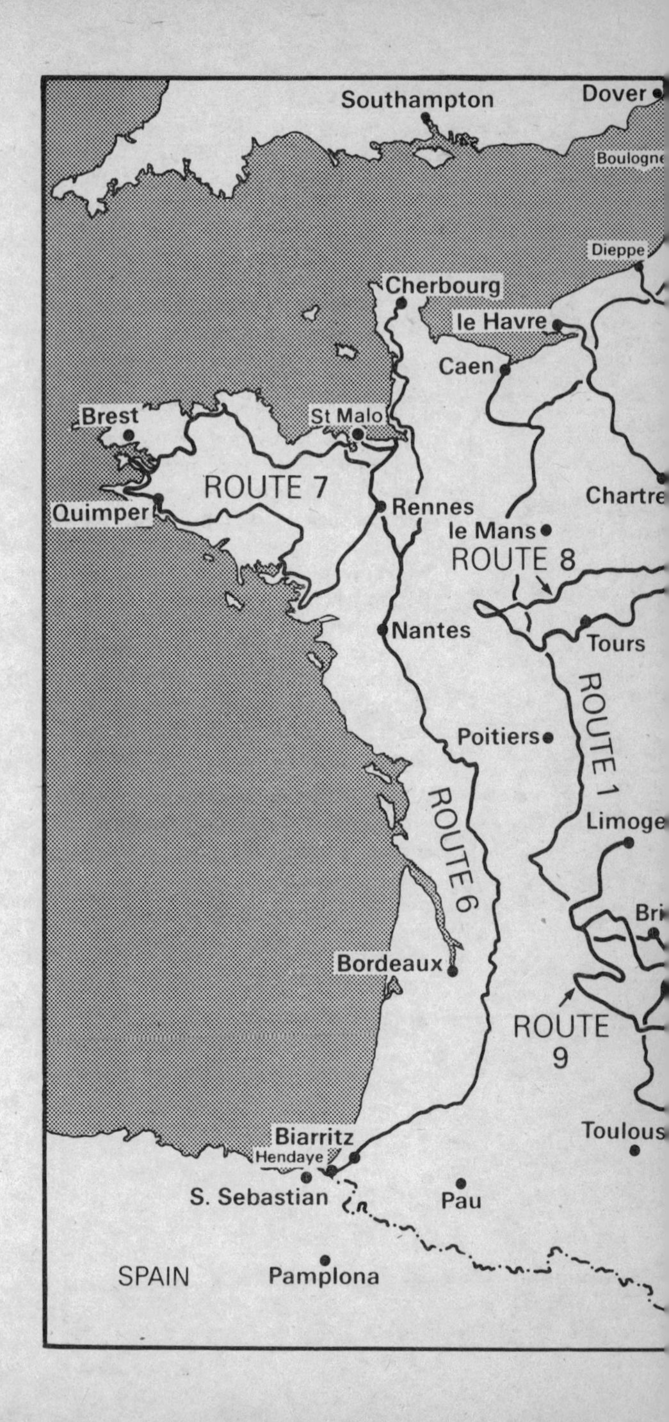

Southampton
Dover
Boulogne
Dieppe
Cherbourg
le Havre
Caen
Brest
St Malo
ROUTE 7
Quimper
Rennes
Chartre
le Mans
ROUTE 8
Nantes
Tours
ROUTE 1
Poitiers
ROUTE 6
Limoge
Bri
Bordeaux
ROUTE 9
Biarritz
Hendaye
Toulous
S. Sebastian
Pau
SPAIN
Pamplona

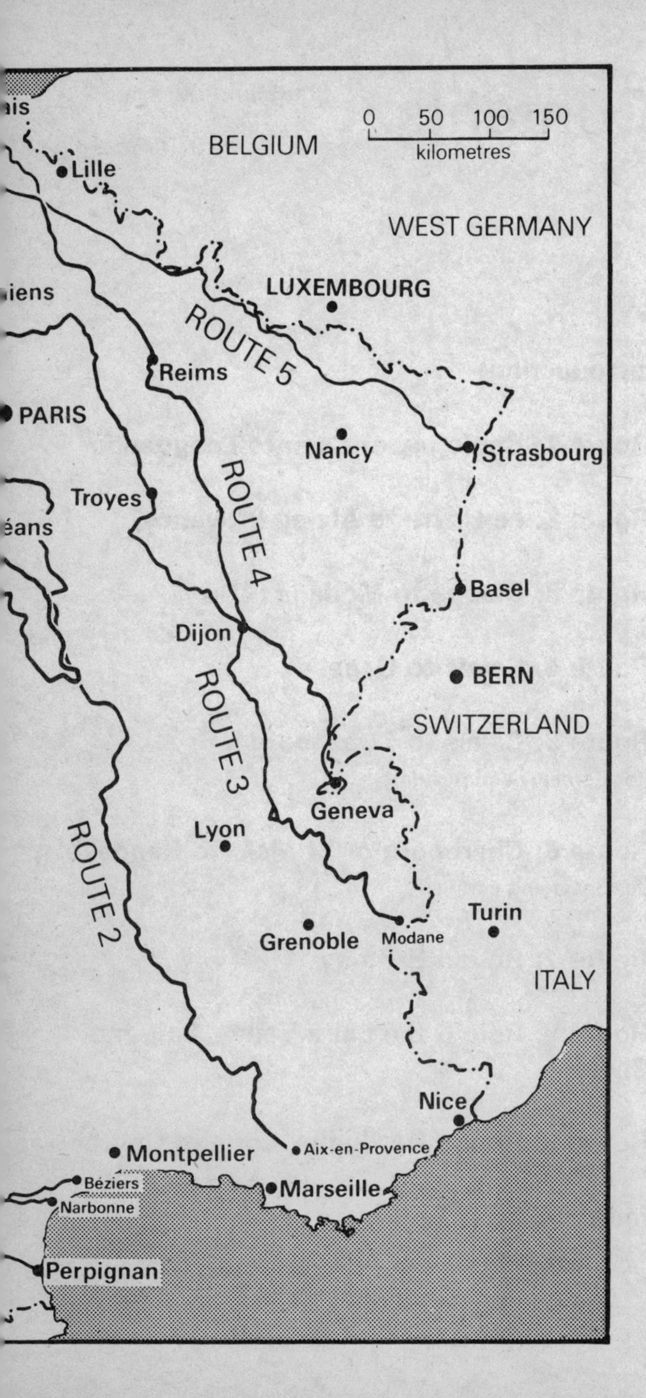

0 50 100 150
kilometres
BELGIUM
Lille
WEST GERMANY
LUXEMBOURG
ROUTE 5
Reims
PARIS
Nancy
Strasbourg
Troyes
ROUTE 4
Basel
Dijon
BERN
ROUTE 3
SWITZERLAND
Geneva
Lyon
ROUTE 2
Turin
Grenoble
Modane
ITALY
Nice
Montpellier
Aix-en-Provence
Béziers
Marseille
Narbonne
Perpignan

Contents

Introduction

To walk the ramparts of old Montreuil as French knights did before the Battle of Crécy, looking across lush lands towards the Channel coast; to compare the deep-toned mediaeval windows in Beauvais cathedral with the new bright windows by Braque; to spend a morning strolling round the loveliest house in the world, Chenonceau, and its superb gardens; to take in the higgledy-piggledy sights and super smells of the country market at St Céré, then cross the stream to the bar where in cool comfort, with a glass of cold wine, you can admire the richly-coloured tapestries of Jean Lurçat, the genius who revived a near-dead art; to watch colts gambolling around mares at Le Pin au Haras, the beautiful stud; to drink the deep red wine beside the hilltop church at Gigondas while grapes grow heavy for the vintage in the vineyards below; to watch mussels and lobsters landed on Carteret quayside, then eat them for dinner; to taste coq au vin in Burgundy, sole Dieppoise in Normandy, fresh-landed sea-bass on the quayside at St Jean de Luz, trout in the Savoie and true pipérade in the Pyrénées; to see the evocative originals of Toulouse-Lautrec's Moulin Rouge posters in the Bishop's Palace at Albi and to watch a patient fisherman beside the rivers of Charente.

That is my way of travelling through France – not dicing with impatient BMWs and evading monster lorries on the accident-prone motorways. I like to see and enjoy France, not belt south to the sun living on a baguette, pâté and my nerves, to collapse exhausted on a beach beside a septic sea. That is why I planned *Travellers' France* in 1977 – to persuade people to meander through France, as I had done for thirty years.

And that is why, in this bigger version of the book, I have included leisurely tours of the Loire, Brittany and the gorgeous hills, woods and valleys of the Dordogne and Quercy. On these I have chosen the lesser-known ways of reaching the well-known sites, such as the great Loire and Dordogne châteaux, as well as leading you to lesser-known treasures.

The enormously increased web of motorways in France has cleared many lesser roads of monster lorries and, with tremendous improvement in lesser roads, travelling off the motorways in France has become an even greater pleasure. Even those tyre-tearing edges to small roads have been smoothed over. And instead of diesel fumes you can once again enjoy the aromas of France which are part of its unique atmosphere.

Not just the obvious smells of fresh-baked bread with farm-fresh butter and local cheese, of coffee and croissants, wine and pastis, and the rich smells of cakes and charcuterie, fresh-baked, in shop windows, but local smells – fresh-landed fish, tangy Atlantic seas, fruits de mer and tempting crêpes in Brittany; cream and butter sauces, trout grilling, and heady Calvados in Normandy; the warm fresh smell of Dordogne hillsides and rivers, the smell of grilled langoustines, pines in the hot sun and herbs of Provence, of lavender covering the hills of Drôme and of herby stockpots from Auvergne kitchens; the intoxicating pure Alpine air around Chamonix and the equally intoxicating perfume as lovely women pass you on La Croissette at Cannes. The smell of beer and spicy sausages from city or mountain bars of Alsace. The smell of fermenting grapes almost anywhere from Champagne to the Rhône and Languedoc, Bordeaux to the Loire and

Burgundy; and everywhere, the magnetic smell of sauces being prepared in the kitchens of small restaurants.

Variety is the essence of France. Scenery varies remarkably from sharp peaks of the Alps to vast forests of Les Landes, lush meadows and fishing streams of Normandy to rugged hills and green valleys of Auvergne, Atlantic rollers breaking on jagged rocks of West Brittany and long sand beaches of the South-West, the Mediterranean lapping more genteelly the organized, fashionable beaches of the Côte d'Azur.

Buildings, too, vary with the scenery – lavish cathedrals and simple village churches; châteaux for gracious living; castles in Dordogne and Gascony built for war, on the Loire for loving, farms for hard working; summer villas, flower-clad for playing.

When the first *Travellers' France* came out in 1979, I was amazed how few holiday-makers had wandered round France to discover these treasures. They went through as fast as possible, as if wary of a trap. Then the book became a best-seller. I had found a gap in the travel market which the trade had inexplicably missed. Only a very few small companies, such as the excellent Vacances Franco-Britanniques, had not missed it.

Since, ferry operators have sought to plug the gap with packaged motoring tours to prebooked hotels. But mostly it is independent travellers who have flooded into France with their cars in one of the biggest travel shake-ups since the big switch to self-catering two decades ago.

These travellers are seeking freedom. They have tired of being 'processed' at airports. They like to discover places of beauty and of historic or artistic interest, even if only as an added bonus to a sea, sand and sun holiday. And they have literally *saved* many little French country hotels. Many owners have told me so. In autumn 1985, a man whose little hotel has been in his family since the 1930s told me: 'We have had very few French bookings. The French are too poor to use hotels and restaurants – or think that they are. But for the British and Belgians, we should have closed'.

That is sad. But at least the hotels are saved for better days. The French have taken to self-catering gîtes and do actually cater for themselves instead of eating out. Incidentally, a lot of French cars outside a restaurant doesn't mean that it is good. The owners may be tourists from Paris who know no more than you do.

Motorways allow the French to drive long distances for a day out, returning home in the evening. So they have fewer weekends in hotels. Parisians drive to the Loire and back for a day out.

The extra tourists travelling in France do mean, of course, that there are often several foreign cars outside hotels or restaurants. This has been grossly exaggerated by some holiday writers who seem often to be trying to discourage as many people as possible from travelling. The problem (if it *is* a problem) is confined mostly to a few hotels in high summer or popular weekends, and mostly within a half-day's drive of ferry ports. You cannot hide a good little hotel away from travellers. We tried it twice. Both were discovered, first by motoring package tour operators, then by another travel writer. The answer is for other little hotels to improve, which is happening, and for new ones to open. Hotel bedrooms have been slowly but definitely improved. Many more have private bathrooms. Though dearer because of inflation, they are still very good value. But *do* look at your room before accepting it. This is normal in France and rooms can vary much in the same hotel.

Meals, too, remain the best value in Europe. Some of us used to pre-inflation prices may think they have become 'expensive' – until we compare them with meal prices in Britain, Belgium or Germany. Some posher restaurants in France *are* charging too much for ordinary wines. Three hundred per cent of the local supermarket price is nonsense.

Thank you very much for your letters, including the very small minority complaining about the hotels and restaurants. It is impossible to answer more than a fraction, but they are truly helpful.

I still get a few letters complaining of a restaurant's cooking in the same week as ten others praising it. It could be a matter of taste – of whether you like classical, regional, 'modern', nouvelle or just old-style French family cooking. But you could have had a bad meal. A wise old French chef said to me recently: 'We chefs must pass a new examination every day.' So true! They have their off-days – even off-weeks. I wish that they didn't. I often get the blame.

I have never claimed to be a true gourmet or Master of Wine. For that you need money or a newspaper expense account. I am just one of the world's most experienced consumers. Too many people nowadays seem to be so busy analysing a meal that they cannot really enjoy it.

French food fashions have made it more difficult to pick a restaurant which suits you. Nouvelle cuisine, with its lightness and pretty patterns, became popular when the French became obsessed with losing weight, even when they did not need to. Offered by a great chef, it can be delicious – as a change. Offered by ordinary chefs, it is unsatisfying, boring and bad value for money.

'Modern' cooking is light, 'inventive', which can mean anything from replacing orange sauce by grapefruit sauce to serve with duck, to genuinely new dishes; but, alas, it still leaves no room for generous helpings of gorgeous lightly cooked vegetables, such as French beans.

'Dégustation' meals of about seven small courses are interesting, sometimes delightful, inevitably expensive, and fine for a night out but *not* very often. It is rather like living on 'starters' (nice for a light lunch). Some portions are minuscule.

Thank goodness many older chefs still offer classical cooking, with tasty rich sauces, and that regional cooking is alive and well all over France. Otherwise fashions could have become the curse of French cooking. Seasons are more important. French cooking made its deserved reputation on seasonal, regional dishes, most carefully cooked, as much as on a few inventions of famous chefs. So long live coq au Chambertin, chicken vallée d'Auge with Calvados and cream, real boeuf Bourguignon, goose cassoulet, and sole à la Dieppoise!

But what do the French think of *us?* Take a bow, gentle and sympathetic readers – according to French hotelkeepers you are nearly all *très gentils, très sympathiques* and even *très corrects*, which is almost as big an accolade as being *très sérieux*.

Not *quite* all of you. Some 'seem not to be happy until they have made a complaint'. They must be readers of those magazines constantly urging travellers to 'complain more', as if the enjoyment of a holiday depends on how quickly the waiter brings the menu or the choice of cheeses.

If some travellers have felt ignored in French hotels and restaurants, maybe they do not know the local rules. I actually saw a man with a large moustache and blazer with regimental badge snap his fingers at a French waiter and shout 'Garçon!' recently. The 'Garçon' became a 'Monsieur' forty years ago and finger-snapping in France ceased with the Revolution.

In France, you still shake hands with everybody. It is polite to wait until you are shown to a table and not just to walk in and sit down. If the patron gives a bigger welcome to regular customers than to you, it is not race-prejudice. The French love to see their friends. Use the same restaurant three times in succession, shake hands, and you will get the same treatment.

If the waiter leaves a menu and does not come back for ten minutes, it is almost a compliment. He assumes that you are taking the menu seriously, as the French do. One French chef complained to me that it took him twelve hours to prepare and cook a four-course meal and that tourists expected to eat it and be out of the restaurant in forty-five minutes, 'almost as if they have to catch the last train'. Waiting between courses is inevitable if dishes are to be freshly cooked.

Please don't expect the same slickness of service from a small family-run auberge as from a heavily staffed, expensive group hotel. But you *will* be treated as a guest – a human being, rather than a room number.

Four hundred kilometres (*not* miles!) is still plenty for a day's run and 250–300km if you want to stop and see things. After all, you are on holiday, not rallying. Most summer accidents in France are on motorways. Most accidents to Britons in France are within 150km of the Channel ports, caused by hurrying to the sun or hurrying to catch a ferry to go home. So, *please* – leave time, wander, *enjoy* France. Be a traveller, not a tourist.

Information

You can follow the routes on Red Michelin France no. 989. But some local diversions are not on these maps and the new Michelin 1:200000 atlas is invaluable (a compendium of 'yellow' Michelin maps from booksellers £7.95).

Many restaurants have a special Sunday lunch with different prices from weekdays, although the ceremonial family Sunday lunch has become rarer.

Check the menu card outside restaurants to see if prices are 'Service, Taxe Compris' (STC) – service and VAT included. These days nearly all *are* STC.

The French eat between 12 noon and 2 p.m. in the week, and in some restaurants lunch orders stop at 1.45 p.m.

French police now apply road laws strictly, and are very tough about speeding. Speed traps abound, fines are enormous for any breach of the law and are collected on the spot. So French drivers are more careful than they were and resent foreigners who are not (especially Belgians!). But they do not always keep to the 130kph (81mph) limit on the toll motorways unless they suspect that the police are about. Speed limits are 60kph (38mph) in town, 90kph (56mph) outside town, 130kph (81mph) on dual carriageways.

Parking laws are rigorously applied. The parking 'clock' system operates in most towns, so get yourself a 'clock' from a tobacconist and always prop it inside your windscreen with the time when you parked indicated. You may not park in front of post offices, police stations or hospitals. You must not cross an unbroken line, single or double, and you will be fined heavily if caught. Seatbelts are compulsory outside towns and children under ten may not travel in front seats.

You must have headlamps altered to dip right. French motorists also object if your beams are not yellow. Do both jobs by using yellow plastic lens converters or plastic stick-on strips with yellow paint provided.

Every year many travellers get into trouble abroad and lose a lot of money by not checking their insurance sufficiently. Legally you no longer need 'green card' insurance to drive in Common Market countries, nor in a host of others. But your own insurance policy will almost certainly give only third-party cover abroad and you may not be covered, for instance, against theft, damage or injury to passengers.

There are still such problems as getting help if the car breaks down or if a member of the party gets ill or is injured and such items as freighting spares from Britain (continental garages do not usually carry spares for right-hand-drive cars, even their own makes), hire car to continue a journey, hotel costs while awaiting repairs.

The nearest thing to comprehensive insurance is offered by the AA, Europe Assistance and American Express Centurion.

In EEC countries such as France Britons are entitled to the same medical treatment as insured nationals of the country. But do get form E111 before you go (you need booklet SA30 from your local social security office to tell you how to apply). I broke four bones in my back in France and ended up in Fréjus hospital. Hospital fees were £70 a day, plus consultant and X-ray charges. I had to pay a fifth of the hospital fees before I left. If I had not had the form, I should have had to pay the whole bill and waited to get the money back when I returned to Britain, after several weeks.

This also shows that it is worth taking out a personal medical insurance. A fifth of £100 a day (average rate), plus the other fees, is a considerable sum of money.

Ferries

Dover/Folkestone–Boulogne
(1hr 40 mins – Sealink, P & O)

Dover–Calais (1hr 15 mins – 1hr 40 mins – Sealink, P & O)

Newhaven–Dieppe (4hrs – Sealink Dieppe Ferries)

Portsmouth–Le Havre (5½hrs – P & O)

Portsmouth–Cherbourg (4¾hrs – Sealink, P & O)

Weymouth–Cherbourg (4hrs – Sealink)

Ramsgate–Dunkirk (2½hrs – Sally Line)

Portsmouth–St Malo (9hrs – Brittany Ferries)

Plymouth–Roscoff (6hrs – Brittany Ferries)

Portsmouth–Caen (Ouistreham) (6hrs – Brittany Ferries)

Poole–Cherbourg (4½hrs day; 6hrs night; end May–mid-September – Brittany Ferries)

Hovercraft–Dover–Boulogne/Calais (35–40 mins – Hoverspeed)

Meal Prices 1988

A = 75 francs or under
B = 75–90f
C = 90–125f
D = 125–150f
E = 150–175f
F = 175–225f
G = over 225f

Nearly all restaurants offer à la carte meals. Most restaurants include service and taxes but a few add '+ service 10%' (up to 15%) so check.

Rooms for 2 people in double room without breakfast and always 'service et taxes compris' (service and taxes included).

A = under 100f
B = 100–150f
C = 150–200f
D = 200–250f
E = 250–350f
F = 350–450f
G = over 450f

Route 1
Boulogne or Caen to Languedoc

An explorer's route which really deserves a week spent on it. It avoids frustrations in cities and towns like Rouen, Le Mans, Tours, Poitiers, Limoges and Toulouse. You could miss out some of the more eccentric detours, but then you would miss some of the most charming places like Montreuil, Le Pin au Haras, Confolens, Brantôme, St Céré, Albi, a lot of fine scenery and good meals.

Crossing the Seine at Caudebec, and the Loire at Saumur, not only avoids much tourist and commercial traffic but takes you to countryside and sights missed by most tours. The route through the Tarn to Carcassonne may add time, but it will also add an extra dimension to your holiday. It is beautiful.

Châteaux of the Dordogne and Lot are not so pretty as in the Loire, but were built by French or English for fighting and are historically more interesting. Their settings are superb. Quercy and the Lot area are as little known or crowded as the Dordogne of twenty-five years ago. For tours of the Loire, Dordogne and Lot, see routes 8 and 9.

Even if you're making for Spain, it is worth a quick look at the Languedoc-Roussillon coast, almost literally remade with bulldozers – canals joining lagoons, marinas, big sandy beaches and new resorts such as St Cyprien, Port-Leucate, Canet-Plage specializing in water sports – but windy and coldish in winter.

A trencherman's route this, with a wide choice of restaurants to suit different tastes and wallets. A route for those who like to take their legs from under the wheel frequently and stretch them under the table.

It's a butter-and-cream route, rather than an oil one. Old-style French cuisine is alive and well in Normandy, with good seafood, including shellfish, dairy products and beef. From the Seine to the Loire and Dordogne, freshwater fish – trout, salmon, eels – take over. The goose and duck are kings from the Loire to Toulouse, with such fungi as truffles, morilles and cèpes. The Loire meat is pork. Lamb is still dear in France and you get little local lamb until the Charente around Angoulême – an area rich in dairy produce, pork, game, poultry, snails and particularly vegetables and fruit, including the Charente melon. Vegetables of the Loire are excellent, even cabbage and especially tender broad beans. Fruit is even better. The food of Périgord and the Dordogne is rich and gorgeous.

In the Languedoc they cook in pork fat, although some oil is used on the coast. The pig and the goose rule most menus, with the haricot bean and more exotic vegetables such as pimentos and aubergines.

Wines of the Loire have gained in popularity and 'lesser' wines have been greatly improved (see route 8).

Strong dark red Cahors wines, loved by the English for centuries, have become more fashionable in France. New lighter wines have been produced to accompany lighter modern dishes but the old-style wines, which should not be drunk younger than five years and are best at ten years or over, are far, far more satisfying. Try Clos de Gamot and Château du Cayrou.

Roussillon wines have been improved enormously by replanting. Languedoc produces 75 per cent of France's Vin du Pays, and Corbières also produces 75 million bottles of the higher rated VDQS wine. Minervois and Fitou (very dark, slightly tannic) have the still higher AOC rating. Lauran Cabaret is my favourite Minervois. Banyuls is sweet, heady and heavy.

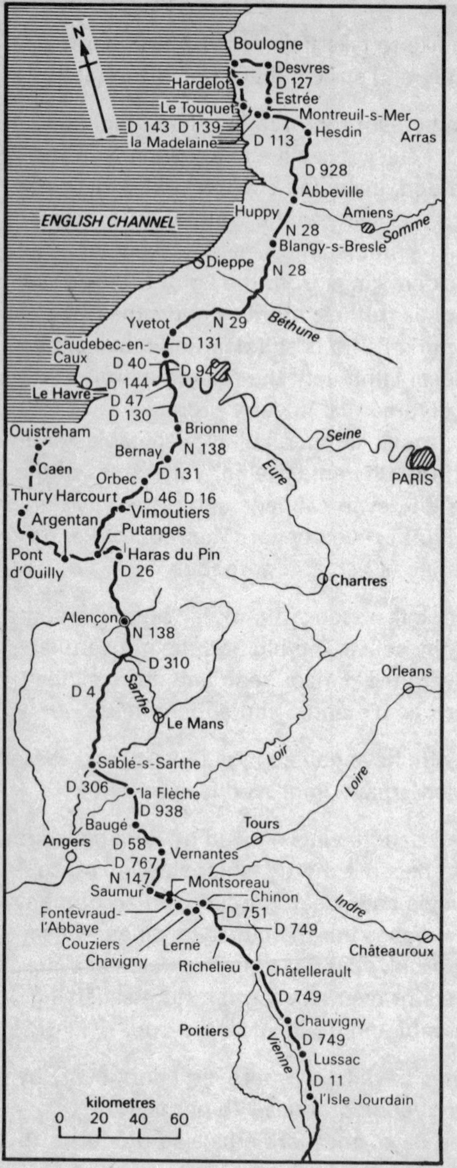
N
Boulogne
Desvres
D 127
Hardelot
Estrée
Le Touquet
Montreuil-s-Mer
D 143 D 139
la Madelaine
D 113
Hesdin
Arras
D 928
Abbeville
Huppy
Amiens
ENGLISH CHANNEL
N 28
Somme
Blangy-s-Bresle
Dieppe
N 28
Yvetot
N 29
Béthune
D 131
Caudebec-en-Caux
D 40
D 94
Le Havre
D 144
D 47
D 130
Ouistreham
Brionne
Seine
Bernay
N 138
Caen
Eure
Orbec
D 131
PARIS
Thury Harcourt
D 46 D 16
Vimoutiers
Argentan
Putanges
Pont d'Ouilly
Haras du Pin
D 26
Chartres
Alençon
N 138
D 310
Orleans
D 4
Sarthe
Le Mans
Loir
Sablé-s-Sarthe
Loire
D 306
la Flèche
D 938
Baugé
Tours
Angers
D 58
Vernantes
D 767
N 147
Montsoreau
Saumur
Chinon
Fontevraud-l'Abbaye
D 751
Indre
D 749
Couziers
Lerné
Châteauroux
Chavigny
Richelieu
Châtellerault
D 749
Chauvigny
Poitiers
D 749
Vienne
Lussac
D 11
l'Isle Jourdain
kilometres
0 20 40 60

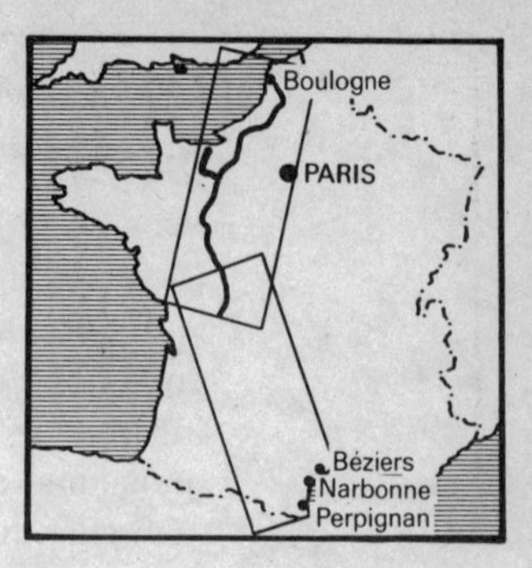
Boulogne
PARIS
Béziers
Narbonne
Perpignan

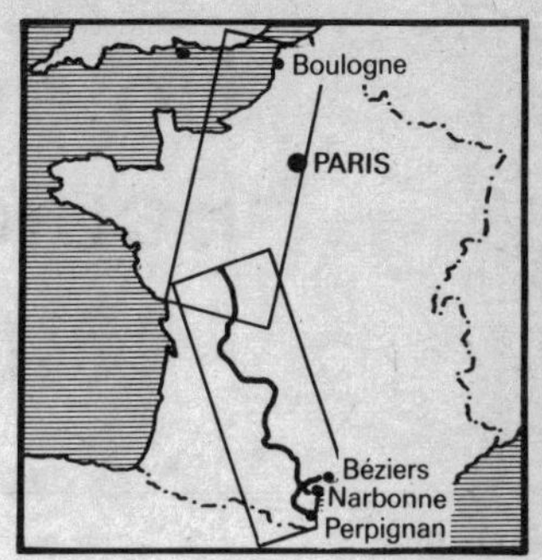
Boulogne
PARIS
Béziers
Narbonne
Perpignan

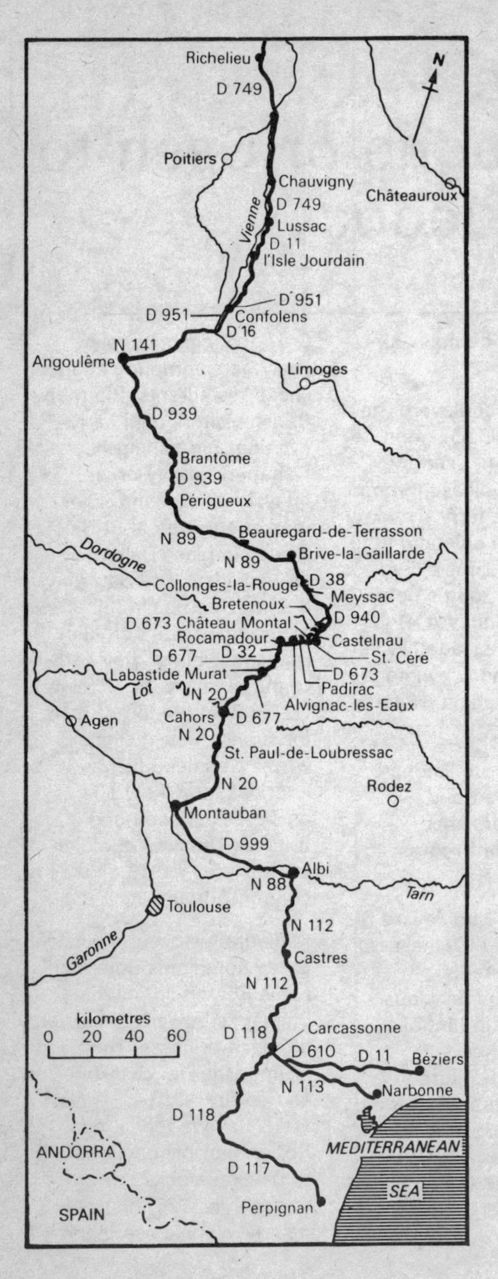
N
Richelieu
D 749
Poitiers
Chauvigny
D 749
Châteauroux
Vienne
Lussac
D 11
l'Isle Jourdain
D 951
D 951
Confolens
D 16
N 141
Angoulême
Limoges
D 939
Brantôme
D 939
Périgueux
N 89
Beauregard-de-Terrasson
Dordogne
N 89
Brive-la-Gaillarde
D 38
Collonges-la-Rouge
Meyssac
Bretenoux
D 940
D 673 Château Montal
Rocamadour
Castelnau
D 677
D 32
St. Céré
D 673
Labastide Murat
Padirac
Lot
N 20
Alvignac-les-Eaux
Agen
Cahors
D 677
N 20
St. Paul-de-Loubressac
N 20
Rodez
Montauban
D 999
Albi
N 88
Tarn
Toulouse
N 112
Garonne
Castres
N 112
kilometres
0 20 40 60
D 118
Carcassonne
D 610
D 11
Béziers
N 113
Narbonne
D 118
ANDORRA
MEDITERRANEAN
D 117
SEA
SPAIN
Perpignan

Route 1
Boulogne or Caen to Languedoc

Boulogne **(Caen route begins on page 35)**

Boulogne can be noisy at night.

La Plage, 124 boulevard Ste Beuve, 21.31.45.35: good value restaurant used by locals; simple pleasant rooms convenient for ferry. Try any fish, especially sole and lotte (monkfish) in saffron, local moules. Front rooms noisy in summer. Menus A, B, D. Rooms A–B. Restaurant shut Mondays, Sunday evenings except July–August. Hotel shut Christmas, January.

Faidherbe, 12 rue Faidherbe, 21.31.60.93: bed and breakfast; refurbished pleasantly. Front rooms noisy. Rooms B–E.

La Matelote, 80 boulevard Ste Beuve, 21.30.17.97: best fish restaurant in area; Tony Lestienne offers delicious light dishes with hint of nouvelle. Try hot langoustine pâté, turbot stuffed with crab, outstanding pastries and desserts. Fine choice of wines. Meals D–G (carte). Shut 23 December–15 January; 15–30 June.

Crowded, chaotic, noisy, lively bars, tempting shops, cheap restaurants, too many British visitors until early evening. Big fishing fleet. Fish market daily on quayside. Food and flower market outside old St Nicolas church in place Dalton (Wednesdays and Saturdays 6 a.m.–1 p.m.). On hill at end of Grande rue is old Ville Haute, surrounded by 13th-century walls with 17 towers. Walk round the top of them for superb views; castle where Napoleon III was imprisoned in 1840 after unsuccessful coup and Britain's Unknown Soldier lay in state in 1919 on way to London burial.

Cathedral whose magnificent dome dominates Boulogne has a Roman crypt where England's Edward II married a French princess. Their son claimed the French throne and started the 100 Years' War. From Gayette tower, de Rozier, first balloonist, tried to balloon across the Channel in 1785; he lies in nearby Wimille cemetery.

La Liégeoise, 10 rue A. Monsigny, 21.31.61.15: famous old restaurant revived by Alain Delpierre's light-modern cooking (not nouvelle); brighter décor, atmosphere; more elegant. Excellent fish, cheeses from great Olivier. Menu D; carte F. Shut Sunday evening; part January.

Brasserie Alfred, 24 place Dalton, 21.31.53.16: 'Old Paris'-style bistro – crowded, noisy, fun. Not for snobs or tête-à-tête meals. Excellent shellfish; very quaffable red house wine and Muscadet. Menus B, C, D, F. Shut Tuesday; 22 December–5 January.

Le Doyen (formerly La Charlotte), 11 rue Doyen, 21.30.13.08: round the corner from Alfred and totally different. Change of name (and sex). Crowded (mostly Britons), booking essential. Good cooking; inventiveness sometimes overdone. Menus B, E, F. Shut Sundays.

Chez Jules, 10 place Dalton, 21.31.54.12: oldest house in Boulogne has long been a popular bar with cosy little restaurant. While young French eat hamburgers from the grill, bargain-seekers go for fish soup, grilled fish or steak or farandol boulonnaise (mixed fish). Keeps open very late. Menus B, C, D.

Best shops in rue Faidherbe, Grande rue and roads joining them – rue Thiers, rue Victor Hugo. Olivier's famous cheese shop and Nouvelles Galeries in rue Thiers. Champion (small hypermarket) almost opposite bridge from car ferry. Auchan hypermarket – 2km on N42.

Sandy beach where bathing started in 1789 has a casino with indoor pool. On D940 (Wimereux road) is a huge cross (Calvaire) dedicated to sailors. Off N1 (Calais road) is Napoleon's premature memorial to his Grande Armée waiting here to invade England.

At nearby Château Souverain Moulin, in Wimereux valley, the chapel (open) has three tapestries by the great modern master Jean Lurçat.

Inland forest and hill roads and paths are a delight.

Boulogne continued	L'Huitrière, 11 place Lorraine, 21.31.35.27: good fish-shop off rue Faidherbe now has a few tables serving superb fresh, simple fish dishes with white wine. Very good value. Menu C and carte. Shut Sunday evening, Monday. At Pont-de-Briques (5km S by D940): Hostellerie de la Rivière, 17 rue Gare, 21.32.22.18: fashionable; Jean Martin and son from Château de Montreuil offer classic cooking with modern touches. Superb desserts. Menus good value, carte expensive. Menus D, F, G. Shut Sunday evening, Monday; all August.	
D119 Equihen Plage, Hardelot (10km)	At Chateau Hesdin–L'Abbé, 4km NE Hardelot, Clery, 21.80.64.31: converted 18th-century chateau. Menu C–E. Rooms D–F.	Hardelot plage: mostly pricey villas along superb sandy beach, dunes, pines. Golf. Riding in forest.
D119/D940 Étaples, Le Touquet (16km)	Étaples – Lion d'Argent, place de Gaulle, 21.94.60.99: simple, very old inn. 1914–18 Tommies carved initials here when convalescing in 'Eat Apples'. Bourgeois cooking, good value (fish, cream, Calvados). Menu B–D. Rooms B. Shut Monday evenings, Tuesdays. Aux Pecheurs d'Etaples, quai de la Canche, 21.94.06.90: fish-only restaurant over modern fish market on quay. Get table near window for views. Menu C plus carte.	Étaples looks across the Canche estuary to Le Touquet but they are worlds apart. The market square is chaotic fun. Fishermen sell catches in quayside market. Le Touquet is pricey, lively Easter–September, especially weekends when Parisians come to their forest villas and promenade flats. Started by the British, who held it until the jet age. Now 'Paris Plage'. Seasonal branches of Paris boutiques, shops. Lively bars, restaurants, night-life.

Le Touquet – Westminster, av Verger, 21.05.19.66: expensive, beautifully furnished 'Grand Hotel' of old Touquet now has a restaurant again. Pleasantly modernized. Menus C–F. Rooms and suites F, G. Restaurant shut Monday evening, Tuesday except July, August.

Côte d'Opale, 99 boulevard Dr J. Pouget, 21.05.08.11: on the front, flowered terrace; good traditional cooking. Priority given to diners-in. Menus D, G. Rooms C, E. Open 20 March–11 November.

Serge Pérard, 67 rue Metz, 21.05.13.33: superb fish – own fish shop. Famous fish soup. Impressionist Sunday-lunch scene of French family parties (book). Menu C, carte. Formidable shellfish platter. Serge thinks my readers 'gentils' – correct and well-mannered.

Cafe des Arts, 80 rue de Paris: fairly new restaurant with good reputation. Try bar (sea bass) braisé à l'orange. Menus C, D. Shut January.

La Chaumière, 80 rue Saint-Jean, 21.05.12.11: renovations recently; 8 studios for 4 planned. Menus A, B, D. Rooms D, E (includes breakfast).

Stella Plage (7km S) – Sables d'Or, 1184 avenue Concorde, 21.94.75.22: happy, slightly nutty hotel; simple rooms

Superb sands, dunes, horse riding, ponies for children, show jumping, tennis (including indoors with natural light), casinos. Griffmode has bargains in cheaper young women's clothes.

At Merlimont (10km): Bagatelle – famous pleasure park, zoo; great for children (open April–end September).

Stella Plage (7km from Le Touquet); dunes almost invade simple family resort. Miles of sands, closes in winter.

	(some family); super cooking, especially fish; modern dishes. Great value. Rooms B–D. Menue A–E. Open 1 May–30 September.	
D143, D139 La Madelaine, Montreuil-sur-Mer	Near St Josse (on D139) – Auberge de Moulinel, 21.94.79.03: nice village inn; charcoal grills; good fish; ficelle Picarde (pancake with creamy stuffing). Menu A–C. Shut January–February. La Madelaine – Auberge du Vieux Logis 21.06.10.92: rustic inn with home cooking: menus change daily. Cheap house wine. Menu A–C. Shut Mondays in winter. La Grenouillère 21.06.07.22: the 'Froggery' is a converted femette by the Canche which I have known for thirty years, during which it has reached the stars (1 from Michelin). Trout and crayfish fresh and succulent. Classic cooking. Fine wine list. Carte meals F–G. Shut February, Tuesday evenings, Wednesdays except high summer, 15 December–end January. Montreuil – Darnetal, place Darnetal, 21.06.04.87: Robert Bureau's warm, happy, unusually decorated little restaurant has been second home to us for 20 years. You will meet many respected citizens who appreciate classic regional meals. Try warm oysters in Champagne, duck, steak	Small winding roads, prettier than N39. Crosses streams, runs beside river Canche. Montreuil is a delight. Not 'sur mer' for centuries but its 700-year-old ramparts give superb views as you walk round their grassy paths (1 hour). In a surviving tower of its castle of stone and brick is a simple board listing local knights killed fighting Henry V at Agincourt. Castle (shut Mondays) has push-button commentaries. Cobbled streets and old squares lined with 17–18th-century houses.  St Saulve abbey and flamboyant 15th-century chapel with rich furnishings. Laurence Sterne began his 18th-century *Sentimental Journey* here at the Hôtel de

Rossini, fish from Boulogne. Six simple, old-fashioned bedrooms. Menus B, C, E. Rooms B–D. Shut Tuesday; Monday evening (except July, August); few days at end of January, June and October.

Château de Montreuil, 4 chaussée des Capucins, 21.81.53.04: Christian Germain, formerly Roux brothers' Chef de Cuisine at Waterside, Bray (3 Michelin stars), has survived a week's 'help' from me in his kitchen to become one of France's best young chefs. One Michelin star – deserves two. Pricey – worth it. Roux's 'New Classic' cooking blended with traditional regional and new ideas. Try sea bass in flaky pastry with fennel sauce; wild duck; chocolate and fruit marquise. Superb! Elegant mansion with lovely garden where his English wife, Lindsay, cossets guests. Meals G. Rooms G. Cheaper mid-week breaks. Restaurant shut Tuesday except July, August; hotel shut mid-December–end January.

Central, 7 rue Change, 21.86.16.04: simple, old-style hotel where Michelle and Monique Megret give smiling service and meals are good value. Bedrooms vary in comfort and price. Menus A, C, E. Rooms C, D, E. Shut Sunday evening, Monday; 20 December–20 January.

France (now reopened) and announced that 'They order these things better in France', (he was talking of begging, not hotels or food). Faded mural of him in courtyard. Napoleon's Marshal Ney set up HQ here for invading England. General Haig's HQ was here in 1916. Nazis used Château hotel as major anti-invasion HQ. Superb Saturday market around place de Gaulle (Haig's statue).

Lush countryside of pretty villages, meadows, trout streams.

Route	Where to stay/eat	Notes
Alternative route **Boulogne – Montreuil D341 to Desvres then D127 to Estrée, D150 to Montreuil (43km)**	Zérables (on D127) – café-restaurant Cocatrix-Gremont, 21.30.73.39: down lane by a lake; simple, superb-value home-cooked meals. Incredibly cheap. Inxent (on D127) – Auberge d'Inxent, 21.06.86.52: pretty old cottage opposite church, long loved by locals, has just changed hands. Menus B–F. Check closing times. Relais Equestre, 21.09.70.34: attractive bed and breakfast rooms attached to riding stables. Horses for hire. Rooms B, C. Shut January. Estrée – Relais de la Course, 21.06.18.04: village inn; simple bedrooms; huge open fire in dining room. Garden, river opposite. Bourgeois cooking (coq au vin; local trout; ham in Madeira). Good choice and value. Menus A, B; rooms A, B. Restaurant shut Sunday evenings.	Through Boulogne forest (walks, picnic spots) to edge of Desvres (famous for porcelain). D127 follows the attractive river Course valley past trout lakes (fishing) near nice hamlets. Estrée (Catholic) and Estrelles (then Protestant) divided by short bridge have hardly spoken since Religious Wars in 16th century. Still have separate schools, mayors, churches, cemeteries for 250 inhabitants! Charming route.
D113 alongside River Canche to Hesdin (23km)	Beaurainville, 12km E of Montreuil – Val de Canche 21.90.32.22: unimpressive-looking inn next to church; cosy inside; garden. André Decobert's meals are fine value; try his local anguilles (tiny river eels). Meals A–D. Rooms B–C. Shut Christmas; Sunday evenings; Mondays. 15–30 October, 1–15 January. Hesdin – La Chope, 48 rue d'Arras 21.86.82.73: old favourite of ours. Relais Routiers and 1-star hotel. Simple, well run, friendly.	Attractive old town at meeting of two rivers, with Renaissance church and pleasant market square. Town hall former palace of Marie of Hungary, sister of Charles V, in 16th century when this was a frontier of the old Habsburg Empire. Her ballroom is now a theatre. Creeper clad Renaissance houses and old walls, secretive cobbled passages to the river recall the TV series of Georges Simenon's detective Maigret – much of it shot here.

Superb cooking by Agnès Samper-Deman. Mostly Flemish, but something from all France. Try carbonnade flamande (beef braised in beer) or her flamiche (leek and cheese tart) Fresh local ingredients. Menu A–D. Rooms B, C. Shut 15–30 October; Christmas, New Year.

Des Flandres, 20 rue d'Arras, 21.86.80.21: modernized Logis; rooms renovated, open spit. Try Canche trout; spit-cooked meat; chicken flambé with genievres cooked in beer. Menu A, B. Rooms B–D. Shut mid-December–mid-January.

Trois Fontaines, 16 rue Abbeville Marionne, 21.86.81.65: modern comfort, lacks atmosphere; outside town, so quiet; nice garden. Menus A–E. Rooms D. Shut Christmas.

At Fillièvres, 12km SE Hesdin on D340 – Vieux Moulin, 21.47.93.42: sweet flowery village with pretty millpond in Canche valley. Watermill now village inn; simple rooms; bar used by locals; good French family cooking. Super trout and old-style dishes. Menu A–B. Rooms B. Open all year.

Lovely forest drives north. Just off D928 to north is Azincourt (Agincourt to us) where Henry V's small exhausted army, racked with sickness, defeated the French army three times its size. Marked simply but poignantly by a cross over French communal graves.

D928 for 15km, right on D938 to Crecy-en-Ponthieu (20km) Forest road D111 to Lamotte Bulleux (11 km), D32, D928 Abbeville (12km)	Crécy – Canon d'Or, 10 ave Général-Leclerc, 22.23.51.14: 16th-century beamed posting inn; bedrooms improved; log fires; very good value. Booking advised. Menus A, C, D. Rooms B, C. Le Maye, 13 rue St Riquier, 22.23.54.35: modern, comfortable. Menus A–C. Rooms B, C. Shut Mondays in winter; mid-February–mid-March.	Crécy forest and the battlefield of 1346 where 1300 French knights fell, mostly to English archers and heroic attacks by the 16-year-old Black Prince, Edward III's eldest son. Moulin Edward III, English HQ, now replaced by a flagstaff. I would not stay in Abbeville – it is too busy and I have not found anywhere satisfactory yet.
N28 Huppy, Blangy-sur-Bresle (25km) N28, then D929 (N29) to Yvetot (86km)	At Lestanville (5km after Totes on D929) take D2 left to Auzouville-en-Caux – Au Bord de la Saane, 35.83.20.12: delightful Mme Clamaron no longer runs this 300-year-old black-and-white Norman inn but Jean-Yves Duval cooks well; delicious trout pâté. Reasonable wine prices. Menus A-C. Shut Mondays.	In château at Huppy a young Colonel set up HQ in May 1940 for an heroic counter attack on the Nazis. His name? Charles de Gaulle. Road skirts beautiful Forest of Eu. Before St Saens, turn right to drive down magnificent avenue called Limousins. It is 22km long and was cut as a fire break. Yvetot – animated market town. Modern round church of St Pierre has superb huge brilliantly coloured glass windows by Max Ingrand defining the walls of the belfry. From 1392 until the Revolution, Yvetot was a tax-free, independent town – called a 'kingdom'.
D131 Caudebec-en-Caux (12km)	Normandie, quai Gilbaud, 35.96.25.11: old-style regional French meals; excellent value; good choice; good service. Menus A, B, D. rooms C. Shut February; restaurant shut Sunday evening.	Once a ferry port for crossing the Seine. Destroyed in 1944, but modern version has matured into a nice small town, with big ships passing. Graceful Brotonne bridge has eased lorry traffic.

Manoir de Retival, rue St Claire, 35.96.11.22; spiky-towered 19th-century manor overlooking Seine valley. Pleasant garden. Tastefully furnished in antiques. I wish it had a restaurant. Rooms D–F. Shut 2 November–15 March.

Marine, 35.96.20.11: a few doors from the Normandie, more formal and comfortable but dearer. Menus B–G. Rooms C–E. Restaurant shut Sunday evening.

At Villequier – Le Grand Sapin, 35.56.78.73: makes me feel old! It's so long since I first sat on the Seine-side terrace tasting 'young' Gérard Octeau's pintade smitane (guinea fowl in cream with mushrooms) or salmon escalope in pike mousse. Some recent criticism of his old-style cooking – but much more praise. Fine value. Simple but pleasant old rooms. Menus A (weekdays), B, C, D. Rooms A, B. Shut Tuesday evening, Wednesday; 15 September–15 June; 15 January–5 February.

Superb 15th-century flamboyant Gothic church built during English occupation. Great organ with 2300 pipes is world famous. St Wandrille (2km E) – named after a monastery founded in AD 649 by Count Wandrille, so physically perfect that he was called 'God's True Athlete'. At his wedding feast, he and his bride vowed to stick to pure love and parted to become monk and nun. Monks have come and gone since. Last century the English Marquis of Stacpool renovated it – as a home, then Maurice Maeterlinck (author of *Life of the Bee*) lived there. Monks returned in 1931. They moved 15th-century barn to convert into a church. You can hear the Gregorian Chant (9.25 a.m. weekdays, 10 a.m. Sundays).

Villequier (3km) riverside beauty spot where Victor Hugo's daughter was drowned.

Over Brotonne bridge (toll) then through Brotonne forest D40, D94, D144, D47, D130 to Brionne (46km)

Logis de Brionne, place St Denis, 32.44.01.73: consistently praised by readers for good cooking of fresh ingredients. Dishes follow seasons; plenty of fish. Menu C–F. Rooms A–C. Shut Sunday evenings, Monday lunch; 3 weeks in January, one week in October.

Brionne is built on isles where river Risle divides.

Bec Hellouin (monastery – 6km on N318, D39) founded 1034 when a young knight, Herluin, changed his charger for a donkey to serve God. Young William the Bastard (William the Conqueror) besieging Brionne, met an

	Bec Hellouin – Auberge de l'Abbaye, 32.44.86.02: beautiful 18th-century auberge, overlooking village green; chintzy country bedrooms; Norman dishes with cider and cream; nice apple tart. Popular with tourists, so 'prudent to book'. You could be summoned by bells at dawn (try ear-plugs). Menus C, E, F. Rooms E. Shut 10 January–28 February; Monday evening, Tuesday low season.	Italian scholar Lanfranc from the monastery, made him his adviser and later Archbishop of Canterbury and virtual ruler of England when William was warring in Normandy. Another Italian Helboin graduate, Anselm, followed him. Abbey (shut Tuesdays) was restored from 1948. Outside the gate is a car museum of cars from 1920. Château d'Harcourt (7km along D26, D137), cradle of a famous family, is a splendid feudal castle, double moated and turreted, with 17th–18th-century alterations, mediaeval and Louis XIV furnishings. Park has many rare trees, labelled.
N138 Bernay (15km)	Angleterre et Cheval Blanc, rue de Gaulle, 32.43.11.75: Logis long famous for Norman cooking of local farm produce; reports vary now from very good to indifferent. Terrace and garden for summer meals. Menus C–F. Rooms B.	Market town where rivers meet; cattle and horse sales. Town Hall was an abbey where troubadour Alexandre de Bernay invented 12-syllable Alexandrine verse. Fine collection of pottery of Nevers, Rouen and Strasbourg and old Norman furniture in abbey lodge.
D131 Orbec (17km) D46, D16 Vimoutiers (21km)	Orbec – France, 152 rue Grande, 31.32.74.02: 18th-century coaching post-house, well run by young patron-chef Georges Corbet; best bedrooms in annexe. Good local trout, beef, chicken, cheese. Menus A, B, D. rooms A, E. Shut 15 December–15 January.	Orbec – delightful old town in the pleasant wooded valley of Orbiquet. Vimoutiers – for butter and cheese; Camembert village is 5km S. Here in 19th century Marie Harel, farmer's wife, perfected a soft cheese which brought a lovely new perfume to Paris. Her statue in Vimoutiers square was presented by a US cheese company.

D26, D305
Haras du Pin
(24km)

National stud in courtyard of elegant 1716 château. Magnificent horses include 100 stallions. Its most famous horse, Furioso, came from England in 1946, died 1967, having sired many racing and show jumping champions including Olympic and World champions. His descendants still prized at sales.

Route from Caen to Haras

Ouistreham (Brittany Ferries port) D514, D515 to Caen (14km)

Ouistreham – Normandie, 71 ave Michel-Cabieu, 31.97.19.57: high-grade Logis; bedrooms much improved. Good Norman cooking. Try marmiton of oysters, duck, trout. Menu B–F. Rooms D, E. Shut Sunday evening, Monday.

Univers Hotel, Broche d'Argent Restaurant, place de Gaulle, 31.97.12.16: attractive; near ferry. Well-equipped little bedrooms (also annexe). Good shellfish – try moules normandes. Menus D–G. Rooms D, E. Shut Christmas.

At Colleville-Montgomery, 4km W on D35a – Ferme St Hubert, 3 rue Mer, 31.96.35.41: charming auberge. Middle menu exceptional value. Menus A, C, D, F, G. Shut Sunday evening, Monday (except July, August) Christmas, New Year.

Brittany Ferries' 'Portsmouth-Caen' boat in fact docks at Ouistreham in mouth of Orne river, linked to Caen by canal. Here Anglo-French Commandoes landed on D-Day 1944. Ouistreham is now a yachting centre with resort of Riva Bella alongside. Super sands, safe bathing. Landing museum (open Easter–mid-September.) Pegasus Bridge, taken by British Airborne troops the night before D-Day, is at Bénouville, down river. Caen was flattened and is totally new; excellent for shopping. Mediaeval churches now restored (beautifully decorated St Pierre), also two abbeys founded by William the Conqueror and his cousin Mathilda as penance for a sinful marriage – Abbayes aux Dames and aux Hommes. Great area for gourmet meals.

Caen continued

At Bénouville (4km S) – Manoir d'Hastings, La Pommeraie Hotel, 31.44. 62.43: 17th-century manor; superb meals by Claude Scavinger, from simplest (ham in cider; local lobster in cider; Norman apple and almond tart; cold tomato soup) to seven-course dégustation. Do try mussel soup with lobster stock or fish pot-au-feu. Lovely expensive bedrooms but book! Menus D–G. Rooms G. Open all year.

At Bavent (8km SE) – Hostellerie du Moulin du Pré, 31.78.83.68: old mill beautifully converted; pretty bedrooms; open country by a park with lake. Meals pricey but good. Menu F. Rooms C, D. Shut Sunday evening, Monday (except July, August); 1–15 March; October.

Caen – Le Dauphin, 29 rue Gemare, 31.86.22.26: Robert Charbedier's cooking has devotees from all France. Norman country dishes – tripe à la mode Caen, apple tart flambé in Calvados, apple charlotte, local lamb – yet foie gras cooked with apples! Californian and Spanish wines – but Auge farm cider. Nice small bedrooms. Menus A, D, F, G. Rooms D, E. Restaurant shut Saturdays. Hotel shut 14–23 February; 14 July–11 August.

Les Echevins, 35 route Trouville, 31.84.10.17: local

favourite Patrick Regnier has moved to a manor house to cook his famous fish dishes and their sauces. Lovely classic and modern dishes. Ex-Benoit, Paris, Oasis at Napoule, tour d'Argent. Menus C–E. Shut Sunday; part February, early July.

La Bourride, 15 rue Vaugueux, 31.93.50.76: in a 17th-century house in Caen's old quarter. Michel Bruneau, formerly at Manoir d'Hastings, cooks meals combining Norman regional and modern cuisine which draw accolades from Michelin, Gault-Millau, the critical Marc Champérard guide and your humble servant. No nouvelle excesses or Kiwicine. 'Cooking, like a woman, has need of love and attention.' Try bourride. Book. Dear but worth every centime. Menus F, G. Shut Sunday, Monday; 1–20 January, 20 August–4 September.

D562 Thury-Harcourt, St Rémy D133A Clécy (34km)

At Goupillières (8km by D6 and D212 from Thury-Harcourt) – Auberge Pont de Brie, Halte de Grimbosq, 31.79.37.84: quiet attractive hotel where lady chef Danielle de Monte produces meals balanced between tradition and invention. Cooks much in cider; superb pâtisserie. Menus A–F. Rooms B, C. Shut Wednesday in winter.

Clécy – Moulin du Vey (annexe Relais de Surosne,

Into lovely Calvados and the Suisse-Normande, land of rocks, gorges and escarpments, rushing rivers, tumbling streams, then suddenly gentle hills, green secret valleys and thick woods. Clecy, a beautiful spot where the Orne river sweeps through slopes and over rapids, is the centre for walks, scrambles, fishermen and canoeists.

	3km), 31.69.71.08: old mill on banks of the Orne. Denise Leduc runs one of my very favourite hotels. Sit on the lawn with a Muscadet watching the river tumble over rapids while son-in-law Michael Choplin cooks a delightful, imaginative meal. Menus C, E, G. Rooms D, E. Shut Friday lunch in winter.	
D168, D167 Le Bô, Pont d'Ouilly (20km)	Auberge St-Christophe (2km by D23 from Pont d'Ouilly), 31.69.81.23: simple Logis in country with good value meals. Path to river Orne from garden. Menus A–E. Rooms C–E. Shut Monday lunch in summer; Sunday evening, Monday in winter; part October; all February.	
D167 to Roche d'Oëtre, D301 through Gorges de St Aubert to Ménil-Hermei D239 Rabodanges, Bge de Rabodanges, GR36, D15 Putanges-Pont Ecrepin (15km)	Putanges – Lion Verd, 33.35.01.86: terrace by river Orne; good value; good cooking with modern tendencies. Menus A–D. Rooms A–C. Shut 24 December–31 January.	Lovely rocky, hilly, wooded country. Superb views from Roche d'Oetre overlooking wriggling gorges of river Rouvre. More wonderful views from narrow roads of St Auberg Gorges. You must walk a short way to some. Putanges is a delightful old market town – fine square, photogenic setting. Bathe in Lac Rabodanges (restaurant by the water).
D15 Argentan (20km) N26 Haras du Pin (16km)	Argentan – La Renaissance, 20 avenue 2e Division Blindée, 33.36.14.20: excellent, fair prices. Michel Moulin, former chef to Duke of Windsor and Rothschilds, here since 1969; individual	Nice little town where lace is still made – thanks to the discovery of 18th-century patterns. Nuns make it in Benedictine Abbey, 2 rue de l'Abbaye (see specimens 2.30 p.m. – 4.30 p.m. except

style, own recipes (sweetbreads in shrimp purée; steamed turbot with asparagus; duck fillet in orange syrup; bitter chocolate cake). Mouth-watering desserts. Smokes own salmon. Menus A–F. Rooms B–D. Shut Sunday low-season.

Sundays). Badly hit in Falaise Gap fighting in 1944. In the market place here. Henry II of England uttered the fateful phrase 'Will no one rid me of this turbulent priest?' that led to Thomas à Becket's murder at Canterbury in 1170.

From Haras du Pin – D26 Château d'O (14km) then through Ecouves forest to Alençon (another 30km)

Alençon – Au Petit Vatel, 72 place du Cdt. Desmeulles, 33.26.23.78: where the modern gourmands of Alençon often mentioned by Balzac would eat today. Not cheap but excellent. Patron-chef Michel Lerat has added a few modern dishes to the regionals (such as salmon in cider) – St Pierre (John Dory) with peaches; confit of duck with crayfish (July/August); mussels in spinach. Everything beautifully cooked, including vegetables. Menu C–F. Shut 15–31 August; part February; Wednesdays, Sunday evenings.

3km S on N138 at Arconnay – Château de Maleffre, 33. 31.82.78/31.73.90: lovely château in parkland with lake. True retreat in family home. Delightful bedrooms. Eat with the family Monday–Thursday evenings only: Menu C including wine. Rooms A–E. Shut Christmas, New Year.

Chateau d'O: 12–18th-century castle with pointed towers of fragile beauty reflected in its moat. Visit inside and park afternoons except Tuesdays.

Écouves delightful forest of mixed trees with deer and wild boar, glades for picnics. Here free French tanks under General Leclerc defeated Nazi Panzers in 1944 and at Carrefour de la Croix stands a memorial tank.

Alençon, market town on the Sarthe river, is famous for 'point d'Alençon' lace started in the 17th century to stop ladies of the court importing lace from Venice. You can see it in Musée de Peinture and École Dentellière (lace school) but not see it being made. Many lovely buildings, including the Préfecture, 17th-century palace of the Guise family. Notre-Dame church, 14th-century, has magnificent stained glass and a very flamboyant porch. Town has good open air swimming pool. Moulinex cookery ware made here.

N138 towards Le Mans turning on D310, D4 to Sablé-dur-Sarthe, then D306 to La Flèche (98km)

Solesmes (4km NE Sablé) – Grand Hotel facing abbey 43.95.45.10: behind a discreet traditional façade, a modern hotel with bow windows and round brick balconies overlooking shady garden. Very comfortable rooms. Regional cooking blended with modern by Bertrand Jacquet, patron and famous chef; huge modern kitchen you can visit, fine vast wine cellars. Try regional dishes, especially chicken (pot-au-feu is delicious) and sandre (delicately flavoured river fish from Sarthe and Loir), sweet and sour duck. Good croissants for breakfast. Menu C–F. Rooms E–F. Shut February.

La Flèche – Le Vert Galant, Grande Rue 43.94.00.51: true 'Old France'. Regulars in bar and dining room, pleasant lounge upstairs. Good atmosphere, but don't expect to be cosseted. Good cooking of food fresh from market. Menu A, C, D, F. rooms B. Shut Thursdays; 20 December–9 January.

Relais Henry IV (2km N on N23), 43.94.07.10: rooms refurbished. Friendlier service. Regional cooking, Loire wines (Chinon, Bourgueil). Good value. Menus A–E. Rooms B. Open all year.

Sablé – pleasantly sited astride river Sarthe where two tributaries flow in. A gloomy, vast castle built in 1711 by the Colbert family (not open). Church has 15th-century windows.

4km NE – Solesmes Abbey, history, started in 1010, chequered; once Benedictine Order's mother church. Associated with revival of Gregorian Chant. (Mass 9.45 a.m. open to public.)

La Flèche – most pleasant small town on Loir (no 'e'). Grew from a castle in the middle of the river. Henry IV gave his château to the Jesuits; now a prep school for military academics, thanks to Napoleon. At W edge of town is delightful Romanesque chapel with Renaissance carved woodwork. 4km SE: Tertre Rouge zoo – 700 animals.

D938 through woods to Baugé (15km), D58 through forest of Chanelais to Vernantes, then D767, N147 to Saumur (40km)

Baugé – La Boule d'Or, 4 rue du Cygne, 41.89.82.12: Logis de France. Menu A–E. Rooms A–C. Shut January; Sunday evenings; Mondays low season.

Saumur – Gambetta, 12 rue Gambetta, 41.67.66.66: a revelation! Christian Moury is patron-chef – local chef who became chef at Savoy, London; head chef Wessex, Winchester; Chef de Cuisine Excelsior, Manchester; 5 years as Executive Chef, Park Lane Hotel, Piccadilly; helped launch Maxim's de Paris, London and Lafayette, King Street, London. Need I say more, except that his cooking is 'creative light classical', his prices low for such expertise. He offers a business lunch, a regional menu, gastronomic menu and carte with superb temptations. His wife, at reception, also owns a vineyard providing Saumur-Champigny for the restaurant. Good reasonably priced Loire wines. Menus C, D, F. Shut Sunday evenings, Monday (except July, August); 4 January–2 February.

Hotel de la Gare, facing station, 41.67.34.24: in the same family since 1919 and Jacques Gaudicheau has the 'Order of French Courtesy' – well deserved. Madame cooks something for everyone, from dish of the day and cheap meals to gourmand.

This woodland route is far nicer than the main road. A Huguenot stronghold astride the Loire, Saumur is now known for wine, religious medals and its cavalry school. The spectacular Louis XV 14th-century castle on a sheer cliff, with lovely views, has a remarkable ceramics museum and a unique museum of the horse.

Cavalry School started in 1763 with the best horsemen in France. Black Squadron still gives horse and tank displays.

Fine tapestries in Hospices Jeanne Delanoue and Notre-Dame church. Delightful Jardin des Plantes of flowered terraces down castle slope, garlanded with vines. At suburb of St-Hilaire-St-Florent taste fruity white wine of Saumur at cellars of Ackerman. Laurence Ackerman, an Alsatian, taught the locals to put sparkle in wine by Champagne method in 1811. Still the best substitute. Also still white – fine aperitif (visits 9.30 a.m.–11.30 a.m. 3 p.m.–5 p.m. 1 May–30 September).

Menu A–F. Rooms B–D. Shut November–April.

At Les Rosiers (15km on D952) pretty spot – Val de Loire, 41.51.80.30: simple, informal, rustic. Straightforward cooking; local duck and fish – brochet (pike), trout. Cheap wines (Champigny, Anjou rouge). Menu B–D. Rooms A–C. Shut Sunday evening, Monday; February.

Auberge Jeanne de Laval 41.51.80.17: Michel, son of the great chef Albert Augeveau, continues the tradition which will outlive all fashions – the best, freshest ingredients, immaculately cooked in butter, varying with the market and seasons. Fish from the Loire (salmon, pike, sandre, perch, angouilles – little eels) and the sea; local poultry and game; best meat and vegetables. Worth every franc. The Queen Mother used to eat here. Menu E–G. Rooms D–F. Shut Mondays.

At Gennes, over Loire bridge from Les Rosiers – Hostellerie de Loire, 41.51.81.03: attractive, beamed. Old Relais de Post; tastefully decorated; bedrooms greatly improved; flowered terrace over river. Traditional cooking (try friture of small Loire fish). Good value. Good local wines. Menus A, B, D. Rooms B–E. Shut Monday evening, Tuesday.

D751
Montsoreau
(12km)

Hostellerie Diane de Méridor and Bussy Hotel, 41.51.70.18: old rustic inn with dining room overlooking Loire; simple bedrooms plus annexe in pleasant old house 500 metres away with better bedrooms. Good cooking; rightly proud of river fish dishes. Super Bourgueil wine. Menus B, C, E. Rooms D. Shut Tuesday; 15 December–7 February.

D947 4km
Fontevraud-L'Abbaye

Croix-Blanche, 7 place Plantagenets, 41.51.71.11: praised by readers for welcome, service, room, bathroom, food and wine. Regional cooking. Old-fashioned bedrooms. Menu A–C. Rooms B–D. Shut February; part November.

La Licorne, allée Sainte Catherine, 41.51.71.11: lovely old house; few tables; a few delicately prepared individualistic dishes superbly cooked. Try sole in oyster butter; house-smoked salmon; excellent desserts. Menus F, G. Book. Shut Sunday evening, Monday; mid-December–1 February.

Abbey, built 1099, run by abbess to annoyance of monks. Fine church (1119) contains tombs and figures of Plantagenets – Henry II, his wife Eleanor, their son Richard Coeur de Lion, King John's wife Isabelle. Britain tried to con the French into sending them to Westminster Abbey but it did not work. Abbey kitchen most interesting.

Nearby on D751 is lovely little Château Petit Thouars overlooking Vienne river, owned by Count whose ancestor was killed fighting Nelson at Aboukir. He lost a leg so had himself stood up in a barrel of sawdust to carry on fight. Present Count makes good red wine. You can taste and buy.

Minor roads SE through Bois de Couziers to Couziers (4km) then to D117. Turn left to Chavigny Lerné, on to D759 right on D751, left on D749 to Chinon (20km)

At La Roche-Clermault (5km before Chinon on D759) – Haut Clos 47.95.94.50: old country house, modern annexe. Good views; cooking over huge log fire. Menus B, C, E. Rooms A–D.

Chinon – L'Océanic, 13 rue Rabelais, 47.93.44.55: simple bistro serving outstanding fish. Menu B. Shut Sunday evening, Monday; 21 December–5 January.

Grand Hotel, Restaurant Boule d'Or, 66 quai Jeanne d'Arc, 47.93.03.13: Logis with 'casserole' for good regional cooking. Convenient situation. Menus A–F. Rooms A–D. Shut Sunday evening, Monday in winter; 19 December–31 January.

Au Plaisir Gourmand, 2 rue Parmentier, 47.93.20.48: Jean-Claude Rigollet now firmly established as best chef in the area, so you must book. Regional cooking. Excellent river fish. Good wine list. Attractive house. Menus D, F. Shut Sunday evening, Monday; two weeks mid-November and mid-February.

La Thélème, 7 place Mirabeau, 47.93.49.39: wine merchants where you can taste Chinon and other Loire wines, buy, or drink with regional meals or snacks in small restaurant. Shut Monday evening, Tuesday lunch.

Attractive route missing traffic on D751. On D17 – La Devinière where Rabelais, great satirical author of *Gargantua*, spent his childhood. Writer, scholar, Franciscan priest and eminent physician. A near surfeit of history in Chinon. Richelieu owned it. Henry II of England died in the castle; his son Richard Lionheart held it but King John lost it to the French. Charles VII moved the French court here, listened to Joan of Arc's strange story, believed her and gave her an army. The château, partly ruined, is still magnificent (Joan of Arc museum). Old town of alleys and turreted houses – rue Voltaire and Grand Carroi outstanding. Astride river Vienne.

Château de Marçay (7km on D749, D116), 47.93.03.47: delightful 15th-century château with conical towers. Twelve new bedrooms opened. Luxurious, elegant and expensive. Fine grounds with pool. Good straightforward cuisine. Excellent Loire wines. Menus F, G. Rooms G. Shut mid-January to mid-March.

D751, D749 to Richelieu (20km), Châtellerault and Chauvigny (58km more)

Richelieu – Le Puits Doré, place Marché, 47.58.10.59: 17th-century historic monument on corner of market place. More bedrooms added. Good value meals; one very cheap menu. Try hot goat's cheese in flaky pastry, good terrines, coq au vin. Good range of wines. Menus A–C. Shut Thursdays in winter.

Châtellerault – Grand Hôtel (restaurant La Charmille), 70 boulevard Blossac, 49. 21.30.11: grand hotel in town centre; comfortable; gourmet restaurant (shut Wednesdays) and cheap grill (shut Saturday evenings, Sundays). Imaginative cooking. Excellent value. Superb goat's cheese with home-baked bread and fresh fruit sorbets. Menu: restaurant E, F. Rooms C–F. Shut 20 January–20 February.

Le Croissant, 15 avenue Kennedy, 49.21.01.77: friendly, family-run; pure French provincial. Traditional

Richelieu – first planned town in France – by Richelieu. His château has gone, but the beautiful park is open. Sunday morning market sometimes with folk costumes.

Châtellerault on river Vienne has good museum of old cars, including steam, electric, early bikes, trikes, motor bikes (near Pont Henri IV – built 1609). Old château (12 rue Gaudeau Lerpinière – built 1423) has museum.

St Jacques church, rue Sully, consecrated 1066.

Chauvigny – dominating position above Vienne; ruins of five castles. Two mediaeval churches. Château Touffon (7km NW) impressive mediaeval-Renaissance; lovely gardens.

cooking. Menu A–F. Rooms A–D. Shut Christmas, New Year. Restaurant Sunday evenings; Mondays.

D749 Lussac D11 past L'Isle Jourdain to les Six Routes, then D729 Confolens (76km)

Confolens – Belle Etoile, route d'Angoulême, 45.84.02.35: simple auberge still delights readers for value and good bourgeois cooking. Pick a back room to avoid noise. Garden to Vienne river. Menus A–C. Rooms A–C. Shut 1–25 October; 2–25 January; Monday from 1 October–1 July.

Vienne, 4 rue Ferrandie, 45.84.09.24: a dreary façade hides nice restaurant and delightful flowery terrace overlooking Vienne river. Regional dishes. Very good value. Menus A–C. Simple rooms A, B. Shut Friday evening, Saturday in winter; 22 October–11 November; 22 December–2 January.

Tour de Nesle, rue Côte, 45.84.02.35: a famous French food journalist recommended this to me for value, fine old dishes such as boeuf bourguignon and Loire wines. I have not yet tried it but the patron-chef is Roger Bardet, brother of the great Jean Bardet of Châteauroux – now of Tours. Cheap. Menus A–D. Shut Tuesday (low season): 15 February–15 March.

Confolens is a quiet old town on Vienne river where it meets the fast-flowing Loire; with old houses between them. Most photogenic street is rue des Francs-Maçons (Freemasons) with steps lined with overhanging houses. Fine 15th-century bridge crosses Vienne river to 11th-century church of St Barthélemy.

D951, N141 Angoulême (63km)	Grand Hotel de France, 1 place des Halles, 45.95.47.95: a revelation. Superb old house where writer Balzac was born; in town centre, near railway station, in busy street – yet behind is a superb garden by the ancient ramparts with panoramic views of the Charente valley. Classic décor and cooking. A splendid retreat. Menu C. Rooms C–F. Restaurant shut 20 December–15 January. Saturday and Sunday lunch. Hotel open all year. La Marmite du Pêcheur (4km on D72 at Pont de Basseau), 45.91.83.74: Madame Poupelain has retired but blessedly young M. Geisler is a very good cook; we had an excellent lunch. Good desserts. Menus B, C. Shut Sunday evening, Monday.	A pleasant walk round the boulevards replacing the old ramparts gives fine views of river Charente. At promenade Beaulieu, overlooking Jardin Vert, is a plaque to France's first 'para', Général Resnier. In 1806, aged 73, he invented a wing-flapping machine and took off from this spot. He hoped to have found a way for Napoleon's troops to invade England. He landed in the river. Traffic can be heavy and route difficult to find in Angoulême.
D939 Brantôme (58km)	At Vieux Mareuil, 17km before Brantôme – Auberge de l'Étang Bleu, 53.60.92.63: hunting lodge-style auberge beside a lake in big park (open to public July–August). Menus of six prices. Long wine list. Good service. Comfortable rooms. Dining room rather barn-like. Menu B–G. Rooms E. Shut 10 January–1 March. Auberge du Soire, 6 rue Georges Saumande, 53.05.82.93: 18th-century auberge rurale; simple rooms. Popular, so don't expect fast food. Good value	Delightful old town beside river Dronne in Périgord, rich in old buildings, including riverside houses with flowered balconies and vines, and riverside gardens with willows. Alas, very crowded in summer, with parking problems. You enter by a 16th-century elbow bridge leading to the old abbey church, with 12th-century belfry and a fountain garden with a bust of the scandalous 16th-century abbot, diplomat and witty cynical chronicler of court life known as 'Brantôme' (Pierre de

Brantôme continued

cheap menu; good gastronomic (cou farci au foie gras). Menu A, B, D. Rooms B–C. Shut Monday in winter.

Moulin de l'Abbaye, 53.05.80.22: ravishing, romantic, beautifully furnished riverside mill. One reader complained that the water kept her awake. She should have been too busy romancing to notice! New young chef Christian Ravinel came from Roux brothers' Waterside Inn, Bray. Beautiful Périgordian meals. Superb menu Autour du Vin with four wines. Expensive, of course. Menus E–G. Rooms F–G. shut 1 November–30 April.

Chabrol, 5 rue Gambetta, 53.05.70.15: fine position by river bridge. Delicious traditional and Périgordian dishes by Jean-Claude Charbonnel, passionate cook. Enormous choice of meat and fish dishes. Lovely wine list. Menus B–G. Rooms D–E. Shut mid-November–mid-December; second half of February; Sunday evening, Monday in winter.

La Jurande, 25 rue Victor-Hugo, 53.05.78.22: very much cheaper; rustic; at entrance to crowded old town; classical dishes. Menus A, B, D, E. Shut Wednesday (low season).

At Bourdeilles (10km on D78) – Griffons, 53.05.75.61: Denise Deborde still cooks Bourdeilles). Superb riverside strolls. Monastery buildings now town hall, schools and Bernard Desmoulins museum, which includes works by this artist, painted, they say, when under the influence of a medium. He died in 1914.

Bourdeilles: lovely little town of watermills, weirs, narrow streets presided over by a 13th-century castle from which Counts of Périgord once terrorized the country; and a Renaissance mansion built by Pierre de Brantôme's sister, now housing a collection of furniture and works of art.

good meals which please my readers. She converted this 16th-century house by a 13th-century river bridge into an hotel. Menus C–F. Rooms D. Shut 10 October–10 April.

At Champagnac de Belair (6km NE by D78, D83) – Moulin du Roc, 53.54.80.36: wonderful! One of our favourites in the world. Beautiful old mill by Dronne river, delightful garden, lavishly furnished, impeccable service, delicious cooking by Solange Gardillou, possibly France's best woman chef. Book well ahead. Menus F–G. Rooms F–G. Shut 15 November–15 December; 15 January–15 February.

D939
Périgueux
(27km)

Goose liver and truffles, luxuries of Périgordian cooking, are now outrageously dear. But why stuffed goose neck should be so dear is a mystery. It's a sort of sausage. An old peasant proverb says: 'A neck of goose and a bottle of wine and you can ask a friend to a banquet'. Another poor man's dish taken over by gourmets!

Domino, 21 place Francheville, 53.08.25.80: fine old Relais de Poste; old-style furnishings in solid wood. Delightful courtyard of greenery for summer eating. Old regional dishes, some modern; excellent

The white dome of the cathedral, as you enter the capital of Périgordian food, also promises an architectural feast; alas, many old buildings have been destroyed. The curious 12th-century cathedral, St Front, owes its flamboyance to the 19th-century architect Abbadie (called The Wrecker) who, when 'restoring', added seventeen turrets. Mediaeval houses can be seen from Barris bridge and in the old town.

Périgueux changed sides between France and England twice during 100 Years' War, finally opting for France.

Périgeux continued	vegetables. Menus D, F. Rooms E, F. Périgord, rue Victor Hugo, 53.53.33.63: still pleases readers; pleasant rooms, pretty courtyard and garden with tables. Excellent Périgordian dishes. Try beef fillet in Périgueux sauce, duck confit. Good value. Menus A–D. Rooms C, D. Shut last week October; part February; Saturday in winter. L'Oison, 31 rue St-Front, 53.09.84.02: overdue recognition at last for Régis Chioraz for some of the best Périgordian cuisine; try panaché de poissons, his own duck foie gras, and desserts. Good Bergerac wines. Menus B–E. Shut Sunday evening, Monday; 2 February–3 March.	Pleasant drive to two ancient abbey churches, Chancelade and Marlande in Feytaud Forest (back along D939, D710 for very short distance; right on D1; then D2).
N89 Terrasson-la-Villedieu (55 km)	At Montignac (turn right at Lardin on D704; 10km) – Relais du Soleil d'Or, 53.51.80.22; classic Périgordian delicacies with some individual ideas. Service criticized. Fine house, tastefully furnished, in splendid quiet gardens. Menus B–G. Rooms B–E; Shut 1 November–Palm Sunday.	18th-century Palladian Château Rastignac, on right of road, said to have inspired Washington's White House. Burned down by Nazis 1944, considerably restored. Busy little town on slope beside Vezere. Old town up the hill dominated by 15th-century church; old houses. One 12th-century bridge, one modern. Deals in walnuts from local farms and truffles (Thursday market). Roads south towards Souillac almost deserted; silent land of woods, hamlets, farms.

N89 Brive la Gaillard (33km)	La Crémaillère, 53 avenue Paris, 55.74.32.47: local people love it. All the Corrèze specialities, including a menu 'following the goose' – foie gras and cèpes ravioli; stuffed goose neck; Causse cheese and walnut ice cream. Or try cassoulet made with goose confit; coddled eggs with truffle juice. Tables in a flower garden in summer. Outstanding desserts. Long wine list. Menu A–D. Rooms B–D. Shut 15 January–15 February; Sunday evenings, Mondays. La Périgourdine, 15 avenue Alsace-Lorraine, 55.24.26.55: charming restaurant and garden, serving good value meals. Menu B–G. Shut 14 July–5 August. Wednesday evenings; Sundays.	Pleasant busy town on river Corrèze, centre of fruit growing and market gardening area, so Saturday market outside old church of St Martin is lively and interesting. Hôtel de Labenche, 16th-century, now a library, but you can see it from the courtyard. Old city walls now tree-lined boulevards.
D38 (SE) to Collonges-la-Rouge (21km)	Relais St Jacques de Compostelle, 55.25.41.02: most attractive; good variety of dishes, prices and regional wines. Menu A, B, C, F. Rooms A, C, E. Shut 1 December–3 January; Wednesday in winter. Auberge Le Prieuré, 55.25.41.00: charming flower-decked house; willing service; excellent cooking; absolute bargain. Patronne-chef Yvonne Albert is a true mistress of regional cooking; superb confit of goose or duck, cèpes or truffled omelettes; Auvergne coq au vin; lovely potatoes cooked in	Reached through wooded hills and valleys, set among walnuts and vines, this charming old city is called La Rouge for the dark red stone of its mansions, old houses and 12th-century fortified church, which has a gun room from the 100 Years' War. Fortified, too, is the elegant house of the Viscounts of Turenne-Castel de Vassinhae. Leave your car at former railway station and walk. Fine old houses. Can get crowded high-season.

Collonges-la-Rouge continued	goose fat. Super Cahors and Bergerac wines. Menu A–C. Rooms B. Shut 1 December–15 March.	
D38 through Meyssac, D940 to Bretenoux, then D14, D43 to Castelnau (30km)	Hôtel Bureau, Biars-sur-Cère (Bretonoux station), 65.38.43.54: genuine old-style Relais with pavement tables; in same family for 55 years. Super value cheap menu; good cheap wines. Vegetables from own garden; barbecues on lawn in summer. Most readers love it. A few expect miracles. Menu A. A chance to recoup if you have overspent on Périgordian feasts. Rooms A. Shut Sunday; 1 December–30 April.	Meyssac is a nice market-town in red clay, surrounded by rolling country of fruit, vineyards, walnuts and poplars. Old wooden houses and towers. Castelnau castle is three miles round – a formidable red-stone fortress standing guard over the Cère and Dordogne rivers, with lovely views of both from ramparts. Built in the 11th century, extended in the 100 Years' War, it was restored from 1896 to 1932. Once it had a garrison of 1500 men and 100 horses. Its rent was then one egg per year, carried in pomp by four oxen to the Viscount of Turenne. Lovely. Romanesque windows and tapestries of Aubusson and Beauvais (shut Tuesdays).
D14 over river Bavé, left on D30 to D673 past Château Montal to St Céré (10km)	Coq Arlequin, boulevard Dr Roux, 65.38.02.13: we love it; delightful; in Gérard Bizat's family 100 years. His son Eric cooks. Charming furnishings. Superb Jean Lurçat tapestries, including the great 'Coq Arlequin' itself. Paintings by Gérard Bizat who was an artist. Also owns leisure park by Château de Montal (3km) with tennis, bar, grill and free swimming for guests. Hotel speciality for 50 years – chicken and sweetbread in super sauce covered with flakiest pastry.	Château Montal is a 'phoenix' castle. Jeanne de Balsac built it in 1534 for a son who was away at the wars, hiring the greatest artists and builders. Only his body returned, and his grief-stricken mother had her window blocked up. In 1879 an asset stripper auctioned its treasures and sold much of its stone for building in Paris. In 1908 a new owner had it repaired and bought back the treasures from museums and collections at ransom prices. One stone doorway was

Gastronomic menu of Quercy dishes. Excellent Cahors wines of Jean Jouffreau. Menu B, F. Rooms D–F. Shut 10 January–10 March.

Du Parc, faubourg Lascabanes, 65.38.17.29: Good news! My old favourite, Marie Annick, daughter of Gérard Bizat of Coq Arlequin, and husband took over in 1987. Everything cooked in hotel to local recipes except foie gras and duck pâté, cooked by brother Eric at Coq Arlequin. Menus A–D. Rooms B–D. shut Tuesday off-season; 15 December–10 January.

Restaurant Ric J. P., route de Leyne (D48), 65.38.04.08: good new restaurant; young chef-patron. Balcony with fine views. Menus B, C, F. Shut Monday (except July, August).

missing, so Rodin, the great sculptor, made a new one.

St Céré is splendid – a smiling little town with the river Bavé running through its streets and flower-decked riverside houses. St Laurent tower, overlooking the town from a steep hill, was the home until he died of Jean Lurçat, the great tapestry and ceramic artist. Many of his works are permanently displayed in St Céré 'casino', around a big pleasant bar. Super Saturday market.

Coq Arlequin (see hotels) was wartime hideout of British agents arranging air drops to French Resistance. Then called Hotel de Paris.

D673 past Grotte de Presque to Padirac (14km)

Gouffre de Padirac – Padirac Hotel, 65.33.64.23: useful; praised by readers. Quiet, cheap. Bargain ultra-cheap menu. Menus A–D. Simple rooms A–B.

Grotte de Presque is made up of caves pillared with slim and thick stalagmites 10m (30ft) high, and of strangely varying shapes. Gouffre de Padirac is a chasm made, it is said, by the heel of the Devil who taunted St Martin to jump it. He did it – all 325 feet of it – on a mule, a feat worthy of Harvey Smith. A refuge shelter during the 100 Years' War and the Huguenot Wars, it was neglected until 1890. By lift and stairs, you can descend 110m (336ft) to a chamber, then walk to an

Grotte de Presque continued		underground river. Here you board flat-bottomed boats for an unreal trip over strangely translucent waters for half a mile to visit more chambers on foot.
D673 Alvignac Les Eaux (5km)	Grand Hotel Palladium, 65.33.60.23: hotel school; efficient but lost charming atmosphere radiating from Alice Vayssouze. Restful, garden, swimming pool. Best rooms in modern block. Good value. Menus A–F. Rooms E. Shut 1 October–4 April. Nouvel Hôtel, 65.33.60.30: modern, clean, good value for one-star hotel. Meals excellent value. Regional specialities and traditional dishes. Cheap wines. Garden. Menu A, B, D. Rooms A–C. Shut 15 December–1 March; Friday, Saturday, Sunday evenings in winter.	Pleasant, quiet village, with nearby spa waters prescribed for disorders of the liver and digestion. Good centre for seeing Rocamadour, Padirac and other crowded sites.
D673 Rocamadour (10km)	Ste Marie Hotel, 65.33.63.07: recently completely renovated; perched on the rock-face; lovely views from terrace. Some rooms in annexe. All regional dishes such as duck confit; truffled omelette; foie gras; goose; truffled pâtés. Wines reasonable. Six menus A–F. Rooms B–D. Shut 10 October–Palm Sunday. Beau Site Hotel, Restaurant Jean de Valon, 65.33.63.08: superb terrace view, especially when city is lit up. Regional dishes beautifully cooked by Didier Menot.	This tourist cliché of a mediaeval city clamped on a 150m (500ft) rock face is magnificent despite too many tourists and shops. View it first from the road terrace at l'Hospitalet above, preferably at night or in the morning sun. You will never forget it. From the castle at the top, the town works its way down through a maze of old houses, towers, rocks and oratories to a road still high above a river valley. It was founded near the top by St Amadour, a recluse, and pilgrims used to climb the

Menus B–E. Rooms D, E. Shut 1 November–1 April.

Near Rignac (4km SE on N140) – Château de Roumégouse, 65.33.63.81: gorgeous neo-Gothic 'fairy-tale' château with pointed tower above Causse de Gramat. Delightfully furnished. One owner in 1890s bribed locals to rebuild their village out of sight of the castle! Used in war by Resistance, then owned by de Gaulle's hairdresser! Fair prices for Relaise et Châteaux hotel. Best regional cooking. Menus D–G. Rooms F–G. Shut 2 November–1 April; restaurant shut Tuesday.

Route Lacave (4km from Rocamadour on D247 – Auberge de la Garenne, 65.33.65.88: quiet, modern, box-like but comfortable; in gardens. Swimming pool. Regional cooking. Menus A–F. Rooms A–E. Open all year.

At Gramat (10km SE by N140) – Lion d'Or, 65.38.73.18: hotel since 1790 but enthusiastic patron-chef Rene Mommejac, Master Chef of France, has beautifully changed dining room recently and 'remade' bedrooms. He scours area for best ingredients, using many old Quercy recipes. Superb old Cahors wines – Germain Vigouroux cellars nearby. Menus B, D, G. Rooms D, E. shut Monday in winter: 15 December–15 January.

216 steps to the ecclesiastical city on their knees and in chains. Today very few kneel at every step. It would be unwise even to *walk* up the steps after a typical meal in one of the restaurants which abound around here. Chapelle Miraculeuse is where the hermit is said to have hollowed an oratory out of the rock.

D32, D677 Labastide Murat (24km)		They changed its name in honour of Jean Murat, the general whom Napoleon made King of Naples after displays of fanatical bravery on battlefields – and after he married Napoleon's sister Caroline. After Bourbons returned to Naples in 1815, he tried to recapture 'his' kingdom, was captured and shot. His modest birthplace is now a museum. The inn is named after him too.
D677, N20 then little road V10 or N20 into Cahors (35km)	Cahors – La Taverne, rue J-B Delpech, 65.35.28.66: another change of chef-patron; Michelin star has gone. But locals still loyal to Cahors' centre of gastronomy made famous by Pierre Escorbiac. Serge Guillouet still offers careful Quercy cooking, even Escorbiac's own tourte quercynoise and truffles 'en croustade'. But he adds his own delicious dishes, such as creamed haricot with smoked goose and cèpes. Gault-Millau names it the place to taste Quercy cooking and my own French expert, Marc de Champérard, approves happily. Best old Cahors wines. Dining room attractive. Menus C, D, F, G. At Laroque des Arcs (5km on D653) – Beau Rivage, route de Figeac, 65.35.30.58: beautiful views over Lot river from terrace and many bedrooms; big garden to river; own stretch of fishing.	A lovely old town in a superb position in and around a horseshoe of the river Lot, with vine-covered hills behind. The fortified mediaeval bridge with three slim towers, Valentre, is one of the most beautiful in the world. Legend claims that the Devil himself helped to finish it on time, then was tricked out of payment. St Etienne's Cathedral, also fortified, founded 1119 and altered until 1500, has mediaeval paintings and a supremely lovely mediaeval door. The town is rich in old buildings and surrounding country reminds me of the Dordogne twenty-five years ago before the main stream of travellers found it. Magnificent view of town and river from Mont St-Cyr, but reached on foot by steep path from near Louis-Philippe Bridge (1½ hrs).

More sophisticated cooking by new chef. Try red mullet (rouget) poached in red wine. Menus B, C, E, G. Rooms D. Shut 10 November –Easter; restaurant shut Tuesday except mid-summer.

At Mercués (NE 7km on D911) – Château de Mercués, 65.20.00.01: stunning castle with four dunce's-hat turrets, bishop's residence since 12th century, made into expensive, delightful hotel by Georges Vigouroux, vigorous wine-maker. Magnificent views from gorgeous terrace; huge park with pool, tennis and wine caves with free tastings. Young chef Hervé Guerin already famed. Menus C, D. Rooms G. Shut 1 November–1 April.

At Lamagdelaine (7km on D653) – Marco, 65.35.30.64: lovely old farmhouse with terrace and flower garden where Claude Marco (ex-Roux Brothers, Gavroche, London) has become a French favourite for imaginative but sensible dishes – oxtail to lobster with orange and foie gras. Try lamb noisette and kidney with perfect biscuit de cèpes. Menus C, E, G. Shut January, February; Sunday evening, Monday low season.

Dark, strong red wine of Cahors (called 'black') loved for centuries by English. Now popular in France. Keeps 10 years or more. Tastings and audio-visual in English at Chateau Haute-Serve (Georges Vigouroux), 7km South on D6. Other tastings at Puy L'Evêque (Route 9).

N20 St Paul de Loubressac (20km)	Relais de la Madeleine 65.21.98.08: Bernard Devianne's Logis and casserole Relais Routiers popular with readers for cheapness and remarkable value. All great Quercy dishes – duck confit, truffled omelette to foie gras. Very cheap house wine. Peaceful position; pleasant grounds. Menu A–C. Rooms A–B. Shut Saturdays; December 1–7 January.	
N20 Montauban (40km)	Hostellerie les Coulandrières (at Montbeton, 4km on D958 towards Castelsarrasin), 63.67.47.47: very pleasant modern hotel built around garden and swimming pool; balconies or terraces to bedrooms; roofed summer outdoor restaurant; welcoming log fire in winter; 7-acre park. Menus B, D, F. Rooms E. Shut Sunday evenings in winter. Grand Hôtel Midi, 12 rue Notre-Dame, 63.63.17.23: new rooms in annexe. New restaurant in glassed verandah. Convenient position by cathedral. Real confit of goose and duck in earthenware pots; truffle soufflé; goose cassoulet. Menus B, C, F. Rooms C–E. Orsay et la Cuisine d'Alain, facing station, 63.63.00.57: charming 'minotel' with pretty sound-proofed bedrooms and excellent cooking by Alain Blanc. Try local-style cassoulet of duck	On terrace above the river Tarn, this pink-brick market town is one of the most photogenic in France. At the end of the 14th-century bridge with seven arches is the 17th-century Bishop's Palace with many works of the 19th-century artist Ingres, a famous Paris teacher. He painted 'Christ and the Doctors' when he was 82. In place Bourdelle alongside you can taste local fruit free in season. The palace ground floor has modern sculptures of Bourdelle, pupil of Rodin, and some by Rodin himself. Place Nationale is a fine square with 17th-century brick arcades.

confit, outstanding fish dishes. Mouth-watering desserts. Summer meals on garden terrace. Menus C–F. Rooms D. Shut Sundays, Monday lunch.

D999 to Gaillac then N88 to Albi (73km) Alternative route from Montauban D115 Brunique D9, D33 Vaour D33, D91, D600 Cordes, Albi (83km)

Marssac (11km from Gaillac on N88) – Francis Cardaillac (Le Tilbury), 63.55.41.90: Francis Cardaillac is a truly great chef. He has revived old recipes and invented new dishes and sauces, which are not for passing fashion but permanent. Gorgeous vegetables and desserts. Modern building by river Tarn, period furnishings. Piano bar. Menus C–G. Shut 4–16 January; Sunday evening, Monday.

Albi – Hostellerie Saint-Antoine, 63.54.04.04: founded 1734, in Rieux family 250 years, modernized, tasteful, quiet garden. Old recipes such as gras-double (stew of ham, tripe, vegetables, garlic, herbs); also classical dishes; lovely desserts. Guests can use pool at La Réserve (3km). Menus C–F. Rooms E–G.

La Réserve (at Fonvialane, 3km on Route Cordes), 63.60.79.79: Rieux family's modern country cousin to Saint-Antoine. Gorgeous position in park by river Tarn. Pool, tennis. Expensive super bedrooms, terrace by river; traditional dishes; lovely light pastries; famous cellar of Gaillac wines. Menu

Gaillac, wine town and working port on Tarn river, has fine old town of wood and brick houses and squares with fountains.

Wine has been made here for 1000 years. White is best known but red is produced – light for drinking young, heavier, elegant wine for ageing. Taste it at St Michael Abbey or 11km N on D922 at Cahuzac at Domaine Jean Cros (best Gaillac wine).

Albi is an impressive town, especially seen from its bridges; centre of the Albigensian sect, ruthlessly destroyed as heretics by the French kings. The red-brick St Cecilia's cathedral is one of the best Gothic in France, and its 15th-century fresco 'Last Judgement' is France's biggest picture. The walls and windows are covered with Italian frescoes. Archbishop's La Berlie palace alongside contains the most important collection of works of Toulouse-Lautrec, born here 1864. Superb!

Nearby is house where he was born in 1864, son of Count Alphonse de Toulouse-Lautrec, and room where he fell at 14 causing his

	D. Rooms F, G. Shut 1 October–1 April. Relais Gascon et Auberge Landaise, 3 rue Balzac, 63.54.26.51: bedrooms greatly improved in this cosy, beamed auberge in old city. Good old Gascon cooking (daube de boeuf au Gaillac, duck cassoulet). Gaillac, Cahors wines cheap. Menus A, C, D. Rooms B, D. Restaurant shut Sunday evenings, Monday in winter.	deformity. House still owned by family. Cordes – 'Cordes-in-the-sky'–fortified village high above Céron valley. Dying in 1921 when artist Yves Brayer founded a colony of craftsmen and painters. Some still at work. Charming but many tourist boutiques.
N112 Castres (42km)	La Caravelle, 150 avenue Roquecourbe, 63.59.27.72: summer restaurant; eat inside or in garden with massed flowers beside the river Agout. Classic cassoulet (Carcassonne recipe with preserved goose), local charcuterie; Gaillac wines, including red. Good value. Menu A, B, E. Shut mid-September – mid-June; Saturdays. Grand Hôtel, 11 rue Libération, 63.59.00.30: same owner-chef, cuisine, menu prices as La Caravelle. Comfortable rooms. Praised by readers. Rooms C–F. Shut 15 December–15 January. Restaurant shut Friday evening, Saturday.	Beautiful scenery. As a change from Lautrec's dancing girls, Castres museum specializes in the more sedate works of Goya, including four major pictures, and some by other Spanish painters, Velasquez among them. Old balconied houses line the river Agout. Cloth-weaving town since 14th century. Jean Jaurés (1859–1914), Father of French socialism, born and educated here, became local 'M.P.'.
N112, D118 Mazamet (18km)	Mazamet – Château de Montledier (route Anglès at Pont de l'Arn, 4km on D109), 63.61.20.54: spectacular 12th-century castle among gorgeous scenery; brilliantly made cosy and bright inside	

by coloured fabrics and décor. Golf course 2km away and all-in golf overnights or weeks offered. Riding, tennis. Delightful bedrooms. Prices reasonable for such comfort. Menus B, C, F. Rooms F–G. Shut January. Restaurant shut Sunday evening, Monday low season.

D118
Carcassonne
(47km)

Carcassonne – many restaurants in old city aimed at tourists whom they don't expect to see again. Choose carefully.

Auberge du Pont Levis, at city entrance, 68.25.55.23: deservedly renowned. First-floor dining room with summer terrace; views of city towers and mountains. Henri Pautard's gastronomic regional dishes predictably ignored by Gault-Millau and Nouvelle fans (try goose cassoulet, smoked goose, duck confit, sole in lobster sauce). Many local wines. Try white La Clape, red Fitou Carte d'Or. Menus E, F. Shut Sunday evening, Monday; part February, part September.

Donjon (in city), 2 rue Comte-Roger, 68.71.08.80: enlarged, modernized without destroying the mediaeval building. Friendly people. Chef Claude Rodriguez of nearby Logis de Trencavel supervises cooking (cassoulet, lamb fricassé, duck in Fitou wine). Dinner only. Menu C. Rooms D–F.

This mediaeval city, rebuilt in 1844 and called a fake by purists, is superbly done and makes the Middle Ages live again; despite too many tourist shops and cafés, you expect a pikeman lurking round every corner. Original fortified city withstood a 5-year siege by Charlemagne. Restored by famous architect Viollet-le-Duc. For best view of 52 towers, walk round the Lices between inner and outer ramparts from Porte Narbonnaise. See also St Nazaire cathedral, Romanesque Gothic with Renaissance glass. City looks dramatic when lit up at night.

Domaine d'Auriac (2½km SE by D118, D104), 68.25.72.22: delicious, pricey, creeper-clad hotel among vineyards and a huge 300-year-old park. Worth every franc for such a beautiful bolt-hole from Carcassonne crowds. Pool, tennis. 'Gentils' welcome. Bernard Rigaudis, a polished chef, rugby player and wine grower, is not afraid to experiment but his delicious cassoulet and other local dishes are best. Best local wines of Aude. Menu F–G. Rooms H. Shut late January; Monday lunch, Sundays.

From Carcassonne N113, D610, D11 to Beziers (78km)

Compagnie du Midi at Restaurant La Racasse, 13 rue Coquille 67.49.13.43: still renowned for fish and fish soup; try assiette chalot (5 fish). Menu B–D. Rooms C–E. Shut mid–end November; restaurant Saturday lunch, Sunday.

La Croustade, 30 avenue 22 Août, 67.28.26.60: rustic restaurant popular locally. Regional cooking. Menus A–C. Shut Sunday evenings, Monday.

Le Gourmandin, 34 ave Alphonse-Mas, 67.28.39.18: Languedoc dishes with a touch of classic and modern. Super vegetables. Best local wines. A real discovery. Menus B, D, F. Shut Sunday evening, Monday; part July.

13th-century cathedral, canal du Midi. Beach at Valras (13km).

Or N113 to Narbonne (56km)

At Ornaisons (off N113 on to D24 at Lézignan-Corbières) – Relais du Val d'Orbieu, 68.27.10.27; old stone mill attractively converted; garden with swimming pool. Views of the Black Mountain. Classic and lighter modern dishes by young chef Richard Toix (try duck cooked in wine of Banyuls); interesting desserts. Excellent wine list. Menus D–G. Rooms F, G. Shut 25 January–23 February; Sunday evening in winter.

Mapotel du Languedoc (formerly Grand Languedoc), 22 boulevard Bambetta, 68.05.14.74: Madame Lyon's hotel still comfortable, clean, good value. Most readers happy but some problems with dining room closing at 9.30 p.m.! 'English pub' bar opens until 2 a.m. Menus A, C, E. Rooms B–E.

La Réverbère, 4 place Jacobins, 68.32.29.18: Claude Giraud runs one of the best restaurants in south-west France; superb cooking at below Michelin-star prices. Considering he is a devotée of Michel Guérard, the genius who made slimming by expensive eating into a cult, he lets gluttons like me off lightly. His Menu Découverte of seven dishes in small portions is delicious. His pricier six-course Farandole Gourmande meal is a delight.

At Lézignan-Corbières, 34km along N113 – opposite railway station, Caves Saury-Serres, wine caves with interesting museum of how wine used to be produced, with stone press, early tractors. Wine from Corbières, Minervois, Fitou, Limoux bottled, matured here. At 12 p.m. snack lunch of local products with wine.

Narbonne – quiet wine town. St Just cathedral, one of tallest – Gothic, begun 1272, never finished; fine tapestries.

15km SW is 11th-century Fontfroide Abbey – well restored, modern stained glass.

His meal of four oyster dishes with cheese and pastries is expensive gluttony. Frequent changes of 300 recipes. Fine table settings. Menus C–G. Shut February; Sunday evenings, Monday.

Lion d'Or, 39 ave Pierre Semard, 68.32.06.92: 'Mike' Bonnet continues to please my readers. Bedrooms modernized, more added. Regional classic cooking (coquelet en vin de Corbieres, duck cassoulet). Menus A, C, D. Rooms D. Shut Sundays low season.

Or D118, D117 to Perpignan (126km)

La Loge, place Loge, 68. 34.54.84: no restaurant; charming little hotel. Pretty rooms with bathrooms. Rooms B–E.

Route 2
Le Havre to Aix-en-Provence

You can taste the freshwater fish of the Loire on this route, then compare it with the salmon of the river Allier, trout and crayfish of the Auvergne, cooked in good local butter. They are especially luscious around Vichy. Pork is delicately excellent, too, even the salted belly used in potée auvergnate (with cabbage, potatoes and root vegetables). Vegetables are good, especially carrots. Ham is almost as good as in Ardennes, and there is a big variety of sausages large and small; also fungi from cèpes to morilles. Good cheeses are Bleu d'Auvergne, hard tasty Cantal and strong fourme d'Ambert. Vichy's Milliard is excellent (black cherry tart made with batter).

The Ardèche has beautiful river fish, good charcuterie and old-fashioned mutton. You can still taste beautifully cooked, genuine hare in the Auvergne, and coq au vin nearly to Burgundy standard. It is not nouvelle cuisine country.

Vaucluse cooking is nearer to true Provençal – oil, lots of garlic, including aïoli (mayonnaise rich in garlic which is slapped over everything from vegetables to fish – and the name is used for village feasts where pots of it stand on the table and barrels of wine surround you). You can have bourride – lighter, subtler bouillabaisse, with the liquid served as soup, then the fish with aïoli. In Provence you are truly in oil, garlic, fish and tomato country, with some magnificent dishes.

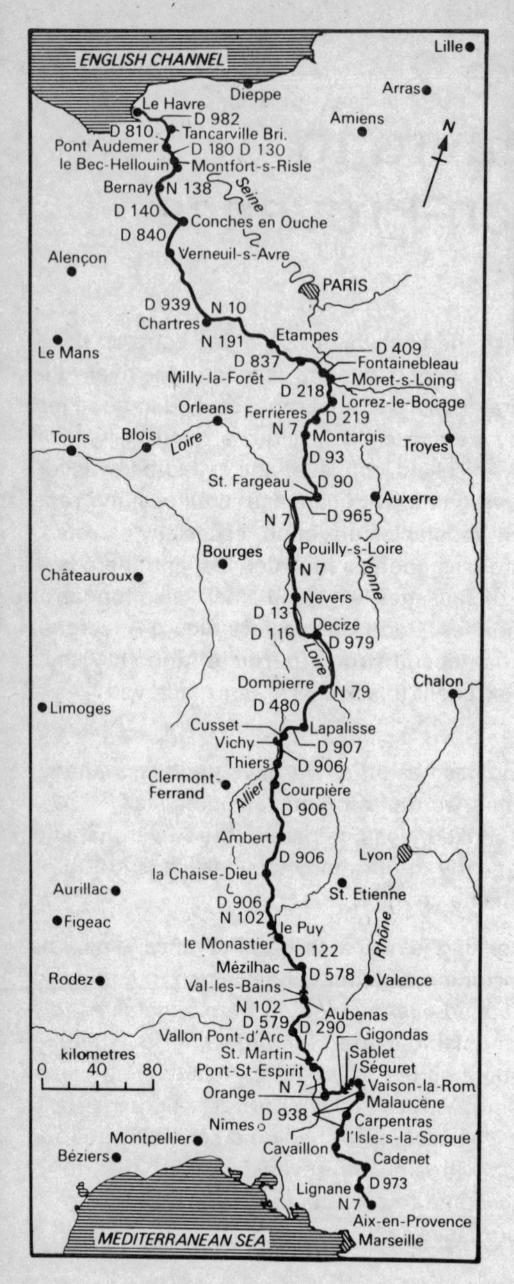
ENGLISH CHANNEL
Lille
Dieppe
Arras
Le Havre
D 982
Amiens
D 810
Tancarville Bri.
Pont Audemer
D 180 D 130
le Bec-Hellouin
Montfort-s-Risle
N
Bernay
N 138
Seine
D 140
Conches en Ouche
D 840
Verneuil-s-Avre
Alençon
PARIS
D 939
N 10
Chartres
Etampes
Le Mans
N 191
D 409
D 837
Fontainebleau
Milly-la-Forêt
Moret-s-Loing
D 218
Lorrez-le-Bocage
Orleans
Ferrières
D 219
N 7
Montargis
Tours
Blois
Loire
Troyes
D 93
St. Fargeau
D 90
Auxerre
N 7
D 965
Pouilly-s-Loire
Bourges
N 7
Yonne
Châteauroux
Nevers
D 13
Decize
D 116
D 979
Loire
Chalon
Dompierre
N 79
Limoges
D 480
Cusset
Lapalisse
Vichy
D 907
Thiers
D 906
Clermont-
Ferrand
Courpière
Allier
D 906
Ambert
D 906
Lyon
la Chaise-Dieu
Aurillac
St. Etienne
D 906
N 102
le Puy
Figeac
Rhône
le Monastier
D 122
Mézilhac
D 578
Rodez
Valence
Val-les-Bains
N 102
Aubenas
D 579
D 290
Vallon Pont-d'Arc
Gigondas
kilometres
St. Martin
Sablet
0 40 80
Pont-St-Espirit
Séguret
N 7
Vaison-la-Rom
Orange
Malaucène
D 938
Nîmes
Carpentras
Montpellier
l'Isle-s-la-Sorgue
Cavaillon
Béziers
Cadenet
D 973
Lignane
N 7
Aix-en-Provence
MEDITERRANEAN SEA
Marseille

Le Havre
PARIS
Aix-en-Provence

Great white wines of the Loire, smoky Pouilly Fumé and Sancerre, have become dear, but Quincy is a fair substitute and Loire Sauvignon has improved greatly. Vouvray is a delight when young, nectar when older. Chinon red and Bourgueil have long been loved by French restaurateurs grown tired of increasing prices for Burgundy and Bordeaux. Gigondas red from the Vaucluse rivals Châteauneuf du Pape and many more red wines near here are excellent value. Baumes de Venise, made from the Muscat grape and fortified, is honey-sweet, delicious and justly fashionable with rich pâtés, fruit, desserts and some cheeses.

A south of Paris route with a chance to see Chartres and Fontainebleau; mostly missing the old N7 it takes in some of the spectacularly rugged Auvergne countryside, the river Allier valley, the superbly lovely hills around Vichy and the valley of the Ardèche river which runs parallel to the Rhône. This canoeing river runs through steep ravines and past little beaches and is excellent for fishing.

Do find time for the diversion from Orange into the Vaucluse to Gigondas – an area of lovely scenery and little wine villages where they see few tourists. A few connoisseurs of 'unknown France' spend their holidays here. Leave time to see Orange, a delightful town.

From other ports you can join the route at Bernay, Conches-en-Ouche or even at Chartres.

Route 2
Le Havre to Aix-en-Provence

Le Havre

I would not stay in Le Havre itself unless necessary. Honfleur, Caudebec, Pont Audemer, Villequier are all so near.

Chaumette, 17 rue Racine, 35.43.66.80: Christine Fréchet is a delightful cook, always experimenting and improving. Fish is local, absolutely fresh, never frozen, fresh cooked for you, so you can't hurry. Try brioches filled with mussels in wine; egg in red pepper and cream jelly; Toulouse ragout. Rather pricey. Menu E–F. Shut Saturday lunch, Sunday; Easter; 15 days August.

Huitrière, 4 rue Paris, 35.21.48.48: opposite P & O ferry. Fish. Readers love it. Try stuffed oysters, moules soubise (mussels in onion purée, after Prince de Soubise, friend of Louis XV). Menus B–D. Shut Mondays.

Charolais, 134 Cours République, 35.25.29.34: useful overnight. 1838 house (once the Mairie), last-century furnishings, modern

Le Havre owes a debt to Auguste Perret, Le Corbusier's teacher, who persuaded planners and architects that reinforced concrete is as acceptable as brick and stone. After terrible war destruction, it was replanned on a gridiron system, with concrete, glass and steel girders. For me it lacks intimacy and the untidy warmth of older French towns.

Perret's huge church of St Joseph, with an 8-sided belfry 116m (348ft) high, looks like a rocket on a launching pad. Inside is an awesome lantern tower and remarkable lighting effects by coloured glass set in the walls. Most interesting.

The Malraux Museum, in glass and steel, facing the sea, has splendid light to show off paintings, including seventy by Dufy (born in Le Havre), others by Sisley and Pissarro, and 200 by Boudin, son of an Honfleur pilot who brought together young painters to give birth to Impressionism. He

plumbing. Friendly. Rooms A–C. Shut 15 February–1 March. English spoken.

Monaco, 16 rue Paris, 35.42.21.01: Max Lucas' cooking still delights Britons. Superb Duclair duck. Menus B(weekdays)–F. Rooms A–D. Shut 20–31 December; Monday off-season.

At Ste-Adresse, posher suburb NE on cape with views – Yves Page, 7 place Clémenceau, 35.46.06.09: delightful; superb fresh fish; live lobster tank. Lovely terrace with fine views of boats and sea. Cosy open fire for winter. Menus D, G (dégustations). Shut 10 August–2 September; Sunday evening, Monday.

Bon Séjour, 3 place Clémenceau, 35.46.19.69: another with sea views, good fish, live lobster tank. Good pâtisseries. Air-conditioned. Varied wine cellar. Menus C, D, G. Open all year.

Phares, 29 rue Gén-de-Gaulle, 35.46.31.86: good b-and-b hotel; friendly, helpful owners speak English. Rooms A–D. Shut 27 December–10 January.

persuaded 15-year-old Claude Monet to switch from caricature to landscape painting.

Avenue Foch, designed to be a modern Champs-Élysées, has shops as smart and expensive as Paris. Arcaded rue de Paris, from the huge town hall square towards the port, is useful for window shopping in rain and wind – elegant clothes, tempting food. Try Rôtisserie Gambetta in place Gambetta for pâté, cheese, wine (open Sundays).

D982 Tancarville bridge (toll) (29km) D810 Pont Audemer (19km)

Tancarville-Ecluse (under bridge) – Marine, 35.39.77.15: old ferry inn of pre-bridge days; attractive garden, lawns by river Seine. Cheaper menu includes half-bottle wine (Gros-Plant or red Bordeaux); good choice on

Little port on several branches of river Risle. One of my favourite hideaways for 40 years; many of its old wood and brick riverside houses blessedly survived war damage; so did the streets and courtyards off rue

second menu. Good value; traditional cooking. Menus C, E. Rooms C, D. Shut Sunday evening, Monday; 15 August–5 September.

Pont Audemer – Auberge du Vieux Puits, 6 rue Notre-Dame du Pré, 32.41.01.48: sheer delight. New rooms added carefully have not harmed the 17th-century house nor lovely garden. Local legend about the well (puits). Delicious cooking of traditional dishes, many Norman, so lots of cream. Try trout, Calvados sorbet, duck with cherries. Meals pricey. Beautifully restored house with antiques, engravings, beams, flagstones, huge fires. Two of 14 bedrooms. Menu G. Rooms B–E. (must take dinner). Shut 27 June–7 July; mid-December–mid-January; Monday evenings, Tuesdays.

At Tourville, 3km S from Pont Audemer – off D139 – Ricardiere, 32.41.09.14: bed and breakfast in charming old country house and pavillon in grounds; all rooms have own bathrooms. Old trees, trout stream in garden. Rooms D.

de la République, and St Ouen church, started in the 11th century. Its superb Renaissance stained glass by no means clashes with modern windows by Max Ingrand, with their unusual use of colour. Market down main street. Mondays and Fridays. Many cobbled streets and little bridges. Walk round.

D180 Corneville-sur-Risle, D130 Appeville-Annebault, Montfort-sur-Risle, Le Bec-Hellouin (28km)	Corneville – Cloches, 32.57.01.04: 'all Normandy on your plate.' Fine old regional cooking; good selection of Loire wines. Fine views from enclosed 'winter garden'. 6km from Pont Audemer. Menu D. Rooms C–E. Shut Monday, Tuesday lunch; 15 February–1 March; 15 November–15 December. For Le Bec-Hellouin and Brionne see Route 1	Through green valley of Risle, with sleepy villages, small towns, Corneville-sur-Risle called jokingly Corneville-les-Cloches (the Bells) after operetta by Planquette of around 1900. Unfortunate Marquis de la Roche Thulon, having donated carillon of 12 bells to the church, could not pay for them. At Hôtel des Cloches you can hear them – on paying a fee (Easter–September). Appeville-Annebault: inside 16th-century church is collection of Brothers of Charity staffs. Montfort is pretty – willows overhanging stream; forest to its streets; overlooked by ruined castle built by King John of England.
N138 Bernay (15km)	See Route 1	
D140 to Conches-en-Ouche (49km)	Conches – Toque Blanche, 18 place Carnot 32.30.01.54: superb Norman cooking in an old Norman building, with staff dressed in old Norman costume. Plenty of cream, but also Fisherman's Dish of steamed salmon, monkfish and plaice in walnut oil, gorgeous grilled oysters with cream of chives; game in season. Super cheeses. With every meal a Trou Normand for the digestion – Calvados sorbet. 'Best apple and pear cider in Normandy' and Calvados 10–100 years old. Menu D–E. Shut Monday, Tuesday evening.	From Bernay you pass Château de Beaumesnil, a 17th-century house, reflected in its moat, in a classical French park; farm maintained since 1640; ponds; labyrinth of yews made from foundations of mediaeval dungeons. Curious line of owners, from Harcourt family to Lord Willoughby (a present from Henry V), Marquis of Nonant, Grand Duke Dimitri of Russia and Jean de Furstenberg. A gorgeous house.

D840 Verneuil-sur-Avre (22km)

Clos, 98 rue Ferté-Vidame, 32.32.21.81: small turreted manor in gorgeous garden. Delightful rooms with antique furniture. Superb classical cooking by Patrick Simon, Master Chef of France. Relais et Châteaux hotel, so not cheap! Charming flowered terrace. Menus F–G. Rooms F–G. Shut December, January.

Restaurant shut Mondays. Saumon, 89 place Madeleine, 32.32.02.36: Alain Simon, son of Patrick at Le Clos, has taken over old post inn. Brightened the dining room, improved the cooking. Very good value. One very cheap menu. Small, simple, charming bedrooms (most with bathrooms). Menus A, D. Rooms C-D. Shut 22 December–4 January.

Flamboyant tower of La Madeleine church as fine as Butter Tower of Rouen, and similarly paid for by rich gourmands who in return could eat butter during Lent. Fine old houses nearby.

D939 Chartres (56km)

Vieille Maison, 5 rue Lait, 37.34.10.67: mediaeval house by cathedral. Attractive restaurant among beams with splendid fireplace and flowery patio. Excellent cooking of fresh market produce. Try Saint-Jacques with asparagus tips, pigeon and mushroom pie. Nice atmosphere. Menus E–G. Shut Sunday evening, Monday; 5–17 January; 25 June–9 July.

Buisson Ardent, 10 rue Lait, 37.34.04.66: excellent value; imaginative cooking; warm atmosphere. Menus A–E. Shut Sunday evening,

The city on the river Eure is dominated by its cathedral on a hill; it is the best-proportioned and one of the most impressive churches in the world; consecrated in 1260, it is rather dark and sombre inside, but has unsurpassable mediaeval stained glass windows. The terrace has good views over the river, and the Bishop's Palace here is now a museum with Flemish tapestries and paintings. The original cathedrals was burned down in 1194, and to build the new one everyone from paupers to princes gave their money and labour; monks, peasants

	Tuesday evening, Wednesday. Écu, 28 rue Grand-Faubourg, 37.21.34.59: country style; pleasant, amiable service. Good value. Try veal Vallée d'Auge, smoked pork, grilled fish. Menu A, C, E. Rooms A–D. Shut 15 days in February.	and ladies of the manor worked together on the scaffolding. Take time to see Renaissance houses around cathedral and wander down to river to see old bridges and houses. A charming town. Good market near cathedral.
N10, then N191 to Étampes (58km)	80km (50 miles) from Paris, so some Parisian prices and summer closures. Europe (A l'Escargot), rue St Jacques, 64.94.02.96: simple family hotel. Cheap meals and wine. Good value; inconvenient closing. Try snails, lamb. Menu A (shut Wednesdays). Rooms B. Shut 20 June–28 July. At Chalo-St-Mars (7km on D21) – Alouettes, 64.95.44.27: stone walls, beams, huge open fire in 18th-century auberge. Traditional French cooking (style of Curnonsky, author of *La France Gastronomique* – 32 volumes!) Menus C–E. Shut February.	In very attractive position on Chalouette river, with riverside walks; many lovely old buildings. In 14th century was seat of ruling regent, Abbé St Denis, while Louis VII was fighting a Crusade, and it rivalled Paris. Lovely drive in Chalouette valley through very pleasant villages – Chalo-St-Mars, Moulinex. Chalou (D21, D160). At Bierville (D49) is L'Épi d'Or, France's first youth hostel (opened 1929).
D837 Milly-la-Forêt (26km)	Milly–Moustier, 41 bis rue Langlois, 84.98.92.52: beautiful 14th-century chapel converted. Good simple cooking of excellent ingredients. Michelin star; rather pricey. Menus D–G. Shut Monday, Tuesday; part February.	Old town on edge of Fontainebleau forest, its fine buildings include market halls made entirely of oak. Chapel of St Blaise-des-Simples (12th-century) restored in 1958. Tomb of Jean Cocteau (1889–1963), one of the greatest writers, artists and playwrights of all

Milly-la-Forêt continued	At Auvers (4km S by D948) – Auberge Auvers Galant, 64.24.51.02: good food at reasonable prices. Menus B–E. Shut Monday evenings, Tuesdays; February.	time. He decorated the chapel in 1959 with lovely drawings of the Crown of Thorns and the Resurrection. 5km north is Château de Courances, magnificent 17th-century building in a park laid out by Le Notre, who also laid out Versailles and Fontainebleau gardens; it is packed with moats, ornamental lakes, waterfalls and fish ponds; you can visit it on Saturdays, Sundays and public holidays.
D837, D409 Fontainebleau (20km)	Most restaurants and hotels are dear and touristy. Ile de France, 128 rue France, 64.22.85.15: attractive 19th-century house in pretty garden; excellent retreat from tourist crowds visiting Fontainebleau palace. Very cheap menus are splendid value. Some Chinese influence by chef from Hong Kong, but classic French dishes, too (coquelet Vallée d'Auge; pintadeau à l'armagnac). Menus A–C. Rooms (some in garden pavillon) D. Open all year. Dauphin, 24 rue Grande, 64.22.27.04; good value. Try duck confit with cèpes; monkfish in cream of red pepper. Menus A, D. Shut February; first week September; Tuesday evenings, Wednesdays.	Charming drive through the wild forest of pines, oaks and beeches; notices name some aged trees as if they were dogs, while others bear legends like 'Stag and Boar Crossing'. Rocks used as climbers' training grounds and torrents rushing between them. The château, not so impressive as Versailles, has as much historic importance and as much atmosphere. Louis VII began it, but the flamboyant Francis I made it into a palace, and brought in Italians Primatice and Rosso to decorate it. Benvenuto Cellini worked here for him and Francis bought the *Mona Lisa* to decorate a room – all for the love of his mistress. Henry II kept his mistress Diane de Poitiers here too, and made her a special garden. When he died, his wife, Catherine de Medici, took it over and sent Diane packing to Château de

Chaumont on the Loire. Louis XIV had the garden laid out; Napoleon I converted part of the château as his living quarters, imprisoned the Pope here, abdicated in the Red Room, and said farewell to his Old Guard in the courtyard. The guided tour shows you most things, but on most weekdays you can also see Napoleon's and Josephine's rooms and those of Pope Pius VII. The château abounds in secretive nooks and crannies and back staircases, ideal for intrigue – or parties.

N6 to Moret-Loing, D218 to Lorrez D219 to Ferrières. Then either N7 or small forest roads to Montargis (51km)

Flagy (left eastward from D218 at Villecerf on D22, 3km) – Moulin, 1.60.96.67.89: idyllic little watermill from 13th century converted into one of our favourite small inns in France. Millstream washes the walls; mill wheels remain in the beamed lounge; the dining room overlooks the stream and garden with huge log fire for winter; eat under the willows in summer. Beamed bedrooms with old country furniture. Good regional cooking with a touch of modern. Excellent value. Try fillet of beef with blue cheese sauce and home-made pasta; fricassé of kidneys and sweetbreads in cider and chervil. Superb cheeseboard. House wine is Beaujolais Villages. Menus C-E. Rooms B-D. Shut Sunday evening, Monday; 15–25 September; 18 December–22 January.

Charming route, once you leave the N6, through farming hamlets with fine old churches, bakers' shops, bars where all the locals put everything on the slate. Even if not staying or eating at the delicious little Moulin, do divert to look at Flagy. See the main square with church, real village shops and bar, walk through the narrow roads over little bridges to main bridge by the mill. Here by the millstream is the lavoir where village women still do their washing.

Montargis – little town of many streams; meeting place of Loing, Puiseaux and Vernisson waterways. Pleasant walks beside them.

Montargis – Gloire, 74 ave Gén-de-Gaulle, 38.85.04.69: fine old house where Jean-Louis Jolly offers menus fairly cheap by Michelin-star standards. One French guide accused him of not being Jolly any more. Certainly his cooking must be taken seriously. Excellent escalope of guinea fowl with sweetbreads and langoustines and sole with lobster sauce. Menus C–F. Rooms A–C. Shut Tuesday evening, Wednesday; 15–28 August; 1–27 February.

Petit Relais, 52 ave Gen-de-Gaulle, 38.98.00.85: small, rustic interior, flowered terrace. Cooking over wood fire. Menu A. Rooms A. Shut Tuesdays; 23 December–15 January.

D93, D90 St Fargeau (51km)

Route beside canal and river Loing to this nice old country town with a rose-pink château, reconstructed in 1752; a pentagon with huge round towers and an elegant interior courtyard which can be visited (shut Tuesdays and February); so can the beautiful park, with a large lake.

D965, N7 Pouilly-sur-Loire (59km)

See Route 8

(Round the Loire, page 242)

N7 Nevers (40km)

See Route 8

(Round the Loire, page 243)

On the Loire where the river Nièvre joins it, Nevers is still famous for beautiful glass and enamelcraft introduced from Italy in 1575 (see

Museum, rue St Martin); it is also steeped in church history and has yet another much-visited cathedral, plus a modern church looking as solid as a Nazi West Wall but interesting inside; it is called Ste Bernadette du Banlay, after Ste Bernadette of Lourdes, whose uncorrupted body is displayed macabrely in a coffin of bronze and glass in the Convent of St Gildard in Nevers where she died. I liked the convent story of their 18th-century parrot called Vert-Vert who was so highly educated in Christian doctrine that the monks of Nantes asked to borrow him. Alas, *en route*, the Loire sailors taught him so much blaspheming that the monks sentenced him to solitary and silence. He died of indigestion, probably bottling up his comments on the Brethren of Nantes.

Lovely Renaissance Ducal Palace with slim towers.

D13, D116 Decize (34km) D979 right on N79 to Dompierre then D480 through Besbre valley to Lapalisse (87km)

Decize – Agriculture, 20 route des Moulins, 86.25.05.38: simple Logis with good value meals. Menus A–D. Rooms A–C. Shut Sundays in winter; 1–20 October.

Lapalisse – Lion des Flandres, 40 rue Pres-Roosevelt, 70.99.06.75: pleasant simple, modern; good value; good traditional cooking. Menus A, C, E. Rooms B–C. Shut Mondays; 15–30 December, 1–31 January.

Decize – built on an island in the Loire river on a steep hill where the Dukes of Nevers once had their castle, it has a lovely half-mile promenade of massive plane trees. On route, Chevenon Castle, poised to control the valley. Built in 14th century by a commander of Charles V regime; later centre for looting and brigandry, typical of the Wars of Religion in France. (D480 follows Besore valley, from where river joins

Lapalisse continued

Loire past several mediaeval châteaux. Gardens of Château Beauvoir open.)

Lapalisse straddles river Besbre; dominated by 12th-century fortress converted to Italian Renaissance style in 15th century by craftsmen from Florence. Renaissance furniture; Flemish tapestries.

D907 to Cusset (23km) 3km to Vichy

Nièvre, 17 ave Gramont, 70.31.82.77: old-style bistro with rooms. Old-style cooking. Menus A(weekday)–C. Rooms A–C. Shut 7–15 November; restaurant Mondays.

Petit Vichy, 22 place Epinat, 70.59.86.42: little restaurant with good regional cooking. Try sauté Auvergne chicken. Menu C. Shut Wednesday.

At Bellerive over river bridge – Marcotel et Restaurant Châteaubriand, 70.32.34.00: modern, with very traditional cooking. Delicious entrecôte St Claude (with spinach, cream, Armagnac). Lovely rich sauces. Very good meat. Outstanding wine list, from local to grand crus; 'almost all Champagnes'. Views over Allier river. Very comfortable. Menus C–F. Rooms E. Shut Sunday evening; Monday lunch in winter; 13–29 December.

At Abrest (4km on D906 to Thiers) – Colombière, 70.98.69.15: lovely views

Vichy – elegant, fashionable and expensive spa with full season of shows in the Grand Casino, May–September, and many nightclubs and pricey restaurants where the well-loaded undo the good done to them in the thermal establishments. Parc des Sources is lovely. Allier lake, 4km (2½ miles) long, is a famous water-sports centre for sailing, water-skiing, canoeing, pedalos, trout fishing, a biggish sandy beach. The Romans discovered the advantages of the strongly alkaline waters of the Célestine spring. Madame de Sévigné, whose home is now the Hôtel Pavillon Sévigné, said in the 18th century that 'the countryside alone would cure me', and I feel the same today; but Napoleon III, spa addict, started the real vogue for Vichy in 1861. Lovely public gardens beside the river Allier.

	over Allier valley; new façade. Very good cooking by Michel Sabot (10 years in kitchen) lures readers. Some modern touches to traditional dishes. Excellent value. Menus A–D. Rooms C. Shut Sunday evening, Monday in winter; mid-January–mid-February. Eperons, ave Hauterive, 70.32.24.86: I cannot resist a riverside friture with attractive summer terrace, such low-priced menus, and such a distinguished name. Menus A, C. Shut 10 November–10 December.	
D906 Thiers (35km)	Pont-de-Dore, 6km SW by N89 – Avenue, 73.80.10.14: known for regional cooking. Menus A, D. Rooms A, B. Shut Sunday evening, Monday lunch; 20 December–10 January.	An attractive road to Thiers, which is beautifully sited above a gorge of the river Durolle, with super views; well worth spending time looking at the very beautiful and photogenic 15th-century timbered houses, especially in place du Pirou and surrounding streets; best views with orientation table from Terrasse du Rempart; you can see the mountains of Dore and Dombes.
D906 Courpière (16km)	Clef des Champs, route d'Ambert (3.5km on D906), 73.53.01.83: Serge and Claudette Helstroffer, who speak English, have run this wayside restaurant with nice view and lovely garden for ten years. My readers are very happy with their regional cooking with fine old dishes like boeuf Bourguignon, and their fish specialities;	At the entrance to a gorge of the river Durolle, it is loved by fishermen – also by gourmets for its raspberries and the dishes produced from them. Château de la Barge, on D906, is beautifully kept and, with huge round towers, makes a fine picture, but can be visited only on Tuesday afternoons – exterior and chapel.

Courpière continued

cheapest menu a real bargain. Auvergne wines cheap, too. Menu A, B, C. Shut first week July; Mondays.

For Château d'Aulteribe you turn off D906 6km before Courpière and take D223, winding uphill; the château was rebuilt to replace a severely practical feudal castle once owned by Lafayette; contains beautiful Louis XV and Louis XVI furniture, Flanders tapestry, and portraits by well-known artists of Henry IV, Richelieu and the unfortunate Mademoiselle de Fontages, mistress of Louis XIV; described as 'beautiful as an angel, stupid as a basket', she died in childbirth when 20 'from wounds received on active service' as the bitchy Madame de Sévigné said.

D906 Ambert (39km)

Livradois, 1 place Livradois, 73.82.10.01: Extraordinary! My favourite French gastronomic writer Marc de Champérard is very rude about Christian Parrain's cooking. Most of my readers love it. 'A memorable meal' writes one. Depends whether you like rich Auvergne dishes cooked the *old* way. Chance to try Ambert blue cheese with Auvergne wine. Menus A, C, E, G. Rooms A–C. Shut 5–12 January; 10–30 November; restaurant shut Sunday evening, Monday in winter.

La Dore, 58 ave Mar-Foch, 73.82.00.58: very good cheap 4-course menu and very cheap house wine. A bargain. Menus A–C. Rooms A–C. Shut Wednesday except July, August.

Papermaking centre since 15th century, with 300 papermills. Moulin Richard de Bas has been renovated. Watch paper being handmade (5½km E by N496 and D57).

Odd round town hall. In Religious Wars Protestant leader Merle kept Catholics out by manning walls with statues from local churches.

D906 La Chaise Dieu (33km)

Tremblant, 71.00.01.85: Jean Boyer's touch of old France in a modern Logis still delights readers. Bargain 4- and 5-course meals. He makes all his own charcuterie, desserts, pâtisseries, ice-creams, cooks lovely old dishes like local trout in almonds, guinea fowl, chicken liver soufflé, salmon mousse, coq au vin. Cheapest menu is incredibly good value. So is red Ventoux house wine. Garden terrace. Menus A–D. Rooms A–D. Shut 15 November–15 April.

Lion d'Or, 71.00.01.58: Mme Chambon has taken over from her husband in this pleasant, friendly hotel opposite the abbey. Offers the same honest, traditional meals at low prices. Menus A, C. Rooms A–C. Shut 1 November–Easter.

A hilltop village; the 14th-century abbey is like an ecclesiastical art museum, with magnificent 16th-century tapestries of Bible scenes from Brussels and Arras and a huge mural 'La Danse Macabre'. The abbey boasted some colourful abbots – two royal bastards: one, son of Henry II, an assassin, later killed in a duel; the other, son of Charles IX, appointed when aged 13. Cardinal Rohan, 'not very strong in Devotion, strong in love of women', hid there. Richelieu 'added it to his benefices' – i.e. stole it.

D906 N102 Le Puy (44km)

Cygne, 47 boulevard Maréchal-Fayolle, 71.09.32.36: town centre. Pavement terrace, another viewing old town. Reasonably priced meals with good choice. Traditional cooking. New rooms with bathrooms. Menus A–F. Rooms B–F. Shut December, January, February. Restaurant Thursdays.

At Bizac (12km S on N88) – Diligence, 71.03.11.50: comfortable rooms with bathrooms; modern. Near Lake Bouchet. Good family cooking; salmon, duck, mountain sausage. Good

Hilly winding road through the extraordinary volcanic hills. Le Puy is an incredible place, surprising even the most sophisticated traveller; volcanic peaks stand within the town; on top of one, Le Rocher St Michel, is an 11th-century Romanesque chapel, reached by steep steps and looking almost like a minaret. On the biggest peak, Rocher Corneille, 750m (2460ft) high, is a 112,000kg (110-ton) statue of Notre-Dame de France, made from 213 cannons captured from the Russians at Sebastopol in the Crimean War. The cathedral, a Romanesque

Le Puy continued	value. Menu A. Rooms A–C. Shut Friday evening, Saturday lunch; January.	building of the 12th century, also has a slightly Oriental look and is impressive inside and out. I find the old abbey cloisters most attractive with tranquil arcades, lawns, and a glimpse of the cathedral. They make a monk's life seem quite alluring. Strange contrast in this town between its oddly attractive moon-like rocks and lush, green country around; a lacemakers' town for centuries, lace shops abound; its lace is exquisite – and very dear.
D535 to Le Monastier, D122 to Mézilhac D578 Vals-les-Bains (92km)	At Antraigues, 8km before Vals on D578 – Lo Podello, 75.38.71.48: Hélène Baissade, painter, interior decorator, still cooks old country dishes from fresh local Ardèche produce in her home, beautifully decorated in old local style. Nothing from the freezer. Permanent exhibition of her own paintings. My readers love her and her cooking. Meals B–F (book). Shut Thursdays in winter.	A winding mountainous route with wonderful scenery, but harder driving than the main road through Aubenas, Vals is a charming town on the river Yolane near where it meets the Ardèche and surrounded by lovely hills varying from deep woods to open pastures, sweeping down to rivers which flow through tiny villages and meadows to deep spectacular gorges.
	Vals les Bains – Grand Hôtel des Bains, 75.94.65.55: I love it. Elegance of the 1860s with bedrooms beautifully furnished, high ceilings, big terrace overlooking gardens and park by a forest of cedars. Good cuisine, good choice; outstanding river fish. Old-style service. Menu D–F. Rooms C–F. Shut early October–mid-May.	Suddenly rediscovered, Vals can get full in midsummer; a pretty place with gardens, swimming pools, a casino, curative baths and a 'bar' on the river promenade offering spa water, which is prescribed for 'sedating the stomach and stimulating the liver'; but note also, inscribed in the pavement of the main shopping street (rue

Europe, 86 rue Jean-Jaurès, 75.37.43.94: over 38 years Albert Mazet has become an institution and example to other hotelkeepers. My readers love his hotel. He cooks with the same enthusiasm and still in the great French manner, still does his own shopping, accepting nothing but the best, relying on fresh seasonal dishes. And everyone smiles. Attractive dining room and lounge. Sensible wine list, good Côtes-du-Rhône, including St Joseph and Gigondas. Menus B–E (book). Rooms D. Shut 10 October–10 April.

Vivarais, rue C.-Expilly, 75.94.65.85: in a charming dining room, chef-patron Christiane Giuliani offers a wide choice of dishes, including a 'slimmer's' meal, another with fine local wines, and a card of Ardèchoise dishes including dish of local hams and sausages, such as Cervelas and Jésus. Terrace overlooking gardens, with grill. Menus C–E. Rooms E–F. Restaurant shut 2 January–3 February.

Lyon, 11 avenue Farincourt, 75.37.43.70: pleasant house with arcaded dining terrace. Sunbathing terrace. Comfortable. Bedrooms improved. Menus C–E. Rooms D, E. Shut 3 October–1 April.

Jeans-Jaurès), this advice: A GOOD MEAL DESERVES A GOOD WINE.

The Ardèche is superb for fishing and canoeing, from open riverside beaches to spectacular steep gorges. A river best seen from a canoe – but for me that was 50 years ago!

N102 Aubenas (6km)	On N104 Privas 16km – Col d'Escrinet (Hotel Panoramique), St Etienne de Boulogne, 75.87.10.11: modern; panoramic views to Cévennes hills over Ardèche valley; garden, park with pool; terraces to most bedrooms. Good meals; try veal kidneys in St Peray wine; local freshwater crayfish tails. Menus B, D, E. Rooms D–F. Shut mid-November–mid-March.	Château owned since the 12th century by famous local families, but altered through the years, is now the town hall. Described by French experts as 'rude', meaning rugged; the courtyard is attractive; you can visit it throughout July and August, Saturdays and Sundays only in June. Aubenas makes delicious marrons glacés. Lovely views as you enter town, also from D259 and from Table d'Orientation 100m (330ft) from château.
N102 right on D579 to Vallon Pont d'Arc Follow D290 through Les Gorges d'Ardèche to St Martin, then D901 to cross Rhône at Pont St Esprit (80km)	Vallon Pont d'Arc – Manoir de Raveyron, rue Henri-Barbusse, 75.88.03.59: in a formidable stone manor, Charles Bataille, well-known Parisian chef, has 'retired' here to cook excellent meals at bargain prices. Dishes as varied as snails in wild fennel, free-range chicken with crayfish sauce, fig tart. Menus A, B, D. Rooms B. Shut 1 October–5 March.	This is a hard driving road over the Corniche, and you can skip it by taking N102 and N86 parallel with the Rhône, but it has truly magnificent scenery, gorges and one splendid view after another. At Vogué, there is a 12th- to 17th-century castle you can visit. Bridge over the Rhône at Pont St Esprit called 'the beginning of Provence'.
D994, N7 Orange (24km)	Arène, place de Langes, 90.34.10.95: hotel now separated from restaurant (Le Garden) alongside; bedrooms much improved – all with bath or shower and WC. Comfortable lounge, good breakfasts. Nice convenient retreat from busy Orange. Rooms C–E. Shut 1 November–15 December.	Orange is one of the most interesting, charming and surprising cities in southern France. It has a Roman theatre which is the best preserved in Europe and holds 10,000 spectators. The city still has its imperial statue of Augustus Caesar, the third biggest triumphal arch in Europe, celebrating Julius Caesar's victories over the Gauls and the Greek-

Pigraillet, chemin Colline-St-Eutrope, 90.34.44.25: reasonable price menus for Michelin-star and such good classical cooking. Carte dearer. Some splendid dishes – cassoulet with goose, duck in honey, crab, ravioli, goats' cheese with walnut bread, super desserts. Pretty, fine position. Garden for summer meals, pool, boules. Menus C–F. Shut Sunday evening, Monday; 1 December–31 January.

Le Forum, 3 rue Mazeau, 90.34.01.09: good value. Menu C. Shut 15–30 September; 20 December–3 January.

At Rochegude, 14km NW by N7, D976, D11, D117 – Château de Rochegude, 75.04.81.88: huge magnificent 12th-century fortress, Relais et Châteaux hotel in park; superb air-conditioned rooms, very costly. Mediaeval dining room, lightened by glass bay. Young chef. Michelin star. Superb local lamb; tempting gâteaux. Excellent Châteauneuf wines. Menus E, F(lunch), G(dinner). Rooms E–G. Restaurant shut early January–early March; Mondays.

Massilian fleet. Orange gave its name to the Dutch Royal family and thus to the Irish Protestant political movement. It has nothing to do with oranges; the name came from the Latin. William the Silent inherited the city in 1559 from the Chalon family and the Dutch prince tore down much of the Roman remains to fortify it, but used the theatre as part of the city wall. After the French got Orange back, under the Treaty of Utrecht, Louis XIV called the theatre 'the finest wall in my kingdom'. The Dutch kept the title 'Prince of Orange'. For a few years during the reign of William of Orange (William III), the town was actually united with England. And in the museum is a room full of paintings by Sir Frank Brangwyn.

Delightful old houses and tree-lined squares and avenues.

Rochegude's Cave des Vignerons has tastings of wine which Thomas Jefferson, when US Ambassador in Paris, sent to George Washington. At Château (see hotels) was discovered a superb Roman statue of Bacchus, now in Paris, museum of St Germain en Laye.

D975 right on D8, then left on D7 (just before Vacqueyras) to Gigondas, Sablet, D23 Séguret D88, D977 to Vaison-la-Romaine (39km)

Montmirail (on D7, 6km before Gigondas), 90.65.84.01: attractive, elegant modern hotel; garden; pool. Excellent cooking. Provençal dishes. Try also tapenade (anchovy paste with capers, olives, tuna). Nice rooms. Remote – 'when you are lost you have arrived'! Menus C–F. Rooms E. Shut 1 December–1 March.

Gigondas – Florets, 90.65.85.01: my old inn made from a remote farmhouse now extended, highly organized and popular, so book. Provençal dishes including pieds et paquets (tripe stuffed with bacon and parsley in sauce with boned trotters). Vacqueyras wine from own vineyards. Menus C–E. Rooms D. Shut January, February; Wednesdays.

Céguret – Table du Comtat, 90.36.91.49: pricey, fashionable, but good flavoursome dishes by Master Chef of France; panoramic restaurant. Regional country style bedrooms, small pool. Book. Menus F, G. Rooms E–G. Shut Tuesday evenings, Wednesdays except July–August; 22 November–8 December; February.

Vaison-la-Romaine – Beffroi (upper town) 90.36.04.71: 16th-century house in old town; shady terrace; large beautifully furnished

Detour worth every kilometre for scenery and experience. Beautiful wild country of Vaucluse, with hamlets, farms and vineyards where you can taste local red wine. Gigondas' hilltop church and village seem to belong to another century. Sablet, too.

Séguret pulls more visitors. Stuck on a cliffside of Dentelles-de-Montmirail: mediaeval village revitalized by craftsmen. Steep streets, superb views. Park car at entrance.

Vaison-la-Romaine is a delightful 19th-century market town; Roman town with excavated villas, theatre, statues, murals, mosaics and public lavatories, and a mediaeval town high on a hill, once abandoned, now inhabited. Single span Roman bridge joins old and newer towns.

Well worth tarrying and exploring villages and hamlets. Wines under-estimated until recently. Not only now well-known Gigondas and Vacqueyras but look for cheaper, less known but very quaffable red Sablet (smooth, fruity), Tricastin red, Roaix red (drink 2–4 years old), Séguret red (robust for travelling, best 3–4 years old), Chusclan rosé (nearly as good as Tavel), Valréas red (velvety, under-rated, drink at least 3 years old). Baumes de Venise

bedrooms. Menus C–D shut Tuesday lunch, Mondays Rooms E. Shut mid-November–mid-March.

Many small excellent-value restaurants in lower town.

Try Théâtre Romain, place Chanoine-Sautel, 90.36.05.87: Menu A–B (shut Thursdays). Rooms A–C. Shut November; 15 February.

At Rasteau (D675, D69 – 9km) – Bellerive, 90.46.10.20: very modern, interesting Relais du Silence. Spectacular views over Ouvèze river to Mont Ventoux. Very comfortable. Pool. Menus C–G. Rooms E. Shut 2 January–15 March.

strong sweet white, fashionable now with foie gras, desserts, cheese. Taste Gigondas at Domaine St Gayon (Roger Meffre).

D938
Malaucène
Carpentras
(27km)

Safari, ave Jean-Henry Fabre, 90.63.35.35: one of few really modern, 'boxy' hotels my readers love. Very well run, happy atmosphere and service. Light, cheerful bedrooms have balconies. In pleasant grounds are self-catering studios (weekly lets). Menus B–F. Rooms E. Open all year.

Rapière du Comtat, 47 boulevard Nord, 90.67.20.03: simple, happy, friendly restaurant with cheap, good value menus. Good fish and fish soup. Open terrace with mountain views. Menus A, C, D. Shut Sunday evening, Monday in winter; Tuesday in April–September; 15 December–15 January.

Through Grozau valley. From Malaucène take D974 up Mont Ventoux (1909m – 6262ft); extinct volcano covered with pine, oaks and beech, giving way to bare rock, murderously hot in summer and hazy midday. To see view in summer, go early morning. You may see Alps, Vercors, Cévennes, even Marseille. Windy all year. I remember 1930s racing car hill climbs up Ventoux. Carpentras is a market town with lively fruit stalls; a wine town, too, and known in France for its 'berlingots', a sweet like a caramel bull's eye. Carpentras has a Roman triumphal arch, built, as in Orange, by retired Roman legionaries who settled in the town. It has also the oldest

Carpentras continued

At Monteux (5km SW on D13) – Saule Pleureur, quartier Beauregard, 90.62.01.35: talented chef Michel Philibert (aged 33) is making French gastronomes sit up with his imaginative dishes made with local ingredients. Tian de brandade (creamed salt cod) much nicer than it sounds, chicken bouillon with truffles delicious. Modern, charming, isolated. Menus B (lunch), E, F, G. Shut Tuesday evening, Wednesday; 2 weeks November; 3 weeks March.

synagogue in France, last relic of a 16th-century ghetto. Market town for grapes, melons, almonds, tomatoes, garlic, herbs.

D938 L'Isle-sur-la-Sorgue to Cavaillon (27km)

Near Belleron, 6km N of L'Isle-sur-la-Sorgue – Grangette, 90.20.00.77: very attractive hotel in big garden with pool; fine views; quiet. A discovery. Menus D–G. Rooms F–G. Open all year.

Cavaillon – Nicolet, 13 place Gambetta, 90.78.01.56: not dear for the fine, careful cooking of Alain Nicolet. Seasonal dishes. Do try his honey profiteroles and his own bread. Nice atmosphere. Polite service. Menus C–F. Shut Sunday, Monday; 10–25 February; 1–13 July.

Fontaine de Vaucluse (E 9km on D25 from just before L'Isle) – small village among rocks which attracts 1 million visitors a year owing to the source of river emerging from a spectacular deep cavern (½-hr walk) and because Italian 14th-century poet Petrarch lived here pouring out his hopeless love for Laura.

Cavaillon – famous for melons, known well for other fruit and for vegetables, it has a splendid market every day in summer in place du Clos. A genuine little country town with the atmosphere of Provence. Behind the high altar of the old cathedral is a picture by Mignard of a bishop getting the better of the Coulobre, a man-eating monster who it was thought inhabited these parts in the Middle Ages.

D973 Cadenet (33km) D943, D543 to join N7 at Lignane (26km) N7 to Aix-en-Provence (6km)

Cadenet – Ombrelles, ave Gare, 94.68.02.40: pleasant modern Logis with good classical cooking and very fair prices. Menus C–F. Rooms A–C. Shut Sunday evening, Monday low season; December, January.

Célony, 3km from Aix on N7 – Mas d'Entremont, 42.23.45.32: readers of this book love this delicious 18th-century farm with 14th-century cloister. Being constantly improved. Rooms now air-conditioned; new bedrooms in bungalows in the grounds. Attractive bedrooms; lovely garden with pool. Lovely views. Wonderful retreat from Aix traffic and gruesome parking problems. Good old-style French cuisine with generous old-style portions. We like its interesting Provence wines. Charming, helpful atmosphere. Menus E, F. Rooms F; half-pension preferred. Shut 1 November–1 March. Restaurant shut Sunday evenings.

Abbaye des Cordeliers, 21 rue Lieutaud, 42.27.29.47: restaurant in 15th-century abbey with tables under trees in garden for summer. Traditional cooking; good fish. Menus C.E. Shut Sunday evening, Monday; 15 January–15th February.

Beautiful route. Aix-en-Provence – one of those tourist clichés which will not let you down; surrounded by lovely landscapes, it has fine old buildings, fountains and majestic avenues flanked by cafés and restaurants; a university town and a spa; Cours Mirabeau, made in the 16th century, is one of the loveliest avenues in France, though named after the scandalous local count who joined the Revolution after a life of debts and debauchery and became a great orator. The Impressionist painter Cézanne was born, worked and died here, and you can visit his studio on avenue Cézanne. There is more to see in Aix than in most big cities, and it is a question of what to leave out unless you are staying; 26 Flemish tapestries in St Sauveur Cathedral are interesting; they were made for Canterbury Cathedral in 1511 and bought by St Sauveur in 1656. Parking difficult in Aix.

Aix-en-Provence continued	Manoir, 8 rue d'Entrecasteaux, 42.26.27.20: 18th-century mansion with 14th-century cloister. Centre of town yet Relais du Silence. No restaurant. Rooms E–G. Shut mid-January–mid-February.

From Aix-en-Provence the motorways and old N7 run behind the coast through the whole Côte d'Azur to the Italian border and beyond. Motorways also to Toulon and Marseille.

Route 3
Dieppe to Modane

(for Italy)

A most enjoyable route with changing pleasant scenery, especially on the smaller roads, most interesting old towns, and a run down the top half of the Burgundy wine road. Finally, mountain scenery with lakes, streams and waterfalls. A dawdlers' route. Few Britons know the hilly forest in Normandy, the beeches of Lyons forest, and the well-groomed park-like forests of Compiègne and Laigue.

You will find all sorts of hidden treasures.

Burgundy is a châteaux country almost as much as the Loire and Dordogne. And the Savoy is one of the loveliest areas of France.

A good start, too. Dieppe is the friendliest of the ferry ports. But you can join easily enough from other ports, though you may miss Eawy forest. Beauvais is the obvious place to join the route, though I would prefer Forges-les-Eaux.

A gourmand will be tempted to stay in Dieppe – Norman cooking at its best, with rich cream and shellfish sauces, wonderful fresh fish, beautiful butter and meat from lush pastures, cream desserts and fresh fruit, all at reasonable prices. And good shopping at small shops in a traffic-free area.

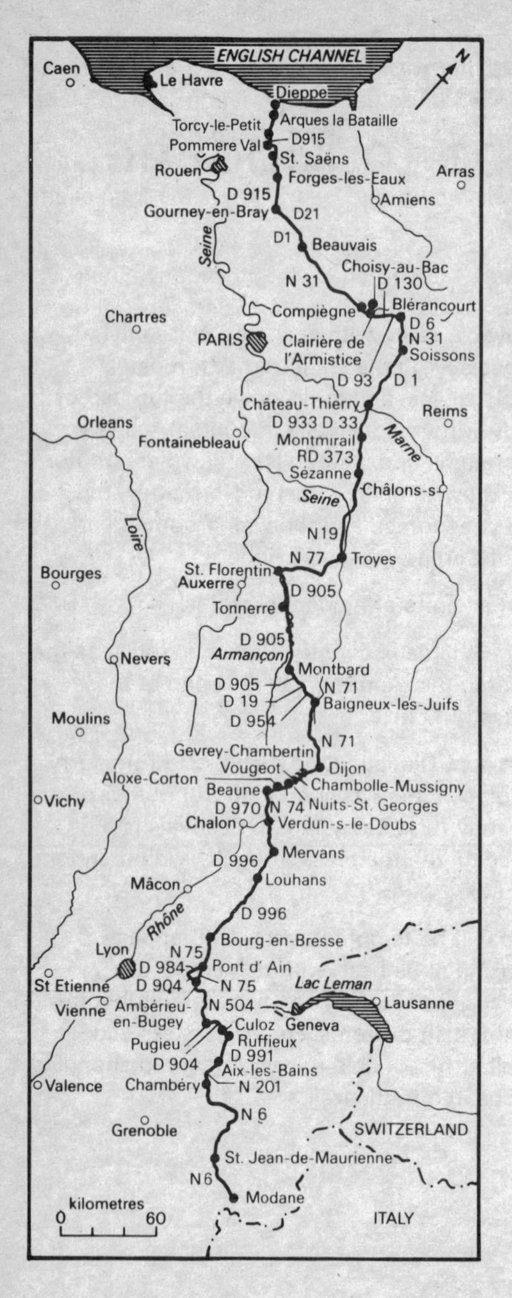
ENGLISH CHANNEL
N
Caen
Le Havre
Dieppe
Torcy-le-Petit
Arques la Bataille
D915
Pommere Val
St. Saëns
Rouen
Forges-les-Eaux
Arras
D 915
Amiens
Gourney-en-Bray
D21
Seine
D1
Beauvais
Choisy-au-Bac
N 31
D 130
Blérancourt
Compiègne
D 6
N 31
Chartres
PARIS
Clairière de
l'Armistice
Soissons
D 93
D 1
Château-Thierry
Reims
D 933 D 33
Orleans
Fontainebleau
Montmirail
Marne
RD 373
Sézanne
Châlons-s
Seine
Loire
N19
N 77
Troyes
St. Florentin
Bourges
Auxerre
D 905
Tonnerre
D 905
Armançon
Nevers
Montbard
D 905
N 71
D 19
Baigneux-les-Juifs
Moulins
D 954
N 71
Gevrey-Chambertin
Vougeot
Dijon
Aloxe-Corton
Chambolle-Mussigny
Beaune
Vichy
D 970
N 74
Nuits-St. Georges
Chalon
Verdun-s-le-Doubs
Mervans
D 996
Louhans
Mâcon
Rhône
D 996
Bourg-en-Bresse
Lyon
N 75
D 984
Pont d' Ain
D 904
N 75
Lac Leman
St Etienne
Vienne
Ambérieu-
en-Bugey
N 504
Lausanne
Culoz
Geneva
Pugieu
Ruffieux
D 904
D 991
Aix-les-Bains
Valence
Chambéry
N 201
N 6
Grenoble
SWITZERLAND
St. Jean-de-Maurienne
N 6
Modane
kilometres
0
60
ITALY

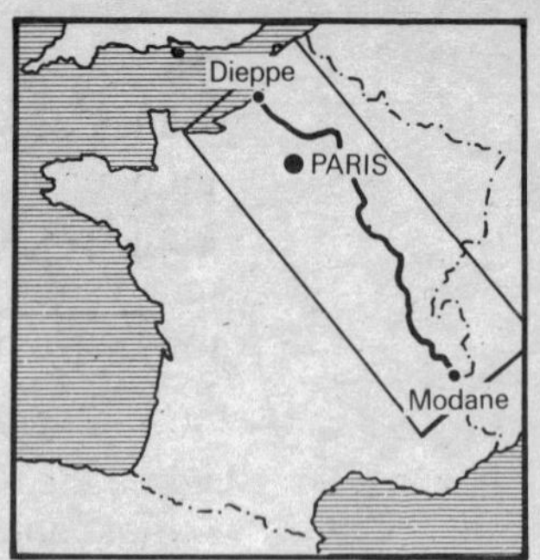
Dieppe
PARIS
Modane

As you leave the coast, you find poultry, especially guinea fowl and duck, game, and river fish, with plenty of good trout. Then more game in the Aisne forests until you reach Burgundy, with fine beef, charcuterie, crayfish, snails and frogs' legs. Dijon is the food capital of this route.

Around Bresse they produce what the French believe to be the best chickens in the world and cook them usually in cream and wine. Savoy's lakes and streams produce crayfish, salmon trout, trout and omble chevalier (small, slim salmon). Hams, salamis and sausages are plentiful in Savoy. Do try the soup of freshwater fish.

Normandy's Calvados (apple spirit) is used in cooking and as a digestive – you sink a glass quickly between courses to settle the stomach (called Trou Normand – the Norman hole). The modern trick is to pour it on apple sorbet. From Dijon south you have a glorious choice of Burgundy wines. Alas, even in Burgundy prices have risen painfully. The weather has hit vineyards, especially Chablis. And the Almighty Dollar and Unyielding Yen have outbid us at auctions.

Few Britons have tried Savoy wines. Whites, looking as pale as water, are mostly sparkling and refreshing. Seyssel wines are best known. Reds are not so good.

Chambéry produces a fine vermouth – light and dry.

Route 3
Dieppe to Modane

(for Italy)

Dieppe

L'Univers, 10 boulevard Verdun, 35.84.12.55: Jean Tilquin is a great chef. His dishes of Normandy, with cream, cider, Calvados, especially fresh local fish, have remained a delight to us for 35 years. Very good Muscadet. Madame Tilquin's family have owned this comfortable, old-style hotel for generations, and Madame is an old-style French lady – enthusiastic, dynamic, excitable, strong-willed. Don't expect faceless, noiseless efficiency. Menu C, D, F. Rooms E–F. Shut December.

Windsor, 18 boulevard Verdun, 35.84.15.23: my old friend Claude Lambert has finally retired. New owners have renovated the upstairs terrace-restaurant with views of promenade and sea. Too early to judge the cooking. Menus A, C, D. Rooms D, E. Shut Sunday evening off-season.

Step off the Newhaven boat and you are truly in France, with bistros opposite, a fish market and pavement cafés for a plate of shrimps or moules marinières to a full meal. Grand' Rue is a pedestrian area, with shops selling a wide variety of things from expensive fashion shoes to cheap chickens and including a Prisunic chain store. There is a good wine shop and hardware store for kitchen equipment. On Saturday mornings, fishermen and farmers bring their produce to market – oysters, butter, farm pâté and prawns are sold from stalls. The sea front has wide lawns, a beachside pool and a casino. Dieppe Castle, where Canadian soldiers in 1942 climbed the sheer cliff face, has a museum with navigation equipment, ivories and paintings, including works by the English Impressionist Sisley who worked gutting fish on this coast when starving.

Aguado, 30 boulevard Verdun, 35.84.27.00: very comfortable, modern concrete and faceless hotel, convenient for sea and ferry. No restaurant. Rooms E. Open all year.

La Présidence, 1 boulevard Verdun, 35.84.31.31: modern, facing sea (get front bedroom), very comfortable, efficient, pricey. Restaurant on fourth floor with fine views. Serves carte meals only. Mostly grills. Bar Anglaise is local meeting spot. Rooms E–G.

Mélie, Grande-rue Pollet, 35.84.21.19: new, in old fishermen's quarter across harbour from ferry terminal. Guy Brachais is already building a reputation for good, delicate cooking of fish. Try créville du pêcheur (small fish, perfectly poached). Interesting choice of lesser-known wines. Menu C; carte F. Shut Monday evenings; February.

Marmite Dieppoise, 8 rue St Jean, 35.84.24.26: Jean-Pierre Toussat's renowned restaurant still gives some of the best value for fish in North France. He knows where to buy fish and how to cook it. Deliberately simple-looking restaurant. Marmite Dieppoise is a Norman soup-stew of fish and shellfish, with leaks, wine and cream. Superb. I am not so fond of choucroute du pêcheur –

Dieppe continued

sauerkraut with fish – but sole Normande and chicken in cider are excellent. Dearest menu (gastronomic) is superb. Menus A, B, E. Shut Sunday and Thursday evening, all Monday; 20 June–5 July; 19 December–15 January.

Port, 99 quai Henry IV, 35.84.36.64: my Dieppoise friends return to the busy, good value restaurant despite its popularity with visitors. I love the coquilles St Jacques (scallops) à la Dieppoise. Four-course cheap menu is excellent value. Menus A, C, F. Shut 3 January–1 February.

Moderne, 21 arcades Poissonerie, 35.84.66.90: 3 storeys, with harbour views from the top. Most dishes are cooked to order, so don't drop in for a rushed meal! It's for serious eaters. Wide choice, Norman cooking with good use of local fish and lots of cream and cider. Good marmite Dieppoise, outstanding fish soufflé in parsley cream. Menus A, C, D. Open all year.

Marine, 1 arcades Poissonerie, 35.84.17.54: the imaginative young chef Marcel Blin has gone, cooking is predictable; 3 menus with good choice and value. A la carte excellent. Nice shellfish quiche, matelote de marine (sole, salmon, turbot, monkfish). Quick 2-course meal (Monday–Thursday) still pulls in young locals. Menus A, C. Shut Tuesday evenings, Wednesdays.

Arcades, 1 arcade de la Bourse, 35.84.14.12: comfortable hotel with chequered history taken over by M. Deligne from La Marine. Menus A, C, E. Rooms B–D.

Normandy, 16 rue Duquesne, 35.84.27.18: memories of romantic, cheap candlelit dinners in rustic charm, with choice of 9 menus! Times change. New décor, 2 menus and carte. Good sole Normande, stuffed oysters, and marmite de poissons. Bargain Roussillon house wine. Menu B, C. Shut Sunday evening, Monday.

At Vertus (76550 Offranville), 4km S on N27 – Bûcherie, route de Rouen, 35.84.83.10: established now as Dieppe's smartest in-place. Shiny place-settings, cocktail bar. Pricey, but excellent cooking, using the very best fish available. Splendid marmite with saffron, lobster from vivier, roast with herbs, and hot apple tart. Book – few tables, Menus C (weekdays), E; carte G. Shut Sunday evening, Monday; 4 days early July; part September.

At Varangeville (76119 Seine-Maritime), 8km on D75 – Terrasse, Vasterival (3km), 35.85.12.54: Delafontaine family here since 1911 and it

At Varangeville (8km) is a clifftop village church with superlative colourful modern window by Braque. His grave, designed by pupils in his

Dieppe continued	is still popular with Britons, especially with those of my readers who love simple old French hotels with old family cooking and welcome. Known for sole Normande. Lovely country position, high above sea, with views. Very reasonable prices. House wine very cheap. Menus A, E. Rooms B–E. Open 15 March–15 October.	style, is in the churchyard. Monet's painting of the church is now in the Barber Institute, Birmingham. He lived at Varangeville when he was too poor to afford canvases. Parc Floralies, Varangeville, is a glorious garden. You can visit Ango Manor, strange 16th-century home of the corsair chief Jean Ango, a French 'Drake' who became Governor of Dieppe after destroying 300 Portuguese ships. Pourville has a museum of the 1942 Dieppe Raid, including tanks.
D54 Arques-la-Bataille, D154, D149 to Torcy-le-Petit, D915 to Pommereval then D12 through forest to St Saëns D929 NE Maucomble D118, Bosc-Mesnil, D83 to join D915 to Forges-les-Eaux (66km)	Forges-les-Eaux – La Paix, 17 rue Neufchatel, 35.90.51.22: a simple exterior hides some of the best value meals in Normandy. Fish straight from Dieppe, eggs, dairy produce, poultry, cider from local farms; beef from Bray farms, beautifully cooked by Remy Michel, in Normandy style. Basic rooms. Menus A, C, D. Rooms A, B. Shut Sunday evenings, Mondays in winter; 15 December–15 January.	A lovely drive through superb beech forest with deep valleys and lovely views. Divert in forest to explore. Forges is a restful small spa; water was drunk regularly by Richelieu and Voltaire (who said it contained more vitriol than ink). Lovely park with sailing lake. Four rivers start here.
D915 Gournay-en-Bray (20km)		On edge of Forêt de Lyons (beeches), 11th-century church. 11km on N30, then a local road, is Gerberoy, fortified hilltop town, almost abandoned in the 17th century until modern painter Le Sidaner (died 1939) and friends restored it.

D21, D1 Beauvais (30km)	La Crémaillère, 1 rue Gui Patin, 44.45.03.13: Daniel Leménager cooks mouthwatering old dishes of the region, like stuffed guinea fowl, ficelles Picardes (rolled pancakes stuffed with cream and ham); lots of cream, cider and Calvados in sauces. Many fine cheeses; interesting desserts. Copious portions. All served in historic auberge with old glass in the dining room. By common consent, best restaurant in Beauvais. Strong wine list. Menu D. Shut Wednesdays (except reservations). Palais, 9 rue St Nicolas, 44.45.12.58: bedrooms modernized; new proprietor; open all year; peaceful; no restaurant. Rooms B–D.	Superb old town regarded too often as half-day's excursion from Paris (76km). The cathedral, begun 1227, was never quite finished but is still magnificent in its new town setting. Highest Gothic choir in the world is awesome. Fine windows both old (14th to 16th centuries) and modern (include Max Ingrand and Braque). Magnificent Renaissance windows (and some modern) in St Etienne church by Angrand le Prince. Do see place Jeanne Hachette, beautifully rebuilt after the war damage and named after the girl who rallied the French to victory by attacking the besieging Burgundy forces with an axe! New National Tapestry Museum (by the cathedral) includes gorgeous tapestries from 15th century to today. The old museum was destroyed by bombing in 1940. Tapestry weaving started in Beauvais by order of Louis XIV. This art form revived in France in last fifty years, mainly through Jean Lurçat, who grew as an artist with Cocteau, Picasso, Matisse.
N31 Compiègne (57km)	Flandre, 16 quai République, 44.83.24.40: totally renovated; solid comfort and reliability; near river. Rooms C, D. Restaurant now separate. Menu A.	In a huge forest 72km (45 miles) north of Paris, Compiègne is a town rich in art treasures. Here the kings of France always had a hunting hideout. Louis XV had a new castle built, rather

Compiègne continued

Picotin, 22 place Hôtel de Ville, 44.40.04.06: traditional French cooking; good value. Menus A, B. Shut Tuesday evening.

At Vaudrampont, 10km S on D332 to Crépy, heart of forest – Bon Accueil, 44.42.84.04: delightful forest hideaway. Jean Edouard Lacroix, formerly chef at the Connaught, London, says: 'We keep up standards of cuisine despite passing fashions'. Lovely meals. In autumn, roebuck, pheasant, hind from the forest. Good wine list – none cheap. Menus D–G. Rooms C–D. Shut Monday evenings, Tuesday; 16 August–29 February.

At Vieux Moulin, 9km E of Compiègne by D973, forest road D14 left; deep in forest – Auberge Daguet, 25 rue St Jean, 44.85.60.72: restaurant in lovely surroundings; built in 1730. Dining room has Louis XIII stained glass, fine old oak, porcelain, silverware, Renaissance sideboard, beautiful ornamental ceiling. Chef-patron André Lousseau is major national and regional award winner. Try vegetable andouillette, turbot ficelle, coq-en-borchon à la bière, omelette soufflé céléstine (baked sweet omelette with apricot preserve – Céléstine was Napoleon III's chef). Good caves – nothing cheap. Menu D plus carte. Shut Wednesday: part February; 1–15 July.

severe but elegant. Louis XVI, when Dauphin, first received his fiancée here (Marie-Antoinette). It became a barracks, but Napolean restored it as his castle home and Napolean III and Empress Eugénie held impressive hunts and balls here. The rooms of Marie-Antoinette and the Napoleans retain their tapestries and furniture. Many Empire period paintings including Boudins.

Vivenel Museum has a vast collection of treasures spanning centuries, with superb Greek vases, and Musée de la Figurine Historique has 80,000 lead, wood and board soldiers. I love the Vehicle and Tourism Museum, with 150 vehicles from a Roman chariot to a Citroën chain-track car and including diligences (stage coaches), a post-chaise, superb sledges, a remarkable steam coach (1885) and early cars.

	At Elincourt-Ste-Marguerite (15km from Compiègne by N32 north then D142 – Château de Bellinglise, 44.76.04.76: delightful 16th-century château with turrets, a warren of rooms; set in a huge park with lake and modern bedrooms in small block on estate. Shut for 6 months until May '87 for total overhaul and opening of 22 bedrooms. Has lost some cosy atmosphere and antique furniture; more efficient, neater, better plumbing. Aimed partly at conferences. Pricey but comfortable. Menu F plus carte. Rooms F (in grounds), G. Open all year.	
N31 D546 to Clairière de l'Armistice (5km)	Choisy au Bac – Auberge des Etangs du Buissonet, 44.40.17.41: very quiet, very attractive. Expensive. Menus F-G. Shut Sunday and Monday evenings.	In this lovely glade, Marshal Foch, commander of Allied Forces, received the German surrender in 1918 in a railway carriage. In 1940 Hitler insisted on receiving the French surrender here. Original carriage taken to Berlin and destroyed when Allies approached. So a replica coach stands in the glade, with genuine objects inside.
D81 Choisy au Bac, D130 through Laigue forest to D934, then right to Blérancourt (32km)	Blérancourt – Griffon, 23.39.60.11: I can't remember when I first went to this charming inn at entrance to the Château. Pleasant garden. Bedrooms improved, more with bathrooms. Pleasant regional dishes. Friendly if not polished service. Menus	Lovely forest run, mostly beeches. Blérancourt was the centre of terrible battles (1916–18). It was rebuilt by Ann Morgan, daughter of the US banker Pierpont Morgan, as a symbol of Franco-American friendship, and its castle dating from the 17th century houses a Franco-

	C, E, F. Rooms E. Shut Sunday evening, Monday; 23–30 December; 1–15 February.	American museum mostly of the Kaiser's war, including a superb Model-T Ford ambulance. Pretty gardens.
D6, N31 Soissons (23km)	Rallye, 10 boulevard Strasbourg, 23.53.00.47: useful bed and breakfast hotel. Rooms B–D. English spoken. At Longpont (14km by D1, D175, D805) – L'Abbaye, 23. 96.02.44: in delightful hamlet with ancient ruined abbey in Retz forest. Nice hideout. Good meat grilled over wood. Five plats du jour. Cheap house wines. Forest game in season. Menu B, F. Rooms B–E. Open all year.	Deeply involved in early French history from AD 486 when Clovis the Frank defeated the Romans. Rubens' superb 'Adoration of the Shepherds' is in the 13th-century cathedral. He painted it in thanks for being nursed through a nasty illness here. Only the frontage remains of the original abbey where Thomas à Becket lived for nine years.
D1 Château Thierry (41km)	Turn left at Grand Rozoy and 12km along D2 at Fère-en-Tardenois is Hostellerie du Château, 23.82.21.13: absolutely magnificent. Superbly furnished castle in a lovely park with 2-star Michelin cooking. True elegance, from table settings to wall hangings. Courteous welcome, immaculate service. Expensive by French standards (not by any other) and worth every franc for such an experience. Château built 1206, owned by the Valois-Orléans family; passed to Condé family; finally to 'Philippe Egalité', Duke of Orléans (friend of our Prince Regent) who joined the French Revolution, knocked down a wing of the château as a gesture of 'equality', but	The writer La Fontaine was born here in 1621 and the house, in a street now named after him, is a museum. Set on the Marne river, round a wooded hill in lovely country, the town has been involved in wars over centuries. The English took it in 1421, Joan of Arc recaptured it and entered through Porte Saint-Pierre which survives. In 1814 Napoleon defeated a force of Russians and Prussians just outside the town towards Montmirail. American units held it bravely and incredibly against a massive German attack in 1918, and hill 204 is part of American history. There is a monument and cemetery (just off N3 west).

	was still guillotined. Ironically his son Louis-Philippe (friend of Queen Victoria) became citizen-king of France. Christopher Blot, member of the family, now at the cooker. Menu G. Rooms G. Shut 1 January–1 March. St Eloi, 27 avenue Soissons, 23.83.02.33: down to earth, after the château; nice little garden; Raymond Barre's good cooking of traditional favourites – boeuf Bourguignon, chicken in Champagne, steak in peppers, trout (from vivier) in Marc de Champagne. Excellent value. Menus A–D. Rooms B. Shut Wednesdays; October; 1–20 February.	
D1, D933, D33 Montmirail (24km)		Pleasant, old, with remains of ramparts, two very old churches and a château which you cannot visit.
D373 Sézanne (24km)	Croix d'Or, 53 rue Notre-Dame, 26.80.61.10: attractive old-style creeper clad inn with pavement terrace; traditional local cooking; good value. Try mussels in Bouzy wine (red still wine of the Champagne), duck liver in Ratafia de Champagne (grape juice in brandy – also a nice aperitif); peach in Champagne. Menu A–D. Rooms A–B. Shut 1–16 January; 10–15 October. Champenois et Lion d'Or, 157 rue Notre-Dame, 26.80.58.03: very old coaching inn with flowery	Market town at meeting of three important roads, but still quite peaceful. Walks by ancient ramparts somewhat tortuous. Interesting flamboyant Gothic church. Westward is a pleasant drive through La Traconne forest (Château d'Esternay, Bricot-la-Ville-Colonne, Barbonne), about 37km.

Sézanne continued

window boxes. New good rooms in annexe. Friendly: Champagne country-style cooking. Try coq au vin (using Bouzy red wine), sole in Champagne and cream; real farm Brie cheese; Marc sorbet. Menu A–C. Rooms A–D. Shut Fridays low season.

France, 25 rue Léon Jolly, 26.81.41.48: old favourite of readers, which shut, now reopened after complete renovation. Bedrooms enormously improved. Old inn popular since last century. Menus C, E, F. Rooms D–E.

D373 N19 Troyes (60km)

Bourgogne, 40 rue de Gaulle, 25.73.02.67: superb classic cooking of Champagne and Burgundy styles. Excellent duck in Bouzy wine, Bresse chicken in Champagne. Wines superb, expensive. A la carte D–F. Shut Sunday and Monday evenings; August.

Valentino, cour Rencontre, 25.73.14.14: charming; terrace and lovely verandah over inside courtyard; in old house in mediaeval quarter. Modern tendencies in cooking – mouthwatering desserts. Menus C, E, F. Shut Sunday evening, Monday; 15 August–2 September.

Royal, 22 boulevard Carnot, 25.73.19.99: fine old-style hotel with iron-railed balconies; comfortable bedrooms. Traditional

Old town with many interests. Centre of hosiery trade for 470 years. Rich in works of art and buildings dating back to 12th century. After victory at Agincourt, Henry V of England married Catherine, daughter of King Charles VI of France in St Jean church, Troyes, and became Regent of France.

Troyes' magnificent cathedral was being built from 12th to 17th centuries and was never finished.

cooking. Good value. Good house wine. Menus B, C, E. Rooms D. Shut 3 weeks in December. Restaurant shut Sunday evening, Monday.

N77 St Florentin, D905 Tonnerre (76km)

Near Venizy, 4.5km NW from St Florentin on D30 – Moulin des Pommerats, 86.35.08.04: pretty, old watermill; riverside garden. Bedrooms comfortable, most modernized recently. Paul Remaux d'Equainville, chef-patron, flew as an RAF pilot 1940–5. Traditional regional cooking of fine ingredients. Trout from the river. For long the hotel which, in all my books, attracted most enthusiasm from readers. So some expected too much of a country hostellerie. Don't expect slick Hilton service! It's a place to relax and forget about time. Menus B, C, E, G. Rooms D–F. Restaurant shut Sunday evening, Monday low season.

Tonnerre – Abbaye St Michel, 86.55.05.99: historic Benedictine abbey on hilltop. Very beautiful, lovely furnishing of fine old rooms. Big pretty park with flowers. Outstanding cooking, regional and traditional, very slightly modernized by patron Daniel Cussac's son, Christophe, who arrived in 1984 from the kitchen of Troisgros. Extremely expensive. Menus G. Rooms G. Shut Sunday evenings, Mondays low season; early January–mid-February.

St Florentin is a small industrial centre, but interesting. At the meeting of two rivers and a canal, it is fishermen's country; church with Renaissance stained glass. Route then follows Burgundy canal to Tonnerre – an old town which deals in wine and is surrounded by vineyards and meadows. A spring (Fosse Dionne) of blue-green water is traditionally used by locals for washing their clothes 'whiter than white'. Tonnerre was the birthplace of Chevalier d'Eon, diplomat and spy, who appeared publicly as both a man and a woman, died in London 1810 and was buried in St Pancras.

East (8km by N65) is Château Tanlay, started in 1547 by the Coligny brothers, Protestant leaders in the Religious Wars, finished 1648 by a tax collector who went broke doing it; moated, very attractive, contains strange allegoric painting of Catholic and Protestant rivalry.

D905 Montbard (47km)	At St Rémy (4km before Montbard on D905 NW) – Saint Rémy, 2 route Dijon, 80.92.13.44: good Bourguignon cooking, sauces like piquant saupiquet of red wine and vinegar; quail in redcurrant sauce. Menu A (not Saturdays)–F. Lunch only except Sundays. No rooms. Shut 22 December–31 January; Mondays. L'Ecu, 7 rue Auguste Carré 80.92.11.66: comfortable, 17th-century house with Louis XVI dining room. Praise from readers for fine classical dishes, including coq au vin, meurette de boeuf (beef in sauce of red wine, bacon, onions, carrots, mushrooms), bacon in cream sauce, marmite d'escargots. Menus (several) B–G. Rooms D–G. Open all year.	Winding, pleasant route alongside Burgundy canal. This is Burgundy château country. One castle not to miss is Ancy-le-Franc – a masterpiece of classical Renaissance and landmark in the history of architecture. Rooms arre sumptuously decorated and the furniture, books, frescos and ancient tapestries are magnificent (18km from Tonnerre). At Montbard, Comte de Buffon knocked down a castle on a hill, built a simple study in a park, and wrote his *Natural History* (first volume 1749). Several of his other buildings are still there. Nearby is the superb mediaeval abbey of Fontenay. A paper factory after the Revolution, it was completely restored after 1902.
D905 for 5km, D19 left, D954 left joining N71 at Baigneux-les-Juifs (32km)		Source of the Seine – at Les Vergerots 2km right on D103 (off N71 8km before St Seine l'Abbaye). Among pines, with statue of a nymph; remains of Roman temple.
N71 to Dijon (49km)	Pré aux Clercs et Trois Faisans, 13 place Libération, 80.67.11.33: historic house opposite Ducal palace. Restaurant for 150 years. Changed hands recently. Traditional Burgundian cooking. Renowned cellar. Wines 60–1500f. Menus B–G. Shut Sunday evenings.	Victor Hugo called Dijon delightful and it still is. Outstanding for food even in this gastronomic area of France; so many interesting things to see that it deserves at least one overnight stay. The chiming clock on St Michel started in the 17th century with a blacksmith. Now he has a wife and two

Thibert, 10 place Wilson, 80.67.74.64: young Jean-Paul Thibert is the rising star of Dijon. Imaginative cooking, without eccentricity. Try pétoncles (scallops), barbu (brill) with chicken livers, pear in white chocolate with passion fruit sauce. Fair prices for outstanding cuisine. Menus C, D, G. Shut Sunday, Monday lunch.

Nord, 2 rue de la Liberté et place Darcy, 80.30.58.58: my sort of traditional French hotel. In same family for four generations. I have known it only 35 years. All bedrooms now have private bathrooms. Warm ambience, décor; old style service; all traditional Burgundian dishes carefully cooked. Charming, moderate prices, superb caves of 80 wines. Show this book when you eat and Dominik Franchot will offer you a Kir. New wine-tasting bar with seventeen Burgundies by the glass. Menus C, F. Rooms C–E. Shut 23 December–mid-January.

Rallye, 38 rue Chabot-Charny, 80.67.11.55: excellent bourgeoise cuisine at reasonable prices. Try panaché of fish, brioche of lamb with tarragon, Bresse chicken. Very good value. Menus B, D, F. Shut Sunday; 15 February–1 March; 14 July–1 August.

children. Among many museums worth seeing is Beaux Arts in the Ducal Palace of Charles de Valois; one of the best in France, with splendid rooms, furniture, kitchen and paintings second only to the Louvre. Don't miss museum La Vie Bourguignonne (partly about wine) at 17 rue Ste Anne. Among many fine old streets, rue des Forges is outstanding. Square Darcy, named after British engineer who gave Dijon clean water supply, is charming; the polar bear statue is by François Pompon, great animal artist.

Superb Gastronomic Fair in November. You can buy Dijon mustard cheaply in plastic buckets. Dijon produces 85 per cent of France's cassis (blackcurrant liquor). Refreshing apéritif Kir (cassis and white wine) was named after Canon Kir, mayor of Dijon and wartime Resistance leader. He served it at functions to promote sale of cassis for his town.

N74 Gevrey-Chambertin (12km)	Vendanges de Bourgogne, 47 route de Beaune, 80.34.30.24: modern hotel, pleasant décor. Traditional dishes well-cooked – trout, salmon, ham en croûte, coq au vin, quail, guinea fowl, snails. Good value. Well-chosen wine list. Menus A–D. Rooms A–E. Shut Sunday evenings, Mondays; 27 January–10 March. Terroirs, 28 route de Dijon, 80.34.30.76: comfortable 3–star Logis with country-style imaginative furnishings. Ten bedrooms added. No restaurant but patron René Leclerc makes and sells own wines. Rooms E–G. Shut 20 December–20 January.	The great wine route starts. It would take a week to taste even a fraction of the good wines, but with a strong-willed or teetotal driver and a few diversions, you could stop at your favourite villages. Chambertin (Champ de Bertin) was Napoleon's favourite tipple, but the Corsican mixed it with water. ('St Peter, ' wrote Hilaire Belloc, 'I cannot remember the name of the village, the girl, or even what we ate for dinner. But, my God, the wine was Chambertin!') And many still call it 'King of Wines'. Gevrey, the village, added the name of its most famous vineyard, Chambertin. Do try this 'Chambertin' itself or Clos-de-Bèze if possible – the original wine produced by Bèze Abbey monks. Bertin bought the field next door (Champ Bertin). Biggest production now is of Charmes Chambertin. Castle (10th-century) worth visiting.
N74 Chambolle-Mussigny (5km on small road on right)		Passing Morey-St-Denis, whose wines we once knew as Gevrey and Chambolle. Best known is Clos de Tart, owned by Mommessin family since 1932 – pale, fruity wine drunk youngish. Try also Clos de la Roche and Clos de la Bussière. Chambolle-Mussigny, whose church has paintings of saints, produces wine almost in Chambertin class. Try Mussigny of Comte

de Vogué; or, if in love, drink Chambolle Les Amoureuses and Les Charmes.

N74 Vougeot (5km)

Gastronomes, 80.62.85.10: nice little restaurant with beams, open fire and real Burgundian cooking. Try sole a la lie de vin, veal kidneys Bercy (wine, shallots, bone marrow). Menus B–D. Shut Monday low season, Tuesday; 16 November–10 December; 15 January–1 March.

Cistercian monks (Trappists) originally planted this vineyard at Vougeot and in the 14th century it was surrounded by a stone wall to protect it from raiders in the 100 Years' War. Now there are 80 owners, making a choice of wines difficult, but all are very drinkable. The 16th-century château was bought in 1944 by the Confrérie des Chevaliers du Tastevin, an organization begun to publicize Burgundy wines; in scarlet and gold robes they hold banquets to enrol new members. At other times you can visit the château. It is spectacularly illuminated on weekends in July and August. Visits July, August.

So highly regarded is Clos de Vougeot that the Revolutionary Colonel Bisson started a tradition by ordering his troops to 'present arms' as they passed the vineyard. Tasting at La Grande Cave on N74.

N74 Vosne-Romanée (3km)

Toute Petite Auberge, 80.61.02.03: simple local auberge but excellent cooking. Menus B, D. Shut Thursdays; December, January.

From here come magnificent wines: deep, rich Romanée-Conti, soft La Tâche, seductive Richebourg, so easy to drink that you tend to quaff it; les Grands Echézeaux, more delicate, for languid enjoyment. Romanée is called Queen of Wines – alas, a costly Queen.

N74 Nuits-St-Georges (3km)

Cultivateurs, 80.61.10.41: simple, charming; locals use it as bar-restaurant. Comfortable sound-proofed bedrooms. Relais Routiers and 2-star hotel. Old France atmosphere. Good cheap wines. Boeuf Bourguignon, poulet chasseur; sauerkraut and couscous in winter. Courtyard for summer eating. Menus A, B. Rooms A–D. Shut 15 December–15 January.

Gentilhommière, W 1.5km route Meuilley, 80.61.12.06: modernized hotel in country. Menus C–F. Rooms D. Restaurant shut Mondays.

A little town almost as important as Beaune in the wine trade. Even has a hospice (founded 1692, caring for old folk) owning vineyards, given by the charitable or conscience-stricken and holding wine sales yearly. Until controls tightened, phoney 'Nuits' sold in Britain spoiled its repute. Prémaux wines are good, reliable, strong. Red wines earthy and irony, mature well. White are scarcer but good. Some lesser wine made into sparkling red Burgundy – ugh! Park the car and explore narrow side streets on foot.

Tastings at Dufouleur, 17 rue Thurot and Henri Remoriquet, 25 rue Charmoise.

N74 Aloxe-Corton (just off N74) (18km)

At Chorey-les-Beaune, between Aloxe-Corton and Beaune – Bareuzai, 80.22.02.90: restaurant owned by wine producer and négociant Robert Voarick, so excellent wine list; panoramic views over wine area and excellent cooking of fine fresh Burgundian dishes, plus home smoked fish. Huge, open grill; snug restaurant. Free wine tasting to help you choose. Also big wine caves in village. Menus A, D, G. Shut January. Rooms being built in 1988.

At foot of Montagne de Corton whose vineyards climb to a wooded hilltop. Wines were made at Aloxe for Charlemagne in 775 and it produces both red and white 'grand cru' wines. Legend says that Charlemagne's wife nagged him because his favourite red wine stained his white beard, so he ordered part of the vineyard to be planted to produce white wine. The red (Aloxe-Corton) is the best wine of Côte de Beaune, full blooded and fit for an emperor. Corton-Charlemagne ranks with Puligny-Montrachet as the finest white Burgundy.

At Savigny-les-Beaune (3km right, of N74) – Ourrée, 80.21.51.52: superb value meals. Four or five courses on cheaper menus. Burgundian dishes. Own wine cellars with tastings. Owner is a producer. Menus A, B, D. Rooms C, D. Shut 1 February–15 March.

At Bouilland, right, off N74 to Savigny-les-Beaune, then on D2 N – Vieux Moulin, 80.21.51.16: very attractive; in open country, nice views; little river alongside. Big garden. Outstanding modern cooking of local produce. Try trout from Vivier; farm chicken in honey and sherry vinegar. Super farm cheeses. Supern list of wines, from leading proprietors – 100 to 3000f! Pretty bedrooms. Lovely hideout. Menus D, F, G. Rooms F, G. Shut mid-December–mid-January; Thursday lunch, Wednesdays.

Voltaire lapped up the red – while serving his guests with Beaujolais! Le Corton red is outstanding, keeps up to 25 years. Top growth wines do not use the word 'Aloxe'.

Tastings at Château de Corton-André. Interesting visit to this old château. Aloxe pronounced Aloss, like dead-loss.

N74 Beaune (34km)

Central, 2 rue Victor-Millot, 80.24.77.24: really central. Some readers complain of noise. After dinner and a bottle of Beaune, I hear no noise! Alas, Robert Cuny is no longer at the cooker but Marie-Josse Cuny runs the hotel sympathetically and chef Jean Garcin cooks Burgundian dishes very well. Good wine list. Menus (good value) C, E, G. Rooms E, F. Shut Wednesday (November –June); 23 November–18 December.

A lot to see in a smallish town, including the Hospice and Hôtel-Dieu (another hospital), both mediaeval, with fine tapestries and other works of art and both kept in funds by the famous annual sale of wines from their vineyards ('biggest charity auction in the world'). Worth a walk round the old ramparts, a visit to the wine museum in the residence of the Dukes of Burgundy, which includes a fine modern

Beaune continued	At Levernois (SE 5km on D970, then D111) – Parc, 80.22.22.51: bed and breakfast hideout from Beaune's traffic; lovely old house in flower garden and park. No restaurant. Rooms B, C. Shut 1–16 March; 22 November–11 December. 	Aubusson tapestry by Jean Lurçat and some superb old glass, and, of course, a visit to a 'cave' (list from tourist office opposite Hôtel-Dieu). Excellent swimming-pool in town, amid rose-beds. Painting of 'Last Judgement' by van der Weyden in Hôtel-Dieu is magnificent. Caves open to public, including tastings, include: Cave des Batistines, 20 rue Fg Madeleine (old cellars; museum of growing implements); J. Calvet, 6 boulevard Perpreuil; Patriarche, Couvent des Visitandines (old convent; 14th-century cellars; tasting fee given to charities). Pommard (6km S) is charming village with château which gives tastings. Wine should be deep rich red, fruity and soft. Tastings at Château de Pommard (20f fee).
D970 Through Verdun-sur-le-Doubs (22km) on to Mervans then D996 to Louhans (39km–61km total)	Turn left off D970 at St Loup on to D183, just past Chaublanc – Moulin d'Hauterive, 85.91.55.56: (postal 71350 St Gervais-en-Vallière): old favourite of ours. Now Parisians go there for amorous weekends. Relais du Silence ('calme, tranquillité, repos') but you can hear a little river tumbling over a weir, bouncing tennis balls and swimming pool splashes. Big park and garden. Fishing. Beams and antique furniture. Fine	A little-used route through river valleys. Verdun-sur-le-Doubs has a lovely tree-lined square facing two rivers. Louhans is a charming, photogenic little town at the meeting of two rivers; quiet except on market days when farmers bring in butter, eggs and poultry. Grande-Rue has fine arcaded houses of 17th and 18th centuries. The old hospital (Hôtel-Dieu) has a collection of glass (glasses, flagons, and Spanish and Moorish pottery).

cooking by Madame Moille: try smoked duck salad, salmon-trout in mustard sauce, Charolais steak, grilled Bresse bleu cheese. Menus F, G. Rooms F–G. Shut Sunday evening, Monday low season; 11 December–3 February.

Just off Nouilly-Louhans road is the beautiful 17th-century Château of Pierre and park.

Louhans – Cheval Rouge, 5 rue d'Alsace, 85.75.21.42: old-style hotel. Best restaurants in France get chickens from this area, so try poulet à la crème. Menu A–E. Rooms A–D. Shut 22 December–4 January; Sunday evenings, Monday low season.

Poularde, 5 rue Jura, 85.75.03.06: pleasant Logis; excellent value meals; try salmon, fricassée de poulet de Bresse. Cheap house wine; all wines reasonable. Menu A, B, C. Rooms A–C. Shut Wednesdays; 20 December–10 January.

D996 Bourg-en-Bresse (56km)

Splendid local dairy products and poultry mean mostly simple cooking – often delectable. Chicken is usually cooked in cream and white wine. Bleu de Bresse cheese is a local speciality.

Mail, 46 avenue Mail, 74.21.00.26: in a world of cooking fashions and innovation Roger Charolles still gets a star from customers and me for roast chicken. Roasting is a great culinary art, far more difficult than making Pernod or

One can tire of looking at old churches in France, but the church at Brou, suburb of Bresse, is one of the prettiest – a meeting of Gothic, flamboyant and Renaissance design, dainty rather than magnificent; the choir stalls, carved by the best local craftsmen, are remarkable. One shows a master enthusiastically beating the bare bottom of a pupil. The nearby tombs were carved by craftsmen brought from Flanders, Italy and Germany.

Bourg-en-Bresse continued

raspberry vinegar sauces or shavings of kiwi fruit. Locals love him, too, for snails and frogs' legs and fish 'as it arrives fresh'. Super wine cellar. Readers say main road and railway can make it noisy at night. We dine too well to notice. Rooms improved. Menus C–G. Rooms B–E. Shut Sunday evenings, Mondays; 14–29 July; 19 December–1 January.

Auberge Bressane, 166 boulevard de Brou, 74.22.22.68: Jean-Pierre Vullin is another chef cooking regional dishes beautifully from superb local ingredients. Comfortable old house. Menus D–G. Shut 24 November–16 December.

Superb windows. The story of the Brou Monastery is, alas, too long and complicated to tell here, but worth reading – a story of an orphan princess used for political power from babyhood, divorced, widowed but so intelligent that she became Regent of the Netherlands and Franche-Comté – wise, liberal, loved by the Comptois people: Marguerite of Austria, daughter of Emperor Maximilian.

Bresse makes fine rustic furniture from cherry, pear and apple trees, and is the market for the great Bresse chickens and dairy produce.

N75 Pont d'Ain (19km)

Alliés, 1 rue Brillat-Savarin, 74.39.00.09: good local cooking (pike quenelles, trout, snails, frogs' legs, Bresse chicken, crayfish). New rooms. Menu C–F. Rooms B–E. Shut Thursday; 20 December–21 January.

N75 to Ambérieu-en-Bugey (12km) (prettier route by Ain river D984 then left on D904 – 19km) N504 to Pugieu (38km) then left on D904 to Artemare (22km more)

At Luthézieu (8km NW from Artemare on D31 and D81) – Vieux Tilleul, 79.87.64.51: traditional cooking of region: try chicken in crayfish sauce; lavaret (fish from Savoie rather like a salmon). Menu A (weekdays) – E. Rooms B. Shut Tuesday evening, Wednesday in winter; January.

From Ambérieu you motor through foothills of the Alps and fine scenery.

At Artemare lovely mountain scenery with a waterfall (Cascade de Cerveyrieu).

D904 to Culoz (15km) Ruffieux (4km) then D991 to Aix-les-Bains (18km)

Ruffieux 79.54.27.38: – Château de Collanges – Fine 14th- to 16th-century turreted manor beautifully furnished. Silent, nice grounds with flowers. Superb views from terrace to Grand Colombier mountain across river Rhône. Rooms renovated. Bourget lake nearby; try any freshwater fish – trout, crayfish, salmon, perch. Cheapest menu very good value. Menu F, G (shut Sunday evenings; Mondays low season). Rooms G, H. Shut 5 January–10 February.

At Aix – Manoir, 37 rue Georges I (behind Thermal establishment), 79.61.44.00: in town but like a country house, in its own grounds, overlooking Lake Bourget. Relais du Silence. Lovely flowers. Comfortable bedrooms vary in size. Salmon and lavaret a speciality. Classical cooking. Menus C–F. Rooms D–F. Shut 20 December–20 January.

Chez la Mère Michaud, 82 rue Genève, 79.35.06.03: old-style, super bistro hotel; quiet shady gardens at back; pavement tables. Family cooking; good value; try lake fish and real gratin Dauphinois (sliced potatoes cooked in cream and garlic). Cheap house wine. Menus A–C; Rooms B, C. Shut December, January; restaurant shut Wednesday.

Lakeside roads with lovely views of distant mountains and Dent du Chat across the waters of Lake Bourget, largest lake in France. It even has a bust of Queen Victoria of England, who spent the spring of 1885 here.

Two sulphur springs are for treating rheumatism, two others less sulphuric for mineral waters. There are two casinos, lovely gardens, good sailing, lake trips and the Fauré Museum with fine modern paintings – Cézanne, Degas, Pissarro, Corot, Rodin (watercolours).

To the French, Aix remains the scene of the great love affair between the poet Lamartine and Elvire, the girl from the French Caribbean married to an old man and in Aix to cure TB. She died in Paris the next year (1817) and he wrote a passionate poem 'Le Lac' when she did not rejoin him at Aix.

Boats take you to Abbaye de Hautecombe; catch the 8.30 a.m. boat in summer to join abbey's Gregorian Chant. Otherwise drive to hear chant at other services.

Aix-les-Bains continued

International Hôtel Rivollier, 18 avenue Charles de Gaulle, 79.35.21.00: period piece, attractive; old furniture; run with old-style courtesy by same family for nearly 80 years. Menus C–G. Rooms E.

Dauphinois et Nivolet, 14 avenue Tresserve, 79. 61.22.56: attractive Logis de France. Family atmosphere; pleasant terrace for dinner on warmer nights; garden. Menus C–E. Rooms C–E. Shut 15 December–15 February.

At Viviers-du-Lac (4km along lakeside) – Week-End Hotel, 79.54.40.22: modern hotel on lakeside with steps to boats and terrace over lake. Bedrooms with balconies. Lake views from dining room. Rooms renovated. Windsurfing. Speciality of friture of small lake fish, lake perch, lavaret with crayfish sauce. Menus A–F. Rooms G–E. Shut Monday low season; 15 December–1 February.

At Bourgét-du-Lac (9km around lake) – Ombremont, 79.25.00.23: former millionaire's gorgeous retreat in steep hillside gardens running down to lake. Magnificent views. Immaculately run, with superb cooking, mainly regional but interesting inventions. Expensive, of course, but gracious living. Menu F, G. (Shut Saturday lunch!) Rooms F–G. Shut 20 December–2 February.

	Also at Bourget (2km route Dent-du-Chat) La Cerisaie, 79.25.01.29: perched high; views of lake and mountains. Cheap. Menu B–D. Rooms B–C. Shut Wednesday; 1 December–6 January.	
N201 Chambéry (16km)	Chaumiére, 14 rue Denfert-Rochereau (facing theatre), 79.33.16.26: Alain Boisson, patron-chef, continues to offer very good value, traditional meals in his rustic restaurant, with reasonably priced wines. Menu A, C. Shut Sundays, Wednesday evenings; 15–22 March, 3–28 August.	Once the capital of the Duchy of Savoy, then an independent state. It did not join France until 1860. Chambéry is dominated by the castle of the Dukes of Savoy, rebuilt in the 15th century and restored later after fires. You can visit it in summer.
	Tonneau, 2 rue St-Antoine, 79.33.78.26: change of chef-patron for restaurant known for real old dishes of Savoie at low prices. Not yet revisited by me. Prices still low. Menus A, C. Shut Monday; 8–31 August.	Magnificent views up here from outside or inside. It is an attractive old town, with narrow arcaded streets surrounded by wide boulevards. It is on the banks of the river Leysse, and is the main centre for Savoy mountain excursions.
	Vanoise, 44 ave Pierre-Lanfrey, 79.69.02.78: in the former restaurant of the old Grand Hotel, opposite the station, Philippe Lenain, a Parisian, offers meals full of new ideas, changing constantly. Menus C–G. Shut Sundays.	Along N542, 2km, is Les Charmettes, a truly charming country house where Rousseau lived for two years with Madame de Warens; he grew flowers, she kept bees.
N6 St-Jean-de-Maurienne (71km)	Modane – Perce-Neige, cours J. Jaurès, 79.05.00.50: small modern family hotel; good value Logis. Menus A, B. Rooms B–D. Shut 1–15 May; 18–31 October.	The route to Modane is up and down but broad and easy with fine scenery. The old town St-Jean-de-Maurienne has yet another cathedral (11th to 13th centuries).
N6 Modane (31km)	Voyageurs, 16 place Sommeillier, 79.05.01.39: Logis. Menus A–E. Rooms B, C. Shut Sunday except mid-summer; 15 October–15 November.	Fréjus road tunnel after Modane to Italy (Bardonecchia) 12.8km long; toll; open all year.

Route 4
Calais to Geneva

A chance to try a variety of French regional cooking. Traditional French cooking to many Britons means the cuisine of Ile de France near Paris, Provence, and Burgundy. That is only part of the feast. The Pas de Calais is influenced by the cream, cider and fresh fish of Normandy. Inland Picardy has a Flemish flavour, with duck, freshwater fish (especially trout and eels), creamy leek tart (flamiche), multitudes of sausages and cooking in beer and Geneva gin – solid food rather than subtle.

Champagne cooking is underestimated and is none the worse for Ile de France and Burgundy influences. Lamb, pork (excellent charcuterie and even breaded baked pigs' trotters). Crayfish and chicken are cooked in still Champagne and some fine dishes in red Bouzy wine. Pike soufflé (pain à la reine) with crayfish sauce is a delicacy we should copy. Chaource is a superb creamy cheese.

In Burgundy they have turned local dishes into gourmet feasts. The Dijon area is known for magnificent beef, game, freshwater fish (try pochouse – mixed fish stewed in wine), coq au Chambertin (a snob coq au vin), snails, gingerbread (pain d'épice) and spicy wine mustard used variously in sauces (usually with cream and called 'à la Dijonnaise'). Meurettes is a spicy red wine sauce with shallots, used for cooking freshwater fish, beef, and poached eggs.

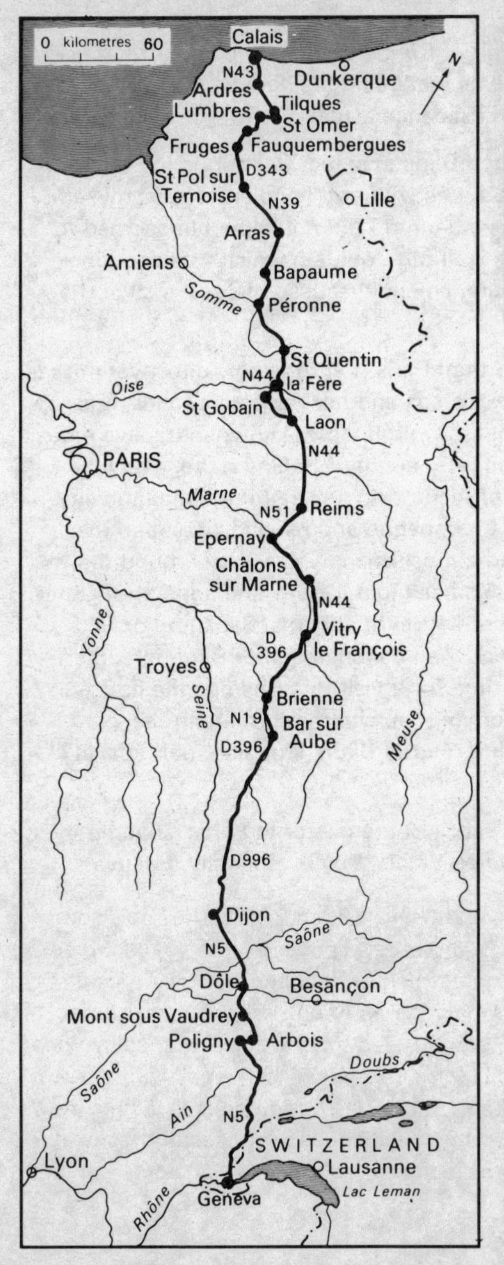
0 kilometres 60
N
Calais
N43
Ardres
Dunkerque
Lumbres
Tilques
St Omer
Fruges
Fauquembergues
D343
St Pol sur
Ternoise
N39
Lille
Arras
Amiens
Bapaume
Somme
Péronne
St Quentin
Oise
N44
la Fère
St Gobain
Laon
N44
PARIS
Marne
N51
Reims
Epernay
Châlons
sur Marne
N44
Yonne
D
396
Vitry
le François
Troyes
Seine
Brienne
N19
Bar sur
Aube
D396
Meuse
D996
Dijon
Saône
N5
Dôle
Besançon
Mont sous Vaudrey
Poligny
Arbois
Doubs
Saône
Ain
N5
SWITZERLAND
Lyon
Lausanne
Lac Leman
Rhône
Geneva

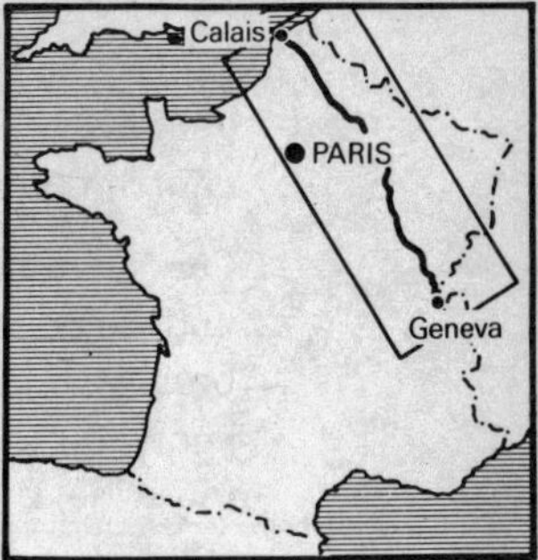
Calais
PARIS
Geneva

Kir, the aperitif of Crème de Cassis (blackcurrant) and white wine, was made famous here by Canon Kir, churchman, Resistance leader and mayor of Dijon.

I once attended Dijon's annual Gastronomic Festival and came home heavier and happier. I found myself breakfasting with a girl I did not know but seemed to know, on the wall of a fountain which was spouting red wine, eating splendid sausage from a stall in the square!

The route north of Paris is surprisingly direct yet misses most industrial areas and heavier traffic roads. It is planned to pass through lesser-known, attractive areas, like the hill country south of St Omer, the lovely countryside of Aisne with its beautiful old hilltop city of Laon, the Champagne and its vineyards, and the delightful and almost unknown country around the Aube valley. You can join it from Boulogne at St Omer; from Dieppe or Le Havre at Arras, Bapaume or St Quentin. Check road conditions after Dijon in winter. Try to leave time for a visit to a Champagne house in Reims or Epernay. You could return along the Burgundy wine road to Dijon, stopping, perhaps, at Chambertin.

A suggested return route nearer to Paris: Chaumont, Troyes, Crépy-en-Valois, Seulis, Chantilly, Beauvais.

Route 4
Calais to Geneva

Calais

Channel, 3 boulevard Résistance, 21.34.42.30: established British favourite; reliable; efficient service; you can see the kitchen; excellent fish. Good value. Menus A–G. Shut 21 December–15 January; Sunday evenings, Tuesdays.

Coq d'Or, place d'Armes, 21.34.79.05; excellent value from bargain cheap menu to dearest. Superb fish (try wild trout, sole Coq d'Or); good meat. Try also soufflé Roquefort. Classical sauces; good choice. Menus A–F. Shut Wednesdays.

Meurice, 5 rue Edouard Roche, 21.34.57.03: most comfortable hotel in Calais; bedrooms Empire to modern. Quiet. Founded 1772 by local postmaster Augustine Meurice to serve London–Paris coach passengers. He also founded Meurice in Paris. Rooms D–E.

Diligence (restaurant attached to Meurice), 21.96.92.89: is under quite different management – the Riechers, who were at Sangatte's Relais. Good fish.

Calais is two towns: the ferry port 38km from Britain, geared for the lucrative trade brought by British motorists and Britons on a day's shopping trip and the manufacturing centre and industrial port where boats from much of the world land cargoes. Signposts from the ferry encourage you to hurry round it to the motorway. Place d'Armes, a mediaeval square until destroyed in World War II, has useful shops including one offering 200 cheeses; also a market Wednesdays, Saturday mornings. Main market is at place Crèvecoeur, off boulevard Lafayette (Thursdays, Saturdays). Local people shop up there beyond the station. Hypermarket at Calais Marck, 3km E. Free bus from ferry terminal (good meals at Crêperie bar). Gro supermarket in place d'Armes is useful.

Outside Calais' Flemish town hall is Rodin's statue to the burghers who defied the English under Edward III. On the islet in the harbour the

Calais continued

Good-value cheaper menu – also carte gastronomique. Meals C–F. Shut Sundays; February.

George V, 36 rue Royale, 21.97.68.00: taken over by Bernard Beauvalot from La Bretagne, St Omer, completely renovated. Bedrooms bigger, sound-proofed; 40 with toilet and bath or shower. A gastronomic restaurant and a bistro (Le Petit George) with a good-value cheap menu. Menu A (bistro); D, plus carte (main restaurant). Rooms B–E. Restaurants shut Saturday lunchtimes, Sunday evenings.

La Duchesse, 44 rue Duc de Guise, 21.97.59.69: Fernand Leroy turned the old tea room into an attractive restaurant three years ago and I wish I had noticed earlier. Very good traditional cooking, with super pastries by Fernand's mum. Lovely grilled fish and very nice sole with smoked salmon in langoustine sauce. Good lobster, too. 250 different wines. Meals C–F. Shut Saturday lunchtimes.

Le Touquet's, 57 rue Royale, 21.34.64.18: bewildering; noisy, chaotic by day, remarkable value for families; calms down later, and from 8 p.m.–3 a.m. is also a casino – roulette, boule, blackjack. Menus A, B, F. Shut Mondays.

Rifle Brigade stood against the Nazis in 1940. Calais' large beach is used by locals, but few tourists.

From Blériot-Plage, 2km on D940, Blériot took off from the beach in 1909. A memorial also to Lambert who ditched in the Channel earlier and was picked up nonchalantly smoking a cigarette.

D127 Guines (10km) D231 Ardres (9km)

Guines – Lion d'Or, 7 place Maréchal-Foch, 21.35.20.51: deliciously old-French. Simple old bar – restaurant looking like a First World War relic in an old square by the town hall. Really good food at bargain prices. Eight bedrooms now have WC and bath or shower (book ahead in midsummer). Menus A, B, C. Rooms A–B. Restaurant shut Sunday lunchtimes.

Brêmes (1km before Ardres) – Bonne Auberge, 21.35.41.09: real country inn, still run by my friends the Desmulies. Informal, no frills, friendly. Most readers think it good value – so do the French, who drive miles to it. This is trout country, so try it braised in Chablis. Or the interesting duck with pears, and tarte-tatin (upside-down apple pie). Good-value wines. Simple bedrooms. Menus A–E. Rooms B. Cheap weekend rates. Shut Sunday evenings, Mondays in winter; 20 December–20 January.

Ardres – Grand Hotel Clément, 91 esplanade Mar.-Leclerc, 21.82.25.25: the Coolen family have been in this delightful little hotel since 1917 and I have known it since the early 1950s. Paul Coolen's son François is now at the cooker, and he learned a lot from the great Georges Blanc of Vonnas (four toques from Gault-Millau, three-star Michelin and one of the great original 'modern' cooks), but

Dull old N43 is also busier than ever now until Ardres with traffic making for new A26 motorway. Old square to right in Guines looks left over from 1914 war; small old shops, cafés, town hall. When Britain owned Calais, Guines was English front line, Ardres was French HQ. Between them (on D231) Henry VIII met Francis I in an ostentatious show of pomp and wealth to discuss an alliance (Field of the Cloth of Gold). They tried to outdo each other in everything. Like most summits, it ended in mutual mistrust. Henry signed a treaty with Charles V, France's enemy.

Lane south from Guines (3km) leads to hilltop memorial to Col. Blanchard and American Dr Jeffries who in 1785 landed here after aerial crossing of Channel by balloon.

Ardres continued

François keeps many old-style regional touches in his cooking. 'Dommage!' says Gault-Millau, 'Thank goodness!' say I. And Michelin gives him a star. Suprême de volaille *truly* supreme. Menu dégustation superb but very expensive. Relais du Silence, pleasant simple bedrooms, very nice garden. Menus C, F, G. Rooms C–E. Shut Mondays; 15 January–15 February.

At Recques-sur-Hem, off N43 7km past Ardres, Château de Cocove, 21.82.68.29: 18th-century château turned into hotel in 1986 by wine merchant. Wine shop in cellar. Charming restaurant. Menu C–E. Rooms E–F.

N43 St Omer (23km)

Tilques (left off N43, 5km before St Omer) – Vert Mesnil, 21.93.28.99: 19th-century château in quiet position with lake – new owners. Used by several package companies. Useful overnight. New bedrooms added. Menus B–G. Rooms E, F. Shut 20 December–20 January.

St Omer – Cygne, 8 rue Caventon, 21.98.20.52: Gérard Maerten-Prévost's little gem opposite an 18th-century swan fountain, which I recommended when it opened in 1983, has been renovated but blessedly is unchanged otherwise. Rather famous now, so book if possible. Splendid value.

Motorway A26 has taken most of N43 heavy traffic. St Omer, once cursed with traffic jams, now a place to explore. Centre of an area of waterways and gardens which lures painters, St Omer has some fine merchants' houses of the 16th and 17th centuries (especially in Grande Place). Rue de l'Escugarie holds Notre-Dame, a former cathedral of the 13th century with same period statue of Christ and tomb of St Omer. Good fine arts museum with works by Flemish, Dutch and French masters, lovely tapestries, ceramics, mosaics, ivories; pleasant boat trips (½-hour) from near station along garden-lined canals and

Lovely duck, including breast fillets (magret) prepared ten different ways. Hot dessert soufflés. Excellent choice of wines. Menus B, D. Shut 10–31 December.

Bretagne, 2 place du Vainquai, 21.38.25.78: very well run by Francis and Sylvie (chef) Beauvalot (see George V, Calais). Attractive grill, plus elegant old-style restaurant (Le Best) known especially for fish, pâtisseries, and a dessert buffet (try boeuf à la moelle and chocolate meringue – but not together!) Wines good value. Menus A–D (wine included). Rooms (very comfortable) B–E. Open all year.

Bollezeele (18km N on D928, D226) – Hostellerie Saint Louis, 47 rue Eglise, 28.68.81.83: charming 18th-century manor, all nicely modernized since we stayed when first opened. Log fires, peaceful garden. Relais du Silence. My readers approve heartily. New games room with 'billiards, TV, musculation' (muscle development exercises – you'll be ready for dinner). I'll stick to wineglass raising. Menus C–G. Rooms D. Open all year.

forest of Clairmarais, with reserve for migrating herons. The park has a good swimming pool and open-air theatre (summer). For bizarre nostalgia, one of the first German rocket bases for attacking Britain (at Wizernes, 4km on N28).

D208 to Wisques, D208, N42 Lumbres (13km)

Wisques – Sapinière, 21.95.14.59: simple inn. Bedrooms much improved (shower, WC, phone, TV). Flemish-style cooking; good vegetables from Marais de St Omer. Local guide says its 'intimacy and discretion lure couples in love, and businessmen'. Menus B–E. Rooms E.

Lumbres (on local road off N42) – Moulin de Mombreux, 21.39.62.44: more than 20 years since we found Jean-Marc Gaudry from Oasis at Napoules (3-star Michelin) converting this delightful old mill. Soon he had a Michelin star. Now he is adding a 3-star hotel with 24 bedrooms to the pretty small rooms in the mill. Expensive meals but his individualistic yet classic cooking is sheer delight. Alas, no cheap wines. Small trout river, the Aa, runs through the garden. Menus E–G. Rooms F–G. Shut 20 December–1 February; Sunday evening, Monday (check).

Trou Normande, 18 route Nationale 42, 21.95.28.63: simple country inn. New chef-patron, more ambitious cooking (try veal fillet in orange sauce, sole with cèpes). More choice of wines. Seven more rooms (very simple). Menus A, B, C. Rooms A. Shut Sunday evenings; part of February.

Benedictine abbey at Wisques in a château and a hilltop building: ancient (15th-century) and modern (1953) architecture; Gregorian Chant at 9.45 a.m. mass. Lovely hill country.

Lumbres, on river l'Aa; old squares, narrow streets; trout fishing but also paper mills, cement works.

At Merck-St Lieven (2km on D225 right off D928) a trout farm with 40 ponds; see them thrash about when fed. Fauquembergues, typical little old market-town with fine 13th-century church, is now missed by D928.

Take D928 on to Ruisseauville (4km) and lane signposted to Azincourt (Agincourt) where in 1415 Henry V's small army beat a French army 3 times its size. Poignantly and simply marked by a cross; an Englishman should count himself accursed for not seeing it.

D192, D193 Cléty (9km) D193, D190 (right) D928 Fauquembergues (10km) D928 Fruges (10km)

At Cléty (on D928) – Truite d'Argent, 21.93.80.57: very simple, incredibly cheap pension – restaurant with bargain meals. Some of my readers are 'regulars'. Menus A. Rooms A. Shut first week February; 1–25 October.

D928, D343 St-Pol-sur-Ternoise (25km) N39 Arras (34km)

At Fillièvres (D101, 17km SW of St Pol) – Vieux Moulin, 21.04.83.42: see route 1 Hesdin.

Arras – this is Flanders and that means Flemish cooking, often in beer or juniper; with sausages, hotpots, delightful flans and big portions.

Chanzy, rue Chanzy, 21.71.02.02: an institution in North France. De Troy family have run it for more than forty years. Dining rooms smarter but the same fine old cooking. Take a good appetite – chicken in beer; sausages; flambés; potée flamande (bacon, ham, sausage, potatoes); hochepot (beef, mutton, pork, vegetables); charcuterie; lovely Flemish leek flan. Huge wine cellars in rock with 120,000 bottles of 1000 appellations dating from 1868. Menus B (regional), C, F (gastronomique). Rooms D. Open all year.

De Troy family due to open b-and-b hotel, Trois Leopards, 47 Grande Place, 21.07.41.41 in 1988. 15th-century façade, modern interior.

Deceptive appearance, for Arras is interesting. Almost destroyed in the 1914–18 war, much of it was rebuilt as before, such as the 15th-century town hall which has a bust of a well-known local lad, Robespierre the French Revolutionary leader; rooms are furnished in 16th-century style. Grande Place and place des Héros have old-style arcaded buildings, and Grande Place buildings have coats of arms of craftsmen and merchants. Good market (Wednesday, Saturday).

At the citadel is a moving memorial to 2000 French Resistance fighters shot by the Nazis, and alongside the graves of 35,000 British killed in World War I. Vimy ridge, where 75,000 Canadians died fighting in 1917, is 8km N just off N17. A huge, impressive memorial, it is sombre and frightening when you consider the confusion and life-wastage of the campaign of that year.

Arras continued

Ambassadeur (Buffet Gare), 21.23.29.80: the old 'station buffet' has lost its Michelin star but its menus are cheaper and good value. Menus C–F. Also has a brasserie 'rapide'. Menus A, B. Shut Sunday evenings.

Faisanderie, 45 Grande Place, 21.48.20.76: Jean-Pierre Dargent (ex-Flavio, Le Touquet) moved from his beamed farmhouse in Pommera to a Flemish 'historic monument' in Arras' main square. You eat on the ground level by a fine old wood fireplace or in the cellar among attractive stone columns. Michelin star for super cooking, basically classical, but imaginative and always with fresh, seasonal food. Menus B, C, E. Shut Sunday evenings, Mondays; part February; 3–24 August.

Univers, 3 place Croix Rouge. 21.71.34.01: delightful, elegant, quiet hotel made from 18th-century monastery. Award winning chef specializes in regional dishes. Menus B, F (gastronomic) Rooms C (small), E. Open all year.

Moderne, 1 boulevard Faidherbe, 21.23.39.57: by station; comfortable old bed-and-breakfast hotel – brasserie below. Rooms (modern, all with bath, WC) E. Shut 24 December–3 January.

N17 D944 N29 through Bapaume, Péronne to St Quentin (70km)

At Péronne – Hostellerie des Remparts, 23 Beaubois, 22.84.01.22: delightfully attractive with flowers, coloured blinds outside; solid comfort within; terrace for good weather. Four menu prices. Local fish includes smoked eel; pike quenelles. Menus A–E. Rooms B–E. Shut 3–13 August.

St Quentin – Grand Hôtel et Restaurant Président, 6 rue Dachery, 23.62.69.77: brilliant conversion of an obsolete hotel; charming furnishings, excellent service; delightful meals. Try roast lamb from Provence hills (les Alpilles); very good fish and chicken dishes. Good desserts. Michelin star; 3 toques and 17–20 from Gault-Millau. Good choice of Bordeaux and Burgundy wines. Menus E–G. Rooms G. Hotel open all year. Restaurant shut Sunday evenings, Mondays; 1–15 February; 3–23 August (check beforehand).

Paix et Albert I (Restaurant le Brésilien), 3 place Huit Octobre, 23.62.77.62: same excellent management as luxury Grand et Restaurant Président (see above). Good for families. Rooms well above expected standard; grills, pizzas, snacks to full meals; oysters; Savoyard specialities (fondue, raclette). Meals carte only, mostly A, B. Rooms E. Open all year.

Motorway A1 has made N17 much easier for driving. Péronne known for local fishing lagoons; specializing in anguilles (freshwater eels), pike. Poor St Quentin was almost totally destroyed in 1914–18. The huge Basillica (12th to 15th centuries) survived with its massive belfry. Industrial town with fine park. Champs-Elysées, on devastated battlefield and lagoon with a beach beside river Somme for watersports.

St Quentin continued	At Neuville-St-Amand (SE 3km by D12) – Château de Neuville, 23.68.41.82: another Michelin-starred restaurant in pleasant rural grounds; eat outside in summer. Fish direct from small boats at Boulogne thrice weekly, very well cooked. Rooms being added. Menus D (weekdays), F, G. Shut August 3 weeks; Christmas; Sunday evenings, Mondays, Wednesday evenings.	
N44 Laon (46km) alternative route N44 to La Fère, D13 to St Gobain then D7 through St Gobain forest to Laon	Bannière de France, 11 rue Franklin-Roosevelt, 23.23.21.44: Lefèvres family have been in this old Relais de Poste over 20 years. We stayed well before that. But it has been here since 1685, anyway! Typical old inn in style and atmosphere despite recent modernization of bedrooms and change of furnishings. We have always loved it and have a boxful of accolades from readers. Suddenly a year ago I started to get criticism of food and service. But meals were excellent on our last visit. French guides are happy and the ultra-critical Gault-Millau talks about 'attentive owners, smiling service and classical cuisine without reproach'! I like veal kidneys in Bouzy wine. Menus C, D, F. Rooms C–E. Shut 20 December–20 January.	A delightful old city, once capital of France (4th to 9th centuries) set high on a steep hill, with magnificent views, especially from mediaeval ramparts; worth an overnight stop to explore and enjoy its old buildings, streets, and rampart walks. Cathedral of Notre-Dame (12th century) is one of the oldest Gothic cathedrals in France. From outside it is beautiful, inside it is magnificent. There are so many historic church buildings in France that they can set me yawning, but this one is not to be missed. Very crowded in tourist season. Paris was a hamlet when Laon was capital. Charlemagne's mother, Berthe Au Grand Pied (Berthe of the big feet), made it her seat.

Angleterre, 10 Boulevard Lyon (in lower town), 23.23.04.62: modern, neat, comfortable, useful. Menus A (weekdays). C, D. Rooms B, D. Restaurant shut Saturday lunch, Sunday in winter.

Petite Auberge, 45 boulevard Pierre-Brossolette, 23.23.02.38: recommended to me by a very distinguished French gastronome but I have not tried it. Chef-patron (aged 22) was at the Château at Fère-en-Tardenois – a great recommendation. Menus C–G. Shut Saturdays.

At St Gobain (alternative route) – Roses de Picardie, 23.52.88.74: useful little modern hotel recommended by readers for exploring forest. No restaurant. Rooms A–C. Open all year.

Parc Restaurant, 23.52.80.58: Menus A (weekday)–C. Shut Sunday evening, Monday; 14 July–15 August.

Alternative route through St Gobain forest much prettier, if slower. St Gobain has 16th-century glass works making the world-renowned St Gobain glass. Named after Irish hermit.

N44 Reims (47km)

Good restaurants are mostly dear. Big choice of small restaurants around cathedral. Study their menus outside. Here are some expensive restaurants.

Boyer 'Les Crayères', 64 boulevard Henry Vasnier, 26.82.80.80: Gérard Boyer is certainly one of the world's greatest chefs, his meals inevitably are very pricey, and if you have not tried one, it is worth saving up to do so. Traditional superlative

Kings of France were crowned in the cathedral and I don't blame them. It can really be called a masterpiece. Begun in 1211, it was badly damaged in World War I, restored in 1938 and it is beautiful. Magnificent 13th-century windows, damaged in that war, were splendidly repaired by the Simon family who also designed new windows. Then Marc Chagall designed three delightful new ones.

Reims continued

cooking of the freshest, best ingredients with individual touches. In a seductively elegant château in a delightful park. Now with beautifully furnished bedrooms (book *far* ahead). Meals carte about 400–600F (1988). Double rooms 900–1400F. Hotel open all year. Restaurant shut Mondays, Tuesday lunch.

Chardonnay, 184 ave Epernay, 26.06.08.60: the Boyers have kept their old restaurant; young chef Dominique Giraudeau serves lovely dishes from old estouffades (stews) and navarin (lamb stew) to modern. One Michelin star to his boss's three, but cheaper. Meals E, F. Shut Saturday lunchtimes, Sundays; August; 19 December–12 January.

Forum, 34 place Forum, 26.47.56.87: 200 metres from the cathedral, but used by locals. Plenty of choice in excellent value cheap menus. Recently renovated. Menus A, B, D. Shut Sunday evenings, Mondays.

Paix et Taverne Maitre Kanter, 9 rue Buirette, 26.40.04.08: very useful; modern; comfortable rooms, garden, pool; good service. Menus A, C, D. Rooms E, F. Open all year.

You can visit Champagne houses here, in Epernay, or, like me, in both. These need no appointment: visiting hours are seasonal, so check: Veuve-Clicquot-Ponsardin, 1 place des Droits-de-l'Homme, phone 26.47.33.60. Mumm (11 miles of cellars; good guiding), 12 rue du Champ-de-Mars 26.40.22.73. Piper-Heidsieck, 51 boulevard Henri-Vasnier 26.85.01.94. Pommery (appointments needed weekends only; 11 miles of cellars include statues). 5 place Général Giraud 26.05.05.01. Tattinger (includes crypt of former abbey), 1 place St Nicaise 26.85.45.35.

N31 west to Thillois, D26 to Gueux, Pargny, then ordinary road to right to St Lié and Ville Dommange: on to D26 to Sacy, Ecueil to Montchenot on N51 to Epernay (27km)

At Champillon, 6km N Epernay on N51 – Royal Champagne, 26.52.87.11: 18th-century Relais de Poste, beautifully furnished, luxurious. Director Marcel Dellinger used to run Château d'Artigny. I don't care what Gault-Millau says, old-style cooking with fine sauces suits me – so do the surroundings, views, ambience. A star from Michelin. 150 different champagnes, 180–850F. Menus F (lunch), G. Rooms F, G. Shut 5–31 January.

Epernay – Terrasse, 7 quai Marne, 26.55.26.05: Menu A (weekdays)–E. Shut 1–15 July; 1–21 February; Sunday evening.

Berceaux, 13 rue Berceaux, 26.55.28.84; wine bar, restaurant, hotel. Chef-patron Luc Maillard an enthusiast for food and wine. Regional cooking, good wines by the glass. Menus (shut Sunday evening) C–G. Rooms C–F.

At Ay (5km by D201) – Vieux Pressoir, 2 rue Gérard-Sondag, 26.55.43.31: nice old house with good value local dishes. Menus B, C. Shut Sunday, Monday and Tuesday evenings; 16–30 August.

Calmer than Reims; Museum of Champagne (31 avenue de Champagne) is historically interesting. Times of visits to Champagne caves and general information from Comité Inter Professional du Vin de Champagne, 5 rue Henri-Martin, 51200 Epernay 26.51.40.47. Moët et Chandon 20 avenue de Champagne 26.51.71.11. has 17 miles of galleries, excellent explanation of wine making. Museum has Napoleon's hat. Open all year but shut weekends. Mercier, 75 avenue de Champagne, 26.51.74.74. tours by electric train, 1 March–1 October. Has world's largest wine cask made in 1889 and holding enough wine for 200,000 bottles – every hostess should have one.

4km N on D386 at Hautvilliers is a Benedictine abbey, vineyard where Pérignon performed his miracle; owned since the Revolution by Moët.

RD3 Châlons-sur-Marne (34km)

Angleterre et Restaurant Jacky Michel, 19 place Monseigneur Tissier, 26.68.21.51: run by a chef from Aux Armes de Champagne (see page 134). Delights my readers for quality. Dining room

Here in AD 451, in a bloody battle in which 200,000 were killed, Attilla the Hun, 'scourge of God', was beaten by Romans, Visigoths and Franks; he fled to Hungary and turned his hordes on to Italy.

Chalons-sur-Marne continued

interestingly transformed by famous decorator Dominique Monnet. Excellent seasonal dishes. I like beef in Ratafia (brandy and grape juice). Hot chocolate soufflé is a favourite. Menus E–G. Rooms E–F. Shut Saturday lunch, Sunday.

At L'Epine, 8km NE by N3 – Aux Armes de Champagne, 26.68.10.43: Jean-Paul Pérardel's hotel, opposite historic church (1400), started by his family as a café in 1907. Luxury auberge, elegant comfort, immaculate table-settings; attractive gardens; superb cooking; magnificent caves (he is a wine merchant, too) – 45 sparkling champagnes, 20 still champagnes. Old-style bar has been updated. Some rooms in quiet annexes. Nothing but praise from my readers. Menus B (weekdays), E, G. Rooms (book) E, F. Shut 5 January–12 February.

Cathedral St Etienne has lovely stained glass spanning 12th to 16th centuries. Superb old books in town library, including *Confessions of St Augustine* and *Romance of the Rose.*

At L'Epine, 7km on N3 is superb Basilique of Notre-Dame in flamboyant Gothic. Pilgrimages go in May.

N44 Vitry le François (32km) D396 to Rosnay, Brienne-le-Château, at Maison Neuve take N19 to Bar-sur-Aube (68km)

At Dolancourt, near Maison Neuve on N19 – Moulin du Landion, 25.26.12.17: delightful old mill with river flowing below restaurant; mill wheels still turn. Trout fishing in river. Big bedrooms with bathrooms. Menus B–F. Rooms D. Shut December.

Bar-sur-Aube – Commerce, 39 rue Nationale, 25.27.08.76: Master Chef of France Claude Paris still offers careful cooking of regional dishes using top-

Napoleon went to military school in Brienne, when aged 9. He could still only speak French in an Italian-Corsican patois, but came top in mathematics and military exercises. Later he called the region 'Ma Patrie'. In 1814 he attacked a Prussian and Russian army here.

Bar is a little market town beside a pretty stretch of river, under wooded and vine-covered slopes. The route misses the main traffic.

	quality ingredients; lovely fresh salmon; quail; fair prices; good choice. Menus A, C, D. Rooms A–D. Shut early January–early February.	15km E of Bar on N19 is Colombey-les-Deux-Eglises. Charles de Gaulle is buried here. La Boisserie, his house (1933–70), is open to visitors.
D396/D996 Dijon (114km)	See Route 3 (page 106)	
N5 Dôle (48km)	Chaumière, 346 avenue Genève, 84.79.03.45: old farmhouse now a cosy rustic hotel. Very pleasant; swimming pool. Good terrines and cheese; good use of various delicate local fungi and river fish (trout, pike, sandre). Bedrooms transformed with bathrooms, TV. Menus C, E, F. Rooms E. Shut Saturday, Sunday in winter; 19 December–19 January. Chandioux, place Grévy, 84.79.00.66: 18th-century coaching inn of charm, attentive service; nicely furnished. Regional dishes (jambon persillé, river fish). Henri Maire's Arbois wines. Menus B–G. Rooms D–E.	Louis Pasteur was born here, son of a tanner, in a street now named after him; there is a small museum. Now an industrial town, it is prettily placed above river Doubs. A long history of fighting for independence against the French kings; it was the first town to be bombarded with howitzer shells – by Prince of Condé in 1636; but Dôle won and the Archbishop, aged 80, watched the French retreat from the roof of the cathedral, thanked God, and dropped dead.
N5 to Mont-sous-Vaudrey D469 Arbois (37km)	Paris, 9 rue Hôtel-de-Ville, 84.66.05.67: Jolly, plump, old-style chef André Jeunet was renovating his hotel-restaurant in February 1988. I hope it doesn't spoil the rustic effect. Son Jean-Paul, a smiling, slimmer modern chef formerly with Troisgros at Roanne, now at the cooker but the lovely old dishes still on the menu – plump local hen in 'yellow' Arbois wine	Arbois – centre of Jura wines; wine growers famous through centuries for independence and hot-headed actions; resenting the importance of Lyon, they declared their little city a republic in 1834. When the police demanded the revolt leaders, they said: 'We are *all* leaders'. Pasteur lived here, went to local primary school and college. His family home

Arbois continued	with morilles, pike mousseline with crayfish sauce, local trout, salmon. Good wine cellar. Menus C–G. Rooms E–F. Shut Monday evening, Tuesday low season; September.	can be visited 15 April–30 September. His vineyard (2km on N83 towards Besançon) bought in 1874 and used for his experiments on fermentation, still produces good wine, drunk on special occasions.
N83 Poligny (10km) N5 Geneva (98km)	Monts de Vaux (4.5km from Poligny) – Hostellerie Monts de Vaux, 84.37.12.50: super old Relais de Poste with old furniture. Very expensive. Menu lunch only E; carte. Rooms E–G. Shut Wednesday lunch, Tuesday low season; end October–end December.	Poligny is an ancient town with fine old Grande Rue. Fine views on this road of the Jura plateau. Just past Poligny, N5 passes La Gulée de Vaux – one of the valleys used by the Romans as a trading route. Lovely views from Monts-de-Vaux. Les Ronses is a winter sports centre. In winter, check this route for weather conditions.

Route 5
Calais to Strasbourg

(for Germany and Austria)

Linking motorways from near Channel ports across Belgium have by-passed this old route to Germany. For the true traveller it has great rewards. Almost direct from Calais or Boulogne, it avoids most northern industrial cities and takes you to lovely scenery, little known to the French.

The beautiful Meuse valley, with small roads running past rocks, ravines and hills, north of Hirson and Charleville to the Belgian border; the pleasant countryside of wooded hills and rivers between Longuyon and Metz; the hillocky road from St Avold to Saverne beneath the Vosges mountains. The industrial towns which you do meet, such as Arras and Metz, have special attractions and interests.

You could return on the more southerly route, back from Metz through Verdun, Reims in the Champagne and either through Compiègne (Route 3) or Laon (Route 4).

By crossing the Rhine into Germany at Strasbourg instead of going through Belgium and crossing into Germany at Aachen, you miss the industrial Ruhr and have a pleasant road to Stuttgart to join the motorway through Frankfurt and Munich and into Austria.

Not many years ago you could find many British tourists in the northern towns through which this route passes – in Arras, Cambrai, Sedan, Metz. They were old soldiers of the 1914–18 War, returning to the battlefields where they had fought and their friends had died. Now most of them have joined their friends, and their sons make pilgrimages to Arnhem and the Normandy beaches. But to anyone with a sense of history these northern battlefields of France are still sadly dramatic and local museums deeply interesting. Read the history of the towns and villages, and you begin to understand the French better.

Much of the route is in Alsace and Lorraine where food is delicious and solid rather than for gourmets – except the pâté de foie gras of Strasbourg, which is superb to taste but sticks in many gullets because the geese have been force-fed.

True *local* quiche Lorraine contains no cheese. A delicious alternative is quiche (or gâteau) au fromage blanc (cream cheese and bacon flan). Sauerkraut (choucroute) appears in many winter dishes in both areas (such as jambon à l'Alsacienne – ham with sauerkraut, Strasbourg sausage and potatoes).

Both provinces have a love of tarts, flans and pastry coverings. Even the delicate freshwater crayfish are often encased in pastry, though they are used in dozens of ways, including as a smooth pink sauce for covering other fish or chicken.

Alsace is pork country, with plenty of good charcuterie, and goose country, with goose fat used for cooking. The German influence has made dumplings popular. Chickens are almost of the Bresse standard. Lorraine's German inspired derentifleisch (smoked rib of beef) is very tasty.

Alsace wines from the French bank of the Rhine are made with similar grapes to the German wines (Riesling, Traminer and Sylvaner) but made dry for French palates, not sugared to suit Germans. Even Muscat grapes are used to make dry white wines, not dessert wines. Moselle wines (quite different from German Mosel) are best when young. Lorraine's rosé wines are often called Vin Gris and are almost red! On labels, Zwicker means wines made with common grapes, Edelzwicker with nobler grapes.

Brandies are made from strawberries (fraise), raspberries (framboise), cherries (kirschwasser), pears (Poire William), plums (Quetsch) and greengages (Reine Claude).

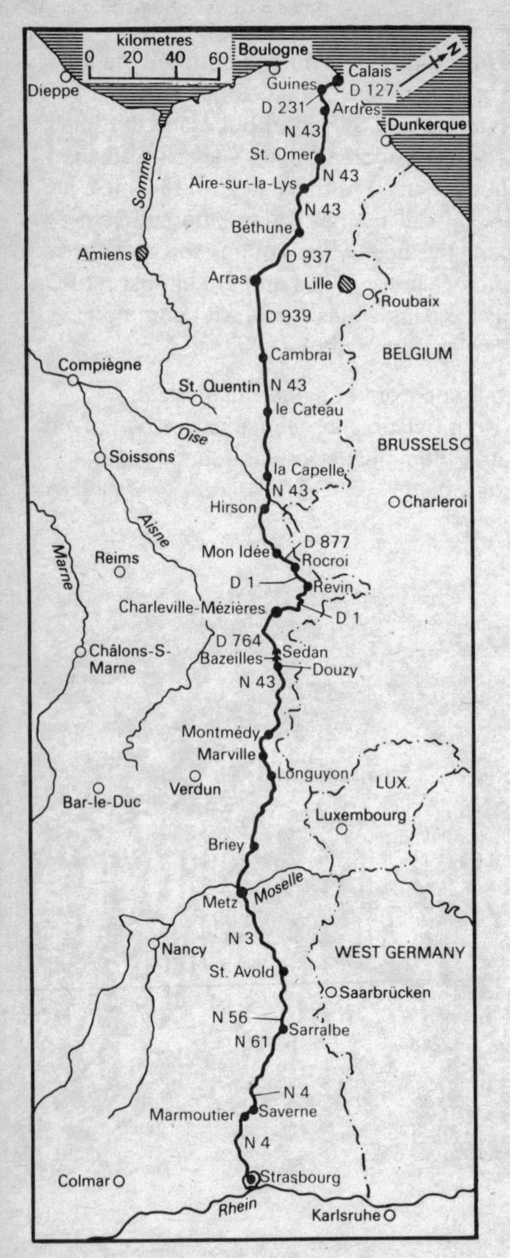
kilometres
0 20 40 60
N
Boulogne
Calais
Dieppe
Guines
D 127
D 231
Ardres
N 43
Dunkerque
St. Omer
N 43
Aire-sur-la-Lys
Somme
N 43
Béthune
Amiens
D 937
Arras
Lille
Roubaix
D 939
Cambrai
BELGIUM
Compiègne
St. Quentin
N 43
le Cateau
Oise
BRUSSELS
Soissons
la Capelle
N 43
Charleroi
Hirson
Aisne
D 877
Marne
Mon Idée
Reims
Rocroi
D 1
Revin
Charleville-Mézières
D 1
D 764
Châlons-S-Marne
Sedan
Bazeilles
Douzy
N 43
Montmédy
Marville
Longuyon
LUX.
Verdun
Bar-le-Duc
Luxembourg
Briey
Moselle
Metz
N 3
Nancy
WEST GERMANY
St. Avold
Saarbrücken
N 56
Sarralbe
N 61
N 4
Marmoutier
Saverne
N 4
Colmar
Strasbourg
Rhein
Karlsruhe

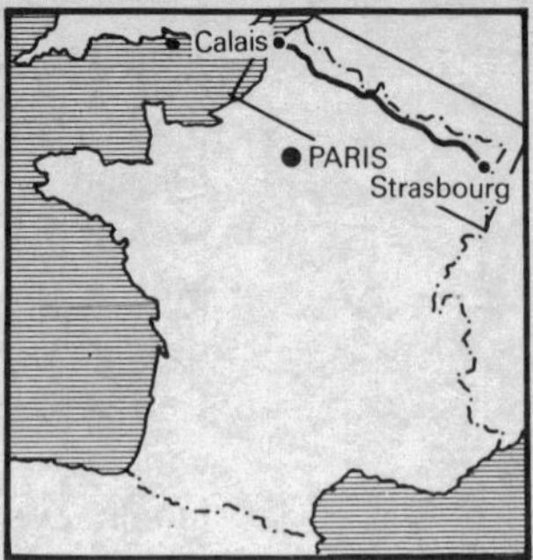
Calais
PARIS
Strasbourg

Route 5
Calais to Strasbourg

(for Germany and Austria)

Calais to St Omer

See Route 4

From St Omer N43 Aire-sur-la-Lys (18km)

Aire – Trois Mousquetaires at Château de la Redoute, 21.39.01.11: thank goodness it will be a little easier to stay in this delightful hotel. Fifteen new rooms are added. A charming gabled 19th-century château with pointed turrets in tranquil grounds to the Lys river. Lake with ducks and swans. Philippe Venet has taken over the kitchen from his father, Marcel, but still cooks in the same traditional way with fine meat grilled over charcoal, super sauces (try contrefilet Dijonnaise). Fine choice of home-made terrines and salads. Lovely fish direct from coast. Excellent value. Cheapest menu is a bargain. Big choice. Excellent desserts. Wines very reasonable. Wonderful welcome, too. Must book. Menus B, C, F, G. Rooms D–E. Shut Sunday evening, Monday; 20 December–20 January.

Well-preserved market town, on edge of industrial belt, where river Lys and Aire canals meet. 18th-century Grand' Place has many old houses; town hall (16th-century) is attractive; 15th-century church of St Peter in flamboyant-Renaissance style. British Army HQ 1917–18. D'Artagnan, only one of Dumas' Three Musketeers who really lived, built the original Château de la Redoute as a fort.

N43 Béthune (25km)	Vieux Beffroy, Grand' Place, 21.68.15.00: well-run, neat auberge with good value meals; hors d'oeuvres buffet impressive. Menus A–F. Rooms B, C. Open all year.	Industrial town, rebuilt considerably after damage in two world wars, but some pleasant 17th-century buildings left. Grand Place rebuilt in Flemish style.
D937 Arras (33km)	See Route 4 (page 127)	
D939 Cambrai (36km)	At Marquion (11km before Cambrai) – Crémaillère, 21.22.50.31: good old classic cooking using fine ingredients. Low prices. Friendly; good service. Menus A–F. Shut Sunday evenings, Mondays; 5–15 September. Cambrai – Escargot, 10 rue de Gaulle, 27.81.24.54: meat and fish grilled over charcoal; vivier of lobsters. Menus A–F. Shut Mondays; December, January. Château Motte-Fénélon, place Château, 27.83.61.38: simply delightful great white country house in a big park. Recommended by French friends. I have not yet stayed. Menu E; carte. Rooms D. Open all year. Beatus, 718 avenue de Paris, 27.81.45.70: quiet, elegant; in a park; attractive Louis XV, XVI. Rooms C–E. No restaurant.	Tank warfare started here; on 20 November 1917, the Tank Corps, 4000 men strong, launched the first tank attack in history, winning a victory and changing the history of war. Linen has been made here since the 15th century. A small town packed with historic and art treasures. Do see the church of Saint Géry, with 85m (250ft) belfry, a Renaissance-style rood screen, and twelve large paintings including 'The Entombment' by Rubens. Fénelon, the churchman, writer and soldier, who got himself badly wounded fighting the Duke of Marlborough, was Archbishop of Cambrai and died there. The massive 14th-century Porte de Paris was part of the old defences. In municipal museum are works of Breughel and Rubens. Handsome covered market.
N43 Le Cateau-Cambrésis (24km)	At Ligny (D74 off N43 or D16 from Caudry) – Château de Ligny, 27.85.25.84: lovely château started in 13th century, completed 17th century. Built round a	The artist Henri Matisse was born here in 1869 and a museum in the 17th-century town hall contains his drawings and engravings. Also birthplace of Adolphe

	courtyard. Renaissance gate leads to a tiny park with deer and ponies; very quiet rooms; very expensive. You dine by candlelight in a room with a big open fire. Menus C (weekdays), F, G. Rooms G. Shut mid-November–mid-February.	Mortier, giant son of a cloth merchant, who became one of Napoleon's best marshals. Made Duke of Treviso, he died protecting King Louis Philippe with his great bulk from explosions of an 'infernal machine'.
N43 La Capelle (30km)	Thierache, 23.97.33.80: Logis with casserole for good regional cooking. Good value meals. Menus A–D. Rooms B, C. Shut 10–25 February.	At La Villa Pasques, 17 rue de l'Armistice (then rue d'Hirson), the German General von Winderfeld came on 7 November 1918 to meet Marshal Foch's staff to arrange the end of the Kaiser's war. The Haudroy Stone, a mile northeast, commemorates the Armistice of 11 November 1918. Capelle has an important race course.
N43 Hirson (14km)	Feutry Restaurant, Hotel Gare, 23.58.16.45: Jean-Luc Feutry, wine merchant and master wine-taster of France, has given this station hotel an excellent wine cellar and better cooking. Try trout in red wine, profiteroles with Cointreau cream. Simple rooms. Menus A–D. Rooms A–B. Shut Sunday evening, Monday; part February. At Landouzy, 7km SW Hirson by D963, D36 – Domaine du Tilleul, 23.98.48.00: delightful; in tranquil park. Young chef from Maxim's in Paris building a deserved reputation. Menus D–G. Rooms E–F. Open 15 March–15 November. Restaurant shut Sunday evening, Monday.	Commercial centre where two rivers meet; superb forest with small lakes right alongside; Etang de Blangy is pretty, with a waterfall. From Etang du Pas Bayard (5km from town) is a summer 'Route Verte', open 1 May to 30 September, through the forest. Fine oak trees. Fine views along ridge road from Hirson. Cheese and cider country.

N43 to Mon Idée, D877 Rocroi, local road D1 to Revin (24km) then right on D1 through Meuse Valley.

At La Neuville-les-Beaulieu, just before Mon Idée off N43 – Môtel du Bois, 24.54.32.55: little modern inn with comfortable rooms (all with shower, WC); regional cooking attracts locals. Try river fish 'soupe'; game in season. Cheap house wine. Menu A, B, C. Rooms B. Shut 15 December–31 January; Monday lunch.

At Auvillers-les-Forges, 1.5km SW Mon Idée on D877 – Hostellerie Lenoir, 24.54.30.11: Master Chef of France Jean Lenoir has over years turned the village café over which he was born into a 2-star Michelin restaurant. He and sister Ginette offer superb regional cooking making best use of fresh local products including game from Ardennes forest. Personal touches (goose liver in honey and jasmine); superb pigeon mousse, soufflé of sandre (river fish). Expensive and worth it. Very friendly. Charming bedrooms. Menus G. Rooms C–F. Three-day cookery courses, too! Shut Fridays; January, February.

At Rocroi – Commerce, place A. Briand, 24.54.11.15: readers love it for value, friendliness and family cooking. You won't go hungry. Traditional dishes such as Flemish cheese tart, coq au vin, kidneys in wine. Wild boar in season. Menus, A–D. Rooms A–C. Shut 5 January–10 February; Mondays in winter.

The French Ardennes, a real wanderers' route, sometimes steep, very beautiful and wild and almost totally unknown to tourists. You pass the massive dark ravine of Les Dames de Meuse. At the bridge of Roches de Laifur are magnificent views of this ravine and the wild rocky cliffs. Montherme, where the Meuse meets the river Semoy, has a fine old town on the Meuse left bank and a 12th-century fortified church. Then you pass the legendary Roche des Quatre Fils Aymon – the legend of the horse Bayard who took four brothers to safety when pursued by Charlemagne's troops. It was Bayard who put his hoof down at Hirson to make Etang du Pas Bayard. Amusing to be in country where, against all the propaganda of school history books, Charlemagne was the villain and local heroes fought against him.

In this country, too, the French fought in the 17th century to free Flanders and the Champagne from Spanish Empire. Revin was once Spanish. At Rocroi, the future Prince of Condé defeated Spain in 1643.

Victor Hugo, George Sand and the poet Rimbaud all lived in the Ardennes and wrote of its beauty – spectacular, sometimes dark and sombre. Country of trout, wild boar and deer.

D764 to Charleville-Mézières (40km from Revin)	On D1 at Monte-Notre-Dame 4km N of Charleville – Auberge de la Forêt, 24.33.37.55: Michel Baudlet was formerly at London's Ritz, so not surprising that tables are most correctly laid, cooking is classical. Menus follow market and season and change daily. 6000 wines in the cellar. Menu A, C, D. No rooms. Shut Sunday and Monday evenings. Heli Port in car park! Charleville – Relais du Square, 7 place Gare, 24.33.38.76: neat, clean, simple hotel, garden. Rooms D. Restaurant now under separate ownership. Buffet de la Gare, 24.33.23.59: recommended to me by a French gourmand for copious value. Wine included. Menu A.	Town-planned by Charles de Gonzague, a well-connected local duke, in the early 17th century, it has the usual planners' trick whereby all main streets meet at right angles; arcaded place Ducal, town centre, is suitably noble. A pleasant town, on both sides of the river Meuse. In the 1914–18 war, the Kaiser and his son, Little Willie, often lived here. It has been the scene of battle after battle through centuries, but in peacetime it produces those splendid heavy French cooking pans. After its terrible battering in 1918 it was adopted by Manchester, England, whose people helped to rebuild it. A main suburb is called Manchester.
D764 Sedan (23km)	Chariot d'Or, 20 place Torcy, 24.27.04.87 cheap simple weekday meals; regional dishes (superb smoked boar ham) and more inventive items like oysters stuffed with almonds, chicken with scallops. Menu A–C. Shut Monday evenings. Bon Vieux Temps, 3 place Halle, 24.29.03.70: good value beautiful regional dishes. Excellent game in season. Menus C–E. Shut Sunday evening, Monday; February.	Road much nicer since motorway was built parallel. Pretty in places. An industrial town now, it has played a big part in French history; its castle, biggest in Europe (15th-century), was studied for centuries by military architects from around the world. Became a Protestant stronghold. Scene of last stand against Prussians by Napoleon III's army under General MacMahon. French surrendered here.

N43 Bazeilles, Douzy, Montmédy (44km)	Montmédy – Mady, 8 place Raymond-Poincaré, 29.80.11.11: in an attractive old square; restaurant favoured by locals. Old-style and regional dishes – coq au vin, steak, duck; trout from vivier. Also Catalan paella. Cheap house wine. Menus A, B, C. Simple rooms A. Shut Sunday evenings, Mondays; February. At Damvillers, 22km S – Croix Blanche, 7 rue Carnot, 28.85.60.12: Logis. Fair value. Menus A-C. Rooms B. Shut Sunday evening, Monday (low season); February.	Château of Bazeilles – built by a Sedan draper 1742; elegant and charming Renaissance building. Open Easter–mid-October. Maison de la Dernière Cartouche (Last Cartridge), where a French marine unit fought incredibly bravely against Germans in 1870. Museum of that Franco-Prussian War, open 1 April–30 September. Douzy has lake for sailing, fishing, swimming. Montmédy citadel was restored by Vauban, the 17th-century military engineer who specialized in conducting sieges, restoring old forts and who invented the socket bayonet.
N43 Marville, Longuyon, Briey, Metz (84km)	Longuyon–Lorraine Hotel-Restaurant Le Mas, opposite station, 82.26.50.07: for my money, the best restaurant for many miles. Gérard Tisserant is truly dedicated to cooking. He even has his fish sent daily by train from Boulogne's fish dock, hence specialities such as scallops in asparagus flan, langoustines in lightest pastry. Inventive, delightful cooking. Charming dining room; excellent wine cellar. Menu C (weekdays)–G (dégustation). Rooms B–D. Shut 6 January–3 February; restaurant shut Mondays low season. Metz – Crinouc, 79 boulevard Gén-Metman (road to Sarrebrucken), 87.74.12.46: Jean-Claude Lamaze, chef-	Marville is an interesting little town with many old houses with carved façades from the Spanish occupation (16th to 17th centuries). Longuyon is set in wooded hills where two rivers meet. Scenery on this run is pleasant, with valleys and plains, and is little known to tourists. Metz, a big commercial centre at the meeting of rivers Moselle and Seille, is extremely pleasant; picturesque islands in the river, a fine old town with narrow streets and old buildings, and a superb Gothic cathedral with a 90m (300ft) tower and fine stained glass. Metz was captured by Germans in 1870, held by them until 1918; they took it

patron, is well-known chef, great sauce-maker, dedicated wine enthusiast. Mouth-watering desserts. Attractive restaurant. Menus D–F. Rooms C–E. Shut 2–15 January; restaurant shut Saturday lunch, Thursdays; 27 August–4 September.

At Ars-sur-Moselle (10km SW Metz on D6) – Auberge de la Gare, 87.60.62.03: original old railway auberge in fine order, with fin-de-siècle décor and old-style Alsatian cooking. Try suckling pig 'en gelée', Roland Moser's own pike quenelles, trout in Riesling. Menus B, C, D, G. Open all year.

again in 1940; it was freed by the Americans in 1944.

N3 to St Avold N56 Sarralbe N61, N4 to Saverne (131km)

Saverne-Geiswiller, 17 rue de la Côte, 88.91.18.51: my readers' favourite has been extended and improved in comfort. Still with Charles Mertz's true Alsatian dishes – sauerkraut, game, wild trout, baekeoff (marinaded beef, mutton, pork, stewed in wine with potatoes and onions). Lobster from a vivier. Desserts include kugelopfs (brioche with Kirsch-steeped raisins, currants, almonds). Reasonable wine prices. Menu A, G. Rooms C–E. Open all year.

Boeuf Noir, 22 Grand'rue, 88.71.12.07: attractive building. Alsatian cooking; interesting fish sauerkraut. Menus A–D. Rooms A–C.

St Avold is on the edge of the coalfields, but this beautiful hilly road across the Lorraine plains is pleasantly wooded in stretches and has fine hilltop views. You cross the river Saar at Sarralbe then after Phalsbourg run up Col de Saverne, then downhill with more good long views. The Col has botanic gardens.

Saverne – in a rocky valley at the foot of the Vosges mountains, where the river Zorn meets the Marne-Rhine canal; well worth a little time. Château des Rohans, built by the dissolute Cardinal de Rohan in the 18th century as cardinal-bishop's residence, is a grandiose, classic building in rose pink – this area is famous for its roses. It faces the canal, in a park where a

Saverne continued	Shut Sunday evening, Tuesday; 1–21 October.	'son et lumière is held on three summer evenings a week from June to August. Many old buildings, including two in wood next to town hall. Château du Haut-Barr (5km by D102, D171): romantic castle ruins; superb views; built 12th century; once HQ of a secret Alsace wine-drinking brotherhood. Member who gave away admission secrets lost his sense of taste and smell for wine for two years!
N4 to Marmoutier then Strasbourg (39km)	At Marlenheim, on N4, 20km before Strasbourg – Hostellerie Reeb, 2 rue Albert Schweitzer, 88.87.52.70: attractive modern hotel in old style with beautifully furnished air-conditioned bedrooms. Grillroom with charcoal open fire and gastronomic restaurant. Garden terrace for summer meals. Views over vineyards. Menus B, E, G. Rooms D. Shut January; Thursdays. Strasbourg has 8 Michelin-starred restaurants, most interesting of which is Maison Kammerzell, 16 place Cathédrale, 88.82.42.14: magnificent tall Alsatian house built 1427 in carved wood with mediaeval staircase in a local institution, luring tourists. Superb windows; interesting frescoes of vineyard scenes in	Between Saverne and Strasbourg is the beautiful Dabo-Wagenbourg country, separating Alsace and Lorraine, Marmoutier has a spectacular Romanesque church with crowded towers. Wasselonne is an ancient fortified city among pleasant hills. The run into Strasbourg is between hop gardens and vineyards. Though one of France's biggest cities, Strasbourg has charm, being on the banks of the Rhine where it meets the river Ill and the Rhône and Marne canals. Cathedral in red sandstone was started in 1176, on the foundations of an earlier church, and completed in 1439. You climb 525 steps up the spire 150m (472ft) high to see town and country beyond. Splendid museum (L'Oeuvre Notre-Dame), a collection of ancient houses with wood galleries and

wine stube Léo Schnug. New director Guy-Pierre Baumann, new chef, with some new versions of sauerkraut dishes but same tasty Strasbourg dishes with goose, smoked bacon, salmon, wild duck, served in big portions, and tempting desserts. Menus E–G. Shut early February.

Buffet de la Gare, 22 place Gare, 88.32.68.28: remarkable value in very pleasant surroundings; choice of two restaurants – 1920s style or modern. Cheap menus. Local dishes. New owners and chef. Menus A, B, C. Open all year.

Chaumière, 2 rue Fonderie, 88.32.35.23: nice intimate restaurant. Classic dishes (pot au feu, shoulder of venison); grills over charcoal. Menu A–C. Shut Sundays, Saturday lunch; 14 July–15 August.

Rohans, 17 rue du Maroquin, 88.82.89.43: attractive, most useful bed and breakfast hotel in pedestrian precinct by cathedral; underground parking nearby. Rooms nicely furnished in period or country style. Rooms E–G. Open all year.

Dauphiné, 30 rue La Première Armée, 88.36.26.61: another good bed and breakfast hotel; garage. Rooms E–F. Shut 23 December–3 January.

containing sculptures from cathedral. Also the Château des Rohans, built for the cardinals, houses three museums and has magnificent rooms; in its beaux-arts departments are masterpieces by Rubens, El Greco, Rembrandt, Van Dyck, Van Goyen, Fragonard, Sisley, Renoir and Corot. Older narrow streets have timbered houses; mediaeval bridges over Ill river.

European Parliament building has a fine old garden opposite.

Strasbourg continued

Ami Schutz, 1 rue Ponts Couverts, 88.32.76.98: delightful restaurant with jolly patronne; all local specialities including baekeoff (marinaded meat stewed). Nice cheap Alsace wines. Menu C; carte. Shut Sundays evenings, Mondays.

Vieille Enseigne, 9 rue Tonneliers, 88.32.58.50: a discovery; quiet charming little restaurant with charming welcome and good cooking – local produce modernish in style. Menus D, E. Alas, shut Saturdays, Sundays; 3 weeks in July; 2 weeks December.

Route 6
Cherbourg or St Malo to Hendaye

(for Spain and Portugal)

A route of discovery, to find places to revisit later, like little seaside resorts of the Cotentin peninsula below Cherbourg, south Normandy, south-east Brittany, the waterways of the secretive Marais Poitevin, the huge sand beaches with Atlantic surfing rollers of Les Landes, backed by vast pine forests, planted to stop blowing sand and drain marshes.

You can save time, especially on the Cotentin peninsula, but its countryside deserves discovering. We have included a route from St Malo to join the road from Cherbourg through a pleasant part of Brittany. More routes from St Malo and Roscoff and a round tour of Brittany are in the next chapter.

We have missed Bordeaux deliberately, though it is a fine place to eat. Traffic is fiercer than ever. Don't miss St Emilion. In summer you can taste wine in place du Clocher by Hostellerie de Plaisance, at other times at various châteaux.

The N10 road has been widened and motorways have cut its traffic but it is best avoided where possible. It is difficult to decide whether to explore the Marais or divert to La Rochelle, one of my favourite places in France. But La Rochelle deserves a week, not an hour or two.

From rich Norman dishes you pass to oysters of Brittany, for Cancale is across the bay from the Granville-Avranches coast and Le Croisic, nursery of Portuguese oysters, is in the Loire estuary near Nantes. The land between is rich in lamb, veal and river fish. Breton crêpes (creamy pancakes) are eaten locally at 5 p.m. with cider – a snack between lunch and dinner.

Poitou-Charente, between Nantes and Bordeaux, has some of the most fertile land and productive water of France; rich dairy and beef pastures, salt-washed sheep pastures, a huge variety of vegetables and fruit, including Charentais melons, oyster beds and mussel farms; and the La Rochelle fishing fleet bringing in a variety of fish. Cooking is in butter, with liberal doses of cream and wine, and dishes are lighter than in Bordeaux. Oysters are served with little spicy sausages, mussels in creamy liquid (called mouclade); moules Bordelaises are mussels in wine and tomato sauce.

True Bordelaise sauce is made with claret, not rough plonk, and butter, tomatoes, beef marrow, shallots, thyme and nutmeg. It goes best with beef, which goes best with Bordeaux wine. Superb Adour river salmon from Les Landes, south of Bordeaux, is cooked in red wine and sauce. Here they often cook in goose fat; game is plentiful in the forests. Goose, duck and pork are served fresh and preserved, but vegetables are poor.

A wine of the Nantes area, Gros Plant, is akin to Muscadet but with an acidity which most French like. In such short space, there is little to say about wines of Bordeaux except: 'Drink them!' Great wines have become impossibly expensive. Recent bad harvests have pushed up prices of medium wines. A good tip is to buy young Côtes de Blayes and Bourg wines from across the Dordogne river – reliable, enjoyable and cheaper.

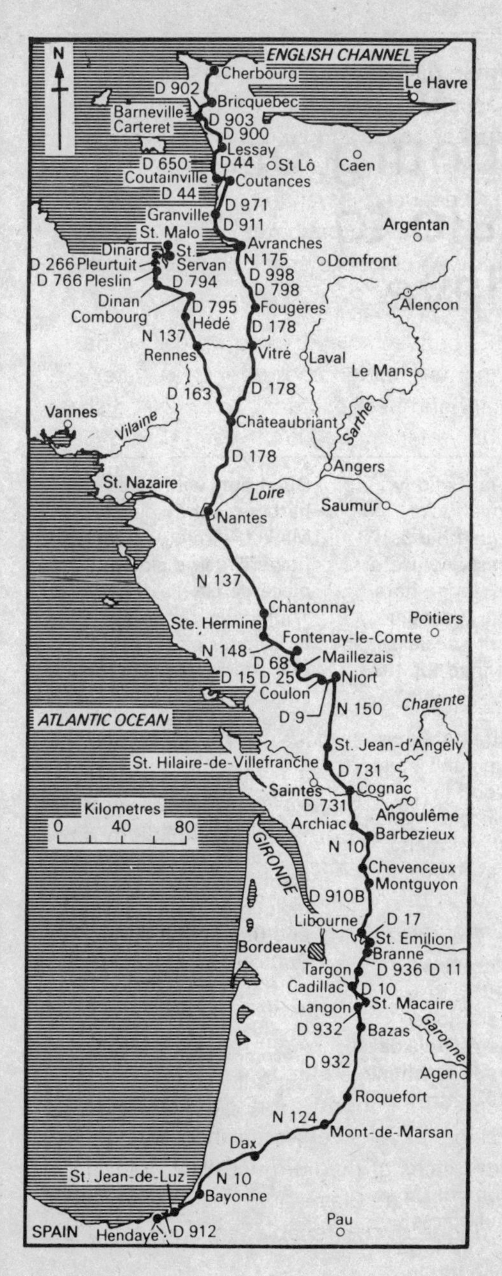
N
ENGLISH CHANNEL
Cherbourg
Le Havre
D 902
Bricquebec
Barneville
Carteret
D 903
D 900
Lessay
D 650
D 44
St Lô
Caen
Coutainville
Coutances
D 44
D 971
Granville
D 911
Argentan
St. Malo
Avranches
Dinard
St.
Servan
N 175
Domfront
D 266 Pleurtuit
D 998
D 766 Pleslin
D 794
D 798
Dinan
D 795
Fougères
Alençon
Combourg
Hédé
D 178
N 137
Rennes
Vitré
Laval
Le Mans
D 163
D 178
Vannes
Vilaine
Châteaubriant
Sarthe
D 178
Angers
St. Nazaire
Loire
Saumur
Nantes
N 137
Chantonnay
Poitiers
Ste. Hermine
Fontenay-le-Comte
N 148
Maillezais
D 68
D 15 D 25
Niort
Coulon
D 9
N 150
Charente
ATLANTIC OCEAN
St. Jean-d'Angély
St. Hilaire-de-Villefranche
D 731
Saintes
Cognac
D 731
Angoulême
Kilometres
0 40 80
Archiac
Barbezieux
N 10
GIRONDE
Chevenceux
Montguyon
D 910B
Libourne
D 17
St. Emilion
Bordeaux
Branne
Targon
D 936 D 11
Cadillac
D 10
Langon
St. Macaire
Garonne
D 932
Bazas
D 932
Agen
Roquefort
N 124
Mont-de-Marsan
Dax
St. Jean-de-Luz
N 10
Bayonne
Pau
SPAIN
Hendaye
D 912

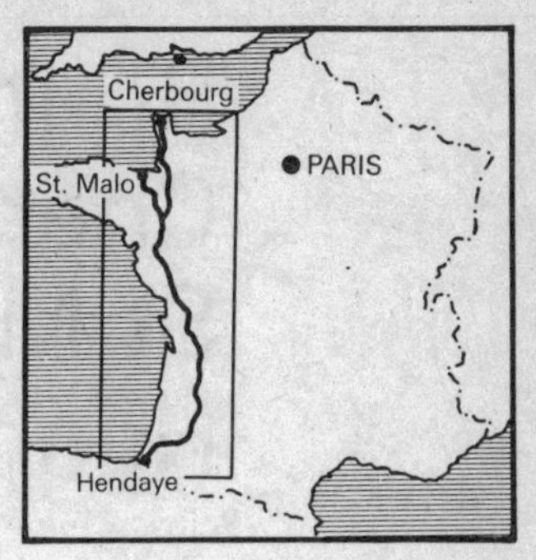
Cherbourg
PARIS
St. Malo
Hendaye

Route 6 Cherbourg or St Malo to Hendaye

Cherbourg

Vauban, 22 quai Caligny, 33.43.14.17: overlooks harbour; changed hands; downstairs brasserie useful for quick meal. Large hors d'oeuvres table. Grander main restaurant specializes in fish. Hotel planned for 1988. Menus B, D.

Pêcherie, 27 rue l'Abbaye, 33.53.05.23: fish and meat grilled over wood fire; popular with locals. Menus A, C, E. Children's menu. Shut Sunday evenings, Monday.

Grandgousier, 21 rue l'Abbaye, 33.53.19.43: Michelin's choice. Bistro style; some very good dishes. Menus A (weekdays), D. Shut Saturday lunchtime, Sundays; 3–16 April; 1–21 September.

Doyen, passage Digard, 33.93.67.04: 'one of those small delightful places you run into when you have taken the wrong turning'

Quiet port with pleasant harbour, sandy beach. Market – fruit, vegetables, flowers, some clothes – in place de Gaulle Tuesdays, Thursdays, Saturday mornings; pavement cafés in this square; small shops in small streets off it. Continent Hypermarket, quai de l'Entrepôt, near harbour. In J. F. Millet museum, works of Millet, peasant who painted country scenes so truly (he lived later in Jersey); also Flemish school paintings including Van Eyck, Van Dyck and Rembrandt and a Botticelli. Fish market off rue au Blé.

In Hitler's war, retreating Germans blew up harbour, but British frogmen cleared debris and mines and it became main Allied supply port, handling twice New York's 1939 capacity. Pluto, Allied underwater oil pipeline, ran here from Isle of Wight.

	writes a reader. Others think it delightful, too. Simple, old, very cheap (a menu at 38f in 1987). Gérard Bellet cooks lovely old dishes (rabbit in cider, coq au vin, veal Vallée d'Auge). Menus A, C. Shut fifteen days in September. Renaissance, 4 rue l'Eglise, 33.43.23.90: useful, pleasant, bed-and-breakfast hotel facing yacht harbour. Friendly hostess. Rooms A–D (all with shower, WC).	
D3 then soon on D900 to Bricquebec (24km)	Vieux Château, 33.52.24.49: in part of the 11th-century château inside castle close. Real favourite with readers. Old rooms recently renovated, six more in annexe. Queen Victoria slept in the biggest, of course. Good regional cooking; all menus excellent value. Try kidneys in cider; moules au Champagne; sauce Victoria served with fish – white wine sauce with langoustines and truffles. Friendly atmosphere. Menus A, B, C, F. Rooms B–E. Shut 20 December–25 January.	Most interesting little place with a 14th-century castle. Queen Victoria stayed here in 1857 after visiting Cherbourg for the opening of the railway to Caen. Climb 160 steps up the keep for fine views of countryside and the Trappist monastery (Abbaye Notre-Dame-de-Grâce) 3km along D121. Market before castle gates on Mondays. Henry V gave the castle to the Duke of Suffolk after Agincourt, but he gave it back to the French later as part of his ransom after capture by Joan of Arc.
D902 Barneville – Carteret (18km)	Marine, Carteret 33.53.83.31: outstanding fish restaurant, especially shellfish, straight from the harbour – turbot, sole, brill, monkfish – whatever the fishermen catch. Lobster from vivier. Seaviews from dining room and attractive bar. Some new rooms beautifully appointed. Good service. Menus C–G (gastronomic). Rooms E–F.	Twin family resorts, with Carteret the lively bit, Barneville with bigger beach. Plenty to amuse children. The estuary harbour – nearest harbour to Jersey – is constantly interesting, with a genuine fishing fleet and the catch sold on the harbourside; yachts coming in from Britain and the Channel Isles, fish being

Barneville – Carteret continued	Shut 5 November–20 December. Les Isles at Barneville, 33.04.98.76 comfortable, most pleasant family Logis above a fine sand beach, with views from garden and some rooms you can see as far as Jersey. Excellent fish direct from boats; lobster from vivier. Menus A, C, E, F. Rooms B–E. Shut 25 November–30 January.	packed, nets drying. A nice small beach and a large sand beach reached across dunes or by a lovely cornice walk over the headland (Customs Officers' Path) with changing views (about 25 mins). Barneville has an 11th-century church with fine painted Romanesque arches inside. Monument to the cutting of Cotentin peninsula by American forces prior to the capture of Cherbourg in 1944. Good Saturday market at Barneville.
D903 then D900 to Lessay (29km)	Portbail (5km along D903, then 3km on small road right – on estuary with sand dunes) – Galiche, place Edouard Laquaire, 33.04.84.18: friendly little inn used by locals; fine old meals (ham in cider and cream; peppered steak; shellfish). Patron-chef Jean-Claude Genest here 20 years. Menus A–E. Rooms (single) A–C. Shut Sunday evenings (except July, August); February. Lessay – Normandie, 3 place St Cloud, 33.46.41.11: remarkable value lures locals. Regional cooking. Menus A (two menus), C. Rooms A, B. Shut Sunday evenings, Mondays (except July, August); October.	A pleasant little town among windy moorland, it has an abbey founded in 1056 by William the Conqueror's family and which is a masterpiece of Norman architecture; it was almost destroyed in the invasion fighting of 1944 but has been carefully and beautifully restored, using original stone and old tools. Benedictines from abbey started Fair of Sainte-Croix, still held mid-September – one of the biggest in Normandy. Vast quantities of sausages, beef and lamb spitroast to be eaten with cider; lovely colts and pied cattle sold in hundreds. Tents and funfair cover the moor.
D650 Coutainville (20km)	Hardy, place 28 Juillet, 33.47.04.11: all spies (and French guides) report that the Hardy is itself again, with Emile Hardy cooking his	Little coast road passing a series of seaside villages with little beaches almost totally unknown to Britons. If you prefer horses to the sea,

superb classical dishes which won him international acclaim a few years back. Good shellfish (the platter is enormous); salt-fed lamb from marshes around Mont St Michel; local sole beautifully cooked in chives. Mouth-watering desserts. Some bedrooms small. Menus B–G (gastronomic). Rooms B–D. Shut Monday low season; 5 January–5 February.

Neptune, Promenoir Jersey, 33.47.07.66: fine old white hotel on sea promenade; comfortable rooms only; bar; no restaurant. Rooms D–E. Shut November; 1–15 March.

you can now take D900 to the St-Lô French national stud with 250 stallions (mostly English and Norman), though most are only there mid-July to mid-February. Visits 10.00–11.30 a.m., 2.30–5 p.m. Then take D972 to rejoin route at Coutances. Coutainville is a quaint *fin de siècle* resort where you expect to see starch-uniformed nannies pushing high prams along the promenade. Still some genuine old bathing huts on the big sand beach; sand dunes; little shops. A friendly place where you can get to know French familes.

D44 Coutances (13km)

P'tit Homme, 4 rue d'Harcourt, 33.45.00.67: little corner restaurant between cathedral and St Nicolas church. Remarkable value. Very cheap. Menus A-C. Shut Monday; 4–23 January.

Relais de Viaduc, 25 ave Verdun, 33.45.02.68: gastronomic Relais Routiers in town centre which we have known for years; super value, excellent chef but gastronomic menu rather over Routiers prices! One all-fish menu. Menus A–F (gastronomic). Rooms (simple) A–B. Shut 4–27 September.

At Montpinchon, 13km on D7, D27, D73 – Château de la Salle, 33.46.95.19: beautiful,

A lovely little town on a hilltop crowned by a really beautiful cathedral, much rebuilt in the 13th century but originally 11th-century, mostly built by the incredible de Hauteville family who went to Italy and became Norman kings of large areas; the famous King Roger of Sicily was one of them. From one tower you can often see Jersey. Fifteen cathedral windows are 13th-century; oldest show St George, St Thomas (à Becket) of Canterbury and St Blaise.

The public flower gardens are beautiful, with magnificent cedar trees; the gardens are illuminated on weekends (1 July–15 September).

Coutances continued

elegantly furnished, immaculate, expensive and worth every franc. Thirteenth-century vaulted dining room; big open fires; fine bedrooms, some overlooking pleasant grounds. New chef. He keeps the Michelin star but we have heard some criticism. His predecessor, Christian L'Haridon, was brilliant. But it's early days yet. Menus D, F. Rooms G. Shut 2 November–20 March.

D971, Granville (29km)

At Montmartin-sur-Mer, right off D971 at Quettreville (12km from Coutances – market village) – Bon Vieux Temps, 33.47.54.44: simple, typical village inn with bargain menus; priciest includes lobster. 2km from sea and vast tidal sands. I like it. You meet local people. Menus A–E. Rooms B–C. Shut only Sunday evening in winter.

At Trelly, 10km from Coutances (follow signs – at hamlet of Chevalier) – Verte Campagne, 33.47.65.33: lovely old hideaway in a stone farmhouse, home of Mme Meredith, widow of a British naval officer. She turned it into an hotel long ago, but it's more like being a paying guest! Don't expect slick service! You will find complete calm and peace, disturbed only by chickens and mooing cows. Lovely walks. Old stone walls, log fires. Some bedrooms tiny.

Nicely protected by rocks, it can be a suntrap. Roc-Point, joined to mainland by a rocky isthmus, was once an English fort (15th-century). If you have no time to explore the historic old town and ramparts, go up to the unpronounceable place l'Isthme for superb views to Brittany. Casino. Narrow beach; best beaches at Donville (15 mins by cliff path) and St Pair au Mer (3km along D911) – golden sands safe for children. Granville museum has fine collection of folk head-dresses.

For centuries, Granville was a big fishing port. In 16th century its ships fished for cod off Newfoundland. Now the industry is dead. From port boats take you to Chaussey Isles (52 islands; another 365 at low tide. Lobster fishermen live on La Grande Île).

I love it. Alas, Madame has been ill but she has taken a partner. Home cooking, Normandy style. Menus A–E. Rooms B–E. Shut Sunday evening, Monday in winter; 2 weeks November and February.

Granville – Normandy-Chaumière, 20 rue Paul Poirier, 33.50.01.71: much-respected British restaurateur told me that Jean-Pierre Dugue is one of the most imaginative chefs he has found in Normandy – ideas without trying to be too clever with fruit and vinegars. Certainly his menus are excellent value, especially if you like seafood. Many traditional Norman dishes, too, with cream and cider. Bedrooms renovated. Menus A, B, D. Rooms B, C. Shut Wednesdays except July, August.

Bains (Restaurant La Potinière), 19 rue Georges Clemenceau, 33.50.17.31: 58 rooms have sea views; modern Norman style; few yards from sea. Lovely shellfish. Menus A, C, D. Rooms B. Shut Mondays in winter.

D911 along coast to Avranches (33km)

St Jean-le-Thomas – Bains, 33.48.84.20: I cannot remember when I first found André Gautier's Logis. Now it is famous among French and British. There's an annexe, 300 metres away beside the sea these days to cope with summer visitors, and heated pool. But friendly family atmosphere unchanged and André's Norman cooking is a delight – crab soufflé in lobster sauce, lobster flambé in Calvados with cream sauce, mussels in cider, local ham in cider, chicken in cider on bed of cream. Alas, shuts 10 October–mid-March. Menus A–E. Rooms A–D.

Avranches – Croix d'Or, 83 rue Constitution, 33.58.04.88: very pleasant; pretty Norman posting inn, authentic old decor; comfortable bedrooms well furnished. Garden. Regional cooking; try crayfish in cream sauce; dodine de canard (boned, stuffed duck, like ballotine). Menu C–G. Rooms A–F. Shut mid-March–mid-November.

Auberge St Michel, 7 place Général Patton, 33.58.01.91: nicely renovated rooms. Good atmosphere and service. Garden. Meals good value; try lotte (monkfish) in cider; pré-salé (salt pasture) lamb. Menus A–D. Rooms A–C. Shut Sunday evenings, Mondays from 15 June–15 September; 15 November–15 March.

This coast road is well worth a diversion for small beach resorts pleasant for future holidays or weekends away: Jullouville (rather exclusive resort with fine sands backed by pine trees); St-Jean-le-Thomas (pleasant village looking across sandbanks to Mont-St-Michel). General Eisenhower, wartime Allied C-in-C, was so impressed he mentioned the view in his war memoirs. Rich in mimosa and wistaria in season.

Avranches, a charming town, is deeply involved in Anglo-French history; here Henry II of England knelt and received absolution from the Pope because his foolhardy knights had murdered Thomas à Becket; you can still see the stone (La Plateforme) on which he knelt. From here General 'Blood and Guts' Patton and his newly formed Third Army of the US Forces launched on 1 August 1944 their first attack against the Nazis which took them right across Europe. The Patton memorial here has an inscription: 'Making the Avranches breakthrough in the roar of its tanks, while marching towards victory and the liberation of France, the glorious American Army of General Patton passed over this crossroads'.

The British and Commonwealth memorial at Bayeaux is more succinct: 'We whom William

		conquered have freed the land of the Conqueror'. Here too in 1639 the French peasants under Jean Quetil (Jean Nu-Pieds – John Barefoot) started a less successful revolt which had repercussions right up to the French Revolution.
N175, D998, D798 Fougères (40km)	Voyageurs, 10 place Gambetta, 99.99.14.17: (restaurant); 99.99.08.20 (hotel): separate management; good regional cooking; deserved local reputation. Charming redecorated dining room. Menus A–D (shut Saturday; 16 August–4 September). Rooms B, C. Shut 20 December–5 January.	Shoemaking town. On a rock above a loop in the river is the shell of a castle captured several times by the English (1166–1499). Now an open air theatre. Walk the ramparts, climb Tour Mélusine for view of town. Cross river Nançon to place aux Arbres, terraced gardens from old ramparts.
D178 Vitré (29km)	Chêne-Vert, 2 place Général de Gaulle, 99.75.00.58: hotel 1789; old furniture. Old-style cooking, too – coq au vin; steak au poivre; apple tart. Menus A–C. Rooms B–F. Shut 22 September–22 October; Friday evenings, Saturdays. Pichet, 17 boulevard Laval, 99.75.24.09: pleasant little restaurant; good value. Menus B–E. Shut part August; Sunday evening, Monday. Petit Billot, 5 place Maréchal Leclerc, 99.75.02.10: outstanding cheap regional menus. Best rooms in new wing. Menus A–C. Rooms B–D. Shut Friday evening, Saturday (except high season); 15 December–15 January.	Lovely view of town as you enter on D178. Then you step into the Middle Ages in a charming town of narrow streets and mediaeval houses, many of timber. Vitré Castle is triangular with big corner towers and town walls attached; splendidly grotesque carvings; drawbridge. Another mediaeval castle – Château des Rochers – on a hill 7km south on D88. Madame de Sévigné, beautiful, witty and bitchy chronicler of French 17th-century life, lived there when not in Paris. Vitré was staunchly Protestant, and the 15th-century Notre-Dame church has an external pulpit from which preachers harangued the Calvinists.

D178
Châteaubriant
(51km)

Ferrière, route de Nantes, 40.28.00.28: 18th-century turreted creeper clad manor in gardens and 7-acre park. One of the Châteaux Hôtels Indépendants as opposed to Relais et Châteaux. Menus A (weekdays)–D. Rooms C–E. Shut 24–28 December.

A sad history to this old fortified town: in the castle which still stands the beautiful Françoise Laval, mistress of King Francis I, was imprisoned by her husband, in a room hung with black, until her death. On 20 October 1941 the Nazis shot 27 local people in a sandpit as a reprisal against French resistance – the first of their mass executions in France. A memorial marks the spot at La Sablière.

Alternative Route St Malo – Châteaubriant

St Malo

Restaurants and hotels 'Intra Muros' – in the old walled port – are mostly small, simple, offering copious meals, mostly of fresh fish from the dock, with family cooking. Do not expect 'grand comfort' or Gault-Millau 'dégustations'. But they are fun, enjoyable and cheap.

Astrobabe, 8 rue Cordiers, 99.40.36.82: St Malo's retreat for nouvelle and modern cooking enthusiasts. Daniel Le Héran was at Bocuse and Maxim's. Personally, I find the 'modernizing' with ginger of St Malo's gorgeous fresh landed sole unnecessary and stuffing of duck with langoustines rather odd. Fresh fish needs simple treatment. Menus C–E.

Delightful fortified old port behind massive walls, with narrow streets. For centuries haunt of French corsairs (royal licensed pirates); curse to English, Dutch and Portuguese shipping from 16th century. Town much destroyed in 1944 battle between Germans and Americans. Superbly restored. Jacques Cartier, discoverer of Canada, born here.

Still a leading fishing port. Leave car outside walls and walk along ramparts. Several small islands include Grande Bé to which you can walk at low tide (45 minutes). Here is tomb of Châteaubriand, brilliant writer, politician, ambassador to England.

Porte St Pierre, 2 place Guet, 99.40.91.27: a little piece of old St Malo which most readers love. A few paces from the old walls and beach. Run by Bertonnière family for more than 50 years. Simple bedrooms, but all with shower or bath and WC, English and French TV, phones. Good straightforward cooking of fresh ingredients (especially fish) by Annaïck, Dame Cuisinière de France. Not for snobs or finger-snappers! Menus A–F. Rooms C–E. Shut 15 November–15 January; restaurant Mondays.

Chiens du Guet, 4 place Guet, 99.40.87.29: neighbour of Porte St Pierre. Taken over in 1987 by Swiss lady, Ingrid Rudin, who speaks English. Very simple old-France style. Wood furnishings, comfortable beds. All fresh produce. Chiens du Guet were fierce guard dogs released at night to discourage invading Englishmen! Menus A–D. Rooms B, C. Shut Monday.

Delaunay, 6 rue Ste-Barbe, 99.40.92.46: Jean-Paul Delaunay's little restaurant, fashionable with young locals. Good, excellent fish. Meals carte C–E. Shut Sunday evenings, Mondays; 2–24 November; 15–28 February.

St Malo continued

Elisabeth, 2 rue Cordiers, 99.56.24.98: nice little hotel without restaurant in a 1600 house in old town which missed the fire of 1661 and destruction of 1944. Most bedrooms with own entrance hall; some small; some in annexe. Rooms E–F. Open all year.

Gilles, 2 rue Pie qui Boit, 99.40.97.25: modern, used by younger locals. Super fish (try vol-au-vents); good value; generous portions. Menus B–C. Shut Thursday; Sunday evening; 1–15 March; 12 November–12 December.

At Paramé, outside walls – Rochebonne, 15 boulevard Châteaubriand, 99.56.01.72: older hotel 80 metres from the sea, changed hands and entirely refitted. All bedrooms with bath or shower, WC, TV. Good traditional cooking. Menus A–D. Rooms C–D. Shut Mondays (low season); 15 January–15 February.

Villefromoy, 7 boulevard Hébert, 99.40.92.20: recommended by readers for beautiful antique furniture, good bathrooms. Private house converted. Bed-and-breakfast only. Rooms E–G. Open 5 March–16 November; 18 December–4 January.

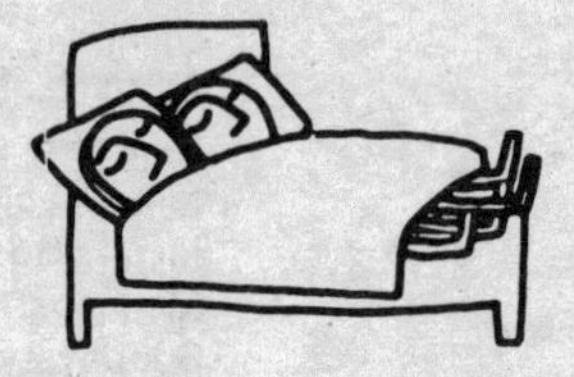

D301 St Servan (5km)	Valmarin, 7 rue Jean XXIII, 99.81.94.76: pricey, charming bed-and-breakfast hotel in 18th-century house probably built for retired pirate. Garden. Rooms E–G. Shut 24 December–1 March. Atre, 7 esplanade Cdt Menguy (Port Solidor), 99.81.68.39: friendly little restaurant where locals get talking to you. Mainly fish. Menus A–C. Shut Tuesday evenings (low season), Wednesday; mid-December–mid-January.	Resort at mouth of Rance; beaches to sea and river. Tour Solidor has model of first round-the-world ship (1519 – 1084 days).
D168 across Rance dam, right D266 Dinard (9km)	Altaïr, 18 boulevard Féart, 99.46.13.58: Patrick Lemenager's good cooking well known to Britons; in the kitchens since he was 14 and follows a family tradition, known for his feuilletage – pastry made of paper-thin leaves – mussel-and-artichoke flan. Fine old Norman furnishings and fireplaces; 100m from beach. Bedrooms totally renovated; all with WC, bath or shower. Menus A, C, D, G. Rooms C–E. Shut Wednesdays (low season); 15 December–15 January. Paix, 6 place République, 99.46.10.38: typical little restaurant in main square with splendid value menus; old-style dishes (grilled salmon with beurre blanc; peppered fillet steak; baked local fish; coq au vin). Menus A, B, D. Rooms A–D. Shut Mondays; 15 November–20 March.	Bright beach resort with good winter temperatures; 3 beaches for wind evasion; casino. Fishing village discovered and adopted by British in 1850. Rance dam, 750m (800yd) long, encloses the estuary for a station using tide for hydro-electric power. Station is in a tunnel 390m (400yd) long; visits 8.30 a.m.–8 p.m. (panels explain the works); generators of 240,000 kw produce 550 million kw a year.

Dinard continued	Dunes, 5 rue Clemenceau, 99.46.12.72: old favourite which faded, has new owner; complete renovation in winter '87–'88. Fine position opposite casino and beach; good garden. Cheap menus A, B. Rooms D, E. Shut 1 November–1 March.	
D266 Pleurtuit **D766 Pleslin** **Dinan (22km)**	Avaugour, place Champ Clos, 96.39.07.49: old house in superb position with garden seemingly suspended above ramparts and castle lawns. Excellent rooms. Georges Quinton makes imaginative dishes from best buys in the market. Good cheap lunch in bar. Summer restaurant in garden tower. Menus C–G. Rooms E. Shut Sundays in winter. Marguerite, 29 place du Guesclin, 96.39.47.65: nice position with balconies overlooking main square; rooms renovated; old style, comfortable; unusual but nice fish dishes. Cheap, good-value menus. Menus A, B, F. Rooms D. Shut December. Terrasses, le Port, 96.39.09.60: most attractive position by Rance river. Try fish terrine, asparagus with pineapple mousse, best end of lamb in orange sauce, oysters, shrimp fricassé, super seafood platter. Menus B–G. Shut Tuesdays.	Dinan – lovely interesting mediaeval town on Rance; old houses in narrow streets enclosed by old walls, 200 feet above river. Alongside Jardin Anglais (river views) is church containing the heart of Bertrand du Guesclin, local lad who died in 1380 after 20 years fighting for French kings. Defending Dinan in 1359 against the Duke of Lancaster he fought and won a duel with Sir Thomas of Canterbury, and the English withdrew. Captured thrice by the English, he lived freely at Court in London.

Pélican, 3 rue Haute-Voile, 96.39.47.05: I found it over 20 years ago when very short of francs and could not believe the portions, choice and number of courses I got for my money; nothing has changed except that you now meet other tourists; incredible value. Very cheap wines. Menus A–C. Shut Sunday evening.

Mère-Pourcel, 3 place Merciers, 96.39.03.80: magnificent 15th-century house (historic monument); strange staircase in middle of dining room. Good service, good Norman cooking (try fresh sardines marinaded in herbs and cider). Nice light lunch A; copious menus C–F. Shut Sunday evenings, Mondays (low season); 4 January–1 March.

D794
Combourg
(13km)

Château, 99.73.00.38: charming, friendly couple, Marie-Thérèse and Christian Pélé, run comfortable, excellent hotel with lovely garden; try Châteaubriand steak with old-style genuine Châteaubriand sauce, lobster in Bourgueil sauce, stuffed amandes de mer (dog-cockle, little shellfish), lamb ragout in cider, mussels in cream with sweet peppers; good desserts. Children's playground. Bedroom modernized. Menus A, C, D, G. Rooms A–E. Shut 20 December–23 January restaurant shut Monday lunch.

Simple old town with little lake, dominated by 11th-century castle; it belonged to Guesclin family, then in 18th century to Count Châteaubriand, father of the great writer who spent an unhappy, lonely youth there. Tour de Chat was haunted by the wooden leg and cat of a former owner. Cat's skeleton was found. Now some swear that the wooden leg walks round looking for it! Open Easter–September.

Combourg continued	France, 18 rue Princes, 99.73.00.01: 6 menus, good value; cheaper menus bargains. Fine wine list from cheap to collectors' items ('67 Château d'Yquem). Menus A–F. Rooms (simple) A. Shut Monday; February. Marché, 12 place des Déportés, 99.73.05.52: little family hotel has sprouted a glassed-in heated terrace. Bargain menus with old-style dishes (coq au vin, duck in orange, snails provençale). Cheap Sauvignon house wine. Very simple bedrooms. Menus A (three prices), C. Rooms A. Shut Friday evenings in winter.	
D795 Hédé (15km)	Vieux Moulin, 99.45.45.70: very attractive old mill, popular with *Le Weekend* and *Travellers' France* readers, so book; garden; good-value meals follow seasons; shellfish from St Malo. Menus A, C, F. Rooms C, D. Shut Sunday evenings, Mondays; 20 December–30 January.	Charming hilltop village with castle ruins, houses with hanging gardens; between canal and pool; countryside dotted with little lakes, windmills and woods.
N137 Rennes (22km)	Piré, 18 rue Maréchal Joffre, 99.79.31.41: Marc Angelle strikes a fine balance between traditional and modern cooking, with personal touches. Excellent value. Super lamb and salmon. Menus B, C, G. Shut Saturday lunch; Sundays. At Betton (9km N on N776) – La Levée, rue Amérique, 99.55.81.18: lovely old house	Rennes has grown in all directions – population, suburbs, industry and university; old town appalling for traffic but good for pedestrians; oddly, centre is 18th-century; narrow, medieval streets with half-timbered houses surround it. Old centre burned down in 1720 by drunk; soldiers brought in to quell flames merely looted.

close to canal and Rance river; open fireplace; fresh and seawater fish; good cheap meals and carte. Menus – 3 in A price! Wines very cheap. Simple rooms A–C. Wonderful value. Shut Sunday evening, Monday; 1–15 July.

Cathedral disappointing. Excellent Museum of Brittany, includes fine historic costumes and first-class audio-visual rooms – but you must understand French. Not a lively city but friendly and bright with flowers. The siege of Rennes in 1491 effectively ended Brittany's independence of France. Charles VIII of France besieged it because Anne, Duchess of Brittany, had refused to marry him. He was morose and slow witted; she was happy, charming and highly educated. The starving citizens of Rennes pleaded with her to marry him. She met Charles, liked him and married him. Breton car museum of old vehicles 2km along N12 Fougères road.

D163 Châteaubriant (55km)

Joining route from Cherbourg – for Châteaubriant, see that route.

From Châteaubriant D178 Nantes (70km)

At Moisden la Rivière (12km along D178) – Chaumière, 2 place l'Eglise, 40.07.61.23: very simple village inn; good value; bargain wine list. Menus A, B. Rooms A. Shut 1–15 August.

Nantes – Colvert, 14 rue Armand-Brossart, 40.48.20.02: super little bistro in a charming street in old Nantes. My readers already love it. Young Didier Maconin, a local lad, cooks flavoursome dishes and is unafraid of spices (he was

For men only – near La Meilleraye, 12km from Châteaubriant, is a Trappist abbey with a restored 12th-century church. Only men may enter. It is beside a big pool. Nantes, on the Breton side of the Loire, is not truly Breton today and is not pretty – an industrial centre, but with very great historic interest and some hidden treasures: Ducal castle (mostly 15th-century) where the Edict of Nantes was issued in 1598 giving many political rights and religious

Nantes continued

chef to the Aga Khan!). Great talent – a big future. Lovely salmon pot-au-feu in vegetable juices. Modern, inventive dishes but not excessive. His wife knows wine, too. Menu C–F. Shut Saturday lunch, Sunday; 1–23 September.

At Les Sorinières (12km on D178) – Abbaye de Villeneuve, 40.04.40.25: 18th-century abbey beautifully restored by the Savry family, whose ancestor started France's first Academy of Cookery. Talented new chef; immaculate service; nice Loire wines; peaceful park; pool. Relais et Châteaux. Delightful. Range of menus C–G. Rooms F, G. Open all year.

At Haute-Goulaine, 11km E on N149 – La Lande St-Martin, 40.06.20.06: reliable, comfortable modernized hotel in pleasant gardens away from Nantes industrial life and traffic. Useful; good value; traditional cooking; high-quality Loire wines. Menus A (weekdays)–F (shut Sunday evening). Rooms B–G.

freedoms to Protestants. Anne of Brittany was mainly responsible for its building. Best part is the Renaissance Tour de la Couronne d'Or, with fine Italian-inspired loggias.

Museum of Popular Art has absorbing collections from Breton culture and life – from head-dresses to furniture, including interesting cooking equipment. Fine Arts Museum (rue Gambetta) contains a big collection of paintings from primitives to moderns, including some fine Rubens. Cathedral is more interesting than it looks from outside. The covered way, with shops, steps and statues, passage Pommeraye, is a lovable piece of ostentation. Pleasant Jardin des Plantes has a statue of Jules Verne (born here). Pleasant trips by boat on river Erdre (from 3–4 hrs).

N137 Chantonnay (73km) Ste Hermine (17km) then N148 to Fontenay-le-Comte (total 112km)

At St Vincent-Sterlanges (on N137 7km before Chantonnay) – Parc (Restaurant Lionel Guilbaud) 51.40.23.17: Lionel Guilbaud is his own man; cooking not classic, nor modern; it is full of ideas, inspired by regional products, lovely langoustines in pastry,

Old town of Fontenay straddles the Vendée river; near place Viete, the centre, is the old part, with 16th- to 17th-century houses. Town hall is on the site of the convent where Rabelais was educated. Château de Terre-Neuve, built for the poet

	petit-gris (snails), duck soufflé with noodles, super desserts. Authentic Vendéenne posting inn 1793. Menus A–E. Cheap wines. Shut Tuesdays; 1–15 March; 1–15 October.	Rapin in the 16th century, has Renaissance statues, chimneypieces and mantels, and fine views from the terrace. Worth seeing.
D938, D68 left to Abbey of Maillezais, then D185 (SW) D25 (E) and local roads along Sèvre-Niortaise river to Coulon (40km) D9 (local) Niort (11km)	Coulon – Central, 49.35.90.20: simple inn; the place to try Marais specialities – crayfish soup; anguilles (little eels) as hot pâté or fricassée in wine, onions, cream; sandres (perch); marsh lamb. Nice summer terrace. Menu A, C, D. Rooms B–C. Shut Sunday evening, Monday; February; October. Niort – Terminus, Restaurant Poêle d'Or, 82 rue Gare, 49.24.00.38: great chef and ambassador of French cuisine Jean-Louis Tavernier predictably gets no accolades from modern guides but remains an excellent exponent of classical cooking and regional dishes. Try his scallops with cèpes and Bayonne ham, his sole Poêle d'Or. Hotel now soundproofed. Menus B, D, E. Rooms D. Shut 20 December–2 January. Relais St-Antoine, place Brèche, 49.24.02.76: young Thierry Fichet is making his mark with the French and my readers. He leans slightly towards modern and pricey dishes (chicken spiked with foie gras; salmon cutlet poached with turmeric) but	Marais-Poitevin – marshes drained in the 11th to 16th centuries to make a delightful 'Green Venice' of waterways among trees and peaceful little villages where people still live as much by freshwater fishing for carp, perch, crayfish and tiny eels (anguilles) as dairy farming with cows and goats. Flat-bottomed boats (*plattes*) propelled by poles still used for moving stock and taking people shopping, to church and to school. Strange, little-known area. Coulon church, in main square, dates back to Charlemagne. Take a *platte* from here for a peaceful water trip, under arches of trees, to see other villages. Abbey of Maillezais, built in the 10th century, has a ruined church, 14th-century abbey buildings and parish church with a superb Romanesque façade. Rabelais spent some time here, and in Religious Wars the abbey was fortified as a Protestant stronghold. Niort – riverside town rich in flowers in season, and with tiny green islands where the river flows into channels. Two enormous towers and ramparts left from the castle

Niort continued

offers two excellent value cheaper menus and old regional dishes – mouclade (mussels in cream), chevreau (kid) in garlic. Pleasing modern décor. Menus B–G. Shut Sunday evening, Monday in winter; 5–25 July.

Charly's, 5 ave Paris, 49.24.07.75: happy little bistro loved by locals. Simple regional dishes – petit salé (lightly salted pork) with cabbage; eel stew. Bargain cheapest menu. Menus A, C, E. Shut Sunday evening.

AT St Rémy (6km on N148) – Relais du Poitou, 49.73.43.99: pleasant modern hotel with good value meals, fair-priced bedrooms. Try mouclade (mussels in cream, wine); local lamb with mogettes (beans in cream). Menus A–F. Rooms C. Restaurant shut Mondays.

At Chavagné-La Crede (11km NE by N11, N5) – Môtel des Rocs, 49.25.50.38: modern, attractive, comfortable; heated pool; in 17 acres. Menus C–F. Rooms E. Open all year.

built by Henry II of England, completed by Richard Lionheart, now a museum of Poitou costumes. Good open air swimming pool and an ice rink. Renaissance former town hall, now museum, was originally Chaumont Mansion where Madame de Maintenon, formidable mistress, then wife, of Louis XIV was born. Market halls lively and interesting.

Rue St Jean (pedestrians) has half-timbered houses, leads to Notre-Dame church (old tapestries).

N150 St-Jean-d'Angély (50km) N150 to St-Hilaire-de-Villefranche D731 to Cognac (36km)

St Jean – Paix, 5 ave Gén-de-Gaulle, 46.32.00.93: very useful little hotel has changed hands. Bedrooms improved, more added. Good 2-star. Old posting house on pilgrims' route to St Jacques de Compostelle. Same chef, traditional bourgeois

11km down N150, at Tout y Faut, well worth taking a diversion on D115 of 7km each way to Dampierre to see the Château of Dampierre-sur-Boutonne; on an island of the river in a lovely valley; an exquisite piece of Renaissance design. From

cooking; try ham in pineau de Charentes (aperitif of cognac and grape juice). Menus A–C. Rooms B–D. Open all year.

At St Laurent de Cognac (6km from Cognac on D732) – Logis de Beaulieu, 45.82.30.50: peaceful, well run; views of vineyards; in park. Most bedrooms big enough for solid *fin de siècle* furniture. But chef has changed and I have not sampled his cooking. Let's hope that it compares with the classic cooking of Georges Biancheri. Menus are cheaper – C–E. Rooms E, F. Shut 15–31 December.

Cognac – Pigeons Blancs, 110 rue Jules-Brisson, 45.82.16.36: delightful 17th-century post house run by two brothers and a sister. Charming décor, pleasant atmosphere, nice bedrooms, interesting cooking by brother Jacques-Henri Tachet. Try cold lobster soufflé with herbs or hot with chives; sole steamed in cognac and herbs. Good cheapest menu. Menus C–G. Rooms C–E (6 only). Shut 1–30 January.

the courtyard see the superb carved friezes; inside are fine Flemish tapestries. St-Jean is an old town with narrow streets and old wooden houses on bank of river Boutonne; beautiful Renaissance fountain (1546) with unhappy name of Pilori as the pillory once stood here. Among explorers' and archaeological items in the museum is the Citroën which was the first car to cross the Sahara, in 1922 – called 'Golden Cross'.

Cognac – overlooking Charente river is Château de Valois where Francis I was born and lived. Remains of cellars and guard room where English prisoners, taken in Canada in Seven Years' War, scratched graffiti . . . now used for maturing Otard brandy. Visit Hennessy (film of brandy production; museum of old instruments; ferry across river to chais with world's largest reserve of old brandy). Brandy was invented when Cognac wine producers distilled it to save freight charges to England and Holland (instant wine – add water!) Dutch called it 'brandewijn' – burnt wine.

D731 to Archiac, Barbezieux (33km)

At Cierzac (13km past Cognac on D731) – Moulin de Cierzac, 45.83.01.32: good value for such good cooking. Very attractive. Menu C. Rooms C–F. Shut Monday, Sunday in winter; February.

Barbezieux's traffic on dreaded N10 much relieved by parallel motorway. Capital of Cognac's Petite Champagne. Only this area and La Grande Champagne (small area nearer Cognac)

Barbezieux continued

Barbezieux – Boule d'Or, 9 boulevard Gambetta, 45.78.22.72: famed for food cooked by Jean Ferrière and lovely flower garden hidden like a hermitage from fearsome N10 traffic. Meals in garden in summer. Classical cooking: try plate of Atlantic fish; sole stuffed with foie gras; hot oysters in pineau; pot roast chicken. Bedrooms attractive. Menus A–F. Rooms A–C. Open all year.

Vieille Auberge, 5 boulevard Gambetta, 45.78.02.61: little bistro we found years ago when Boule d'Or was full is now in Michelin and has won a Prestige d'Or! Readers love it. Restaurant is prettier, flowered terrace enclosed. Bargain menus of bourgeoise cuisine; copious. New pricier menu good value. Menus A–E. Six simple rooms A. Shut Sunday evening, Monday; 1–15 May; 1–20 November.

may call their brandy 'Fine Champagne'. Also produces excellent chickens, marrons glacés and fruits confits (preserved chestnuts and fruit).

N10 Chevenceux (20km) D910B Montguyon, Libourne (47km) (67km total)

Montguyon – Poste, 18 avenue République, 46.04.19.39: little modern logis; reasonably priced; cheap meals; game in season. Menu, A, B. Rooms B.

Libourne – Loubat, 32 rue Chanzy, 57.51.17.58: old railway hotel renovated. Recommended to me by local vignerons – possibly because of its good wine list and Bordelais cooking. Menus B–F. Rooms D.

Libourne was founded by an English knight, Roger of Leybourne, who had been on a crusade with Henry III's son. In Leybourne church, Kent, is a window showing the gate-tower at Libourne and the castle of Leybourne. From the time when the English were here in the 100 Years' War, Libourne, at this point where the Dordogne meets the river Isle, has been the big port for the export of wine; the wine was brought down

the rivers on *gabares* (flat-bottomed boats) which were broken up at Libourne to make wine casks. There was fierce competition each year to see who could get wine to England first – Libourne or Bordeaux. It is still a market centre for wines of its own area – St Emilion, Pomerol and Fronsac.

Local D17 from near Libourne railway station to St Emilion (8km)

Hostellerie de Plaisance, place de Clocher, 57.24.72.32: no longer the little dream hotel of my youth. Modern dining room added; formal service; food still good (especially gastronomic menu), the scene as beautiful, with views from the terrace over rooftops of the town to the hills. Magnificent wines but some overpriced (especially A. C. St Emilion). Rooms renovated but highly priced. Menus C–F. Rooms G. Shut 1–30 January.

Logis de la Cadène, place Marché-au-Bois, 57.24.71.40: lunch only; delightful. Small 18th-century house (near church) where Moulierac family who own Château-la-Clotte (Grand Cru Class wines) serve super value traditional meals and their own wines. I love it. Superb wine list. Menus A–E. Shut Monday; 25–30 June; 1–8 September; January.

One of the most delightful little towns in France. Built on two hills with views across rooftops to the valley of the Dordogne, it has little houses packed together in steep streets – mostly old, with their own wine cellars and built of yellowy stone which shines gold in the sunlight. The marketplace with an old acacia tree called the Tree of Liberty is calm until market days, when it is crowded and fun.

Once fortified, St Emilion still has its ramparts and its old tower left from the days of Henry III, Plantagenet King of England who founded the castle. St Emilion's own 7th-century hermitage is hewn from the rock, complete with bed, table and fountain to make a bathtub. A huge underground shrine nearby, like a ballroom, was hacked out of rock by monks. The atmosphere of the place holds you – helped, of course, by splendid wine.

St Emilion continued	Auberge Commanderie, rue Cordeliers, 57.24.70.19: old house; rooms renovated in 1987. Pleasant cheap meals. Brasserie-crêperie added. Menus B–G. Rooms B–D.	Tastings of AC wines at Union de Producteurs, place du Rocher (9–12 a.m., 2–6 p.m.; shut Saturday). For other tastings see *Eperon's French Wine Tours* (Pan).
D122 to Branne (across Dordogne river) then D936 W, left on D11 to Targon and Cadillac (44km) D10 to St Macaire, over Garonne river to Langon (13km)	At Verdelais (6km N of Langon) – Hostellerie St Pierre, 56.62.02.03: in its bar, Toulouse-Lautrec sketched while his mother was in church. A panel on which he drew himself was found by accident. It is in the hotel hall. Good cooking of South-West France. Real goose-confit cassoulet. Bordeaux wines at sensible prices. Sauternes by the glass as aperitif. Menus B–E. Rooms C. Shut Mondays in winter; 1–15 November. Langon – Claude Darroze, 95 cours Gén.-Leclerc, 56.63.00.48: Claude is a Master Chef of France and rates very high indeed with us and with Champérard. His cooking is local, professional, often simple (superb roast lamb of Médoc) and has great variety, from grandma's recipes of Aquitaine to his own. Tradition with lightness. He hunts out the best in the markets like a detective. Nice summer terrace. Very welcoming atmosphere. Good wine list. Menus D, F, G. Rooms D–F. Shut 15–30 October; 15–30 January.	Cadillac – beautiful gateway leads to arcaded square on bastide (fortified town) 16th-century chapel with tombs of Dukes of Epernon. Formidable castle (17th-century) built by first Duke, colourful friend of Henry IV (Protestant Henry of Navarre). When Henry turned Catholic to get the French throne, the Duke stayed Protestant. Henry persuaded him to build the castle to distract him from making war on the King. Castle has superb tapestries, carved chimney pieces. Headquarters of a wine brotherhood. Cadillac white wine is Première Côte de Bordeaux. Langon, a wine market town on the Garonne, is joined by a bridge to St Macaire, a mediaeval town with ramparts and fortified bridge. Sauterne, the small area producing greatest of sweet wines, starts nearby. Try it as 'elevenses', not as a dessert wine when you are too replete really to enjoy it. And if any wine experts sound horrified, tell them that the idea came from a very famous mayor of Bordeaux.

Grangousier, 2 rue Auros, 56.63.30.59: good cheaper restaurant. Menus A–E.

A vineyard at St Macaire, Malrome, and its château, was bought by the artist Toulouse-Lautrec's mother. She hoped that here he would regain his health. In 1901 he died here and is buried in the churchyard at Verdelais, 6km north. Ste Croix-du-Mont (2km) has wonderful views from terrace at Château de Taste, which produces fine sweet white wine.

D932 Bazas, Roquefort, then Mont-de-Marsan (83km)

Roquefort – Commerce hotel, Tournebroche restaurant, rue Laubanner, 58.45.50.13: Alain Labat's four menus described by a French gastronome as 'sensational'. Certainly, outstanding value, with strong local flavour of Les Landes. Gras-double (gourmet's tripe), goose, renowned local duck in many forms (pâté, liver, confit, magret, roast, pot roast). Friendly atmosphere and service. Grill over wood in restaurant. Six more comfortable rooms in garden. Cheap Tursan wine. Menus A–D. Rooms D. Shut Sunday evening, Monday (except July, August); 3–25 January.

Mont-de-Marsan Midou, place Porte-Campet, 58.75.24.26: pretty, rustic dining room with open fire. Real Landais dishes – cuisse de canard (duck's thigh in wine); pipérade (red peppers, ham, onion, tomatoes, eggs); garbure (rich soup

The road goes through the great Landais forest running to the coast and from the Gironde to near the Spanish frontier. It was planted as part of drainage of marshes in early 19th century. Before, shepherds moved on stilts (now confined to folklore dancers). Roquefort is *not* the cheese Roquefort. Mont-de-Marsan is a strange town; it has a huge hippodrome for various horse shows (trotting to show jumping), a 'gentle' form of bull fighting without a bull being killed, only driven to despair, and a market for chickens and foie gras. Pleasant river scenes. Big mid-July Fête de la Madeleine.

Mont-de-Marsan continued	with preserved fowl, pork, vegetables). Large helpings. Menus A, C, E. Rooms B. Clefs d'Argent, ave Martyrs-de-la-Libération, 58.06.16.45: good, simple cooking of Landais dishes by well-known chef-patron Jacques Porte. Excellent value. Fresh fish from Bordeaux. Menus A, C, D. Shut Monday.	
N124 Dax (50km)	Bois de Boulogne (1km by allée des Baignots), 58.74.23.32: by small lake among trees. New chef; lovely setting. Superb fish. Eat on terrace under oaks in summer. Menus A, C. Shut October; Sunday evening, Monday (low season). Richelieu, 13 avenue Victor Hugo, 58.90.05.78: two famous chefs (Jacques Darc and son Alain) offer excellent value meals. Traditional cooking of fresh regional ingredients. Menus B–F. Rooms C, D.	In the 1st century Caesar Augustus visited this old spa; radioactive hot springs used for treatment of rheumatism; mud baths too. Fine walks and parks by the river Adour. Dax was under English rule from Richard the Lionheart's reign until 1451. Here was born, in 1576, a peasant, Vincent de Paul, who became priest, galley slave in Tunisia, and father of modern hospitals. He started soup kitchens, too, when Paris and then the Lorraine were threatened with famine. He was canonized in 1737.
N124, N10 Bayonne (46km)	Euskalduna, 61 rue Pannecau, 59.59.28.02: true Basque cooking. Speciality of fish from St Jean de Luz and river Adour (trout and salmon); chipirons (cuttlefish) in dark spicy sauce; tripotcha (veal sausage); baudroie (angler fish); piballes (small fried eels); Basque fish soup. Fresh tunny and anchovies in season; gambas. Carte only	Motorway bypass has relieved awful traffic problems. Capital of the French Basques, it became English when Eleanor of Aquitaine married Henry II, and stayed so for three centuries; the Basque fleet fought alongside the English navy. But it was the last place in France to hold out against Wellington. Place de la

around C–F. Good value Rioja wines. Shut Monday; part May; part October.

Bon Vieux Temps, 23 rue Pelletier (in St André church district), 59.59.78.94: small; classical cooking; good value. Menus B–D. Shut February; Saturday lunch, Sunday evening, Mondays.

Cheval Blanc, 68 rue Bourgneuf, 59.59.01.33: intelligent, talented young chef, Jean-Claude Tellechea, still learning from great restaurants (Troisgros); modern, but not nouvelle, with traditional base. Superb desserts. One of oldest auberges in Bayonne. Sensible pricing. Menus C–F. Shut Mondays low season; 4–25 January.

Biarritz – Fronton Hotel et La Résidence, 34 avenue Maréchal-Joffre, 59.23.09.36: old-style hotel with modern addition; comfortable; good value meals; excellent wine list with many cheaper wines. Menus A–C. Rooms D. Shut 20 October–20 November.

Liberté is an excellent and attractive shopping centre with arcades. Bayonne is known for its cured ham, chocolates, Armagnac and salmon from the Adour river. Also a liqueur, Izzara, yellow or green, similar to Chartreuse. A most attractive city with a lovely cathedral and an interesting museum of Basque culture.

8km away is the still elegant, though fading, resort of Biarritz, developed from a fishing village by Napoleon III for his Empress Eugénie, and beloved by Edward VII. It gets crowded high season now. The Hôtel Palais is the original palace built by Napoleon III for Eugénie so that she could be as near as possible to her beloved Spain.

I remember when it was crammed with film stars. Now it draws rich Spaniards. Biarritz is the surfing capital of Europe so bathing is fun but dangerous. So is the beachside casino.

N10 St-Jean-de-Luz (21km)

La Vieille Auberge, 22 rue Tourasse, 59.26.19.61: in little old street with beamed rustic dining room; in Daniel Grand's family since 1954. He serves superb fish from local fleet. Paella, ttoro (Basque bouillabaisse with tomato, onion, garlic), gambas, also chicken Basque style. Good cheap menus: A, B, C. Cheap

A charming resort and busy fishing port. St-Jean sailors and fishermen are known all over the world; they first fished the Newfoundland Banks in 1520, and now have the biggest tuna fishing fleet in France; many old houses towards the port; in the baroque St Jean-Baptiste church, Louis XIV married

St-Jean-de-Luz continued

wines. Shut Wednesday; 11 November–20 March.

At Cibourne, 1km over river, (several good small fish restaurants on dockside) – Arrantzaleak, avenue Jean-Poulou, chemin de Halage, 59.47.10.75: 'rugby teams assured of a great welcome – sporting meals' says the brochure. Retired rugby players like me get quite a welcome, too. Daily fish from quayside, grilled before your eyes. Lovely! Good non-fish dishes, too; jugged wild boar, duck. Summer terrace beside Nivelle river. Menu C (weekends carte only). Good cheap wines. Shut 15 December–15 January; Wednesdays except summer.

Chez Dominique, quai Maurice Ravel, 59.47.29.16: superb fish-only restaurant; very pricey but worth it. Carte only – meals F, G. Shut Sunday evenings, Mondays.

Marie-Thérèse, and the door through which they passed has been closed ever since.

D912 to Hendaye and Spanish border (11km)

Most people are so busy going backwards and forwards between Spain and France that they don't notice Henday's very pleasant beach, backed by magnolias, palms and mimosa, and pretty promenade.

Route 7
Round Brittany

Before jet package holidays, Brittany was the favourite holiday area abroad for British families, and children of my generation met their first foreign friends on the beaches of Dinard, La Baule, Morgat or Benodet. It is still very popular with Parisian families and has renewed its popularity with the British since Brittany Ferries restarted the old St Malo ferry service.

Most visitors to Brittany hug the coast, missing many treasures and uncrowded roads inland. The trick when touring is to hit the coast at key spots and enjoy the uncrowded by-roads, villages, delightful waterways and low hills of the interior.

You never feel far from the sea in Brittany, even on gorse-covered moors or winding inland waterways. The sea rules life. Brittany has 700 miles of coast – sandy beaches, rocky headlands, tall cliffs, little coves reminding us of Cornwall, salt marshes, fens and hundreds of islands, some just little rocks. The Gulf Stream washes it, bringing gentle warmth to protected beaches; the Atlantic hurls fierce rollers at unprotected rocks.

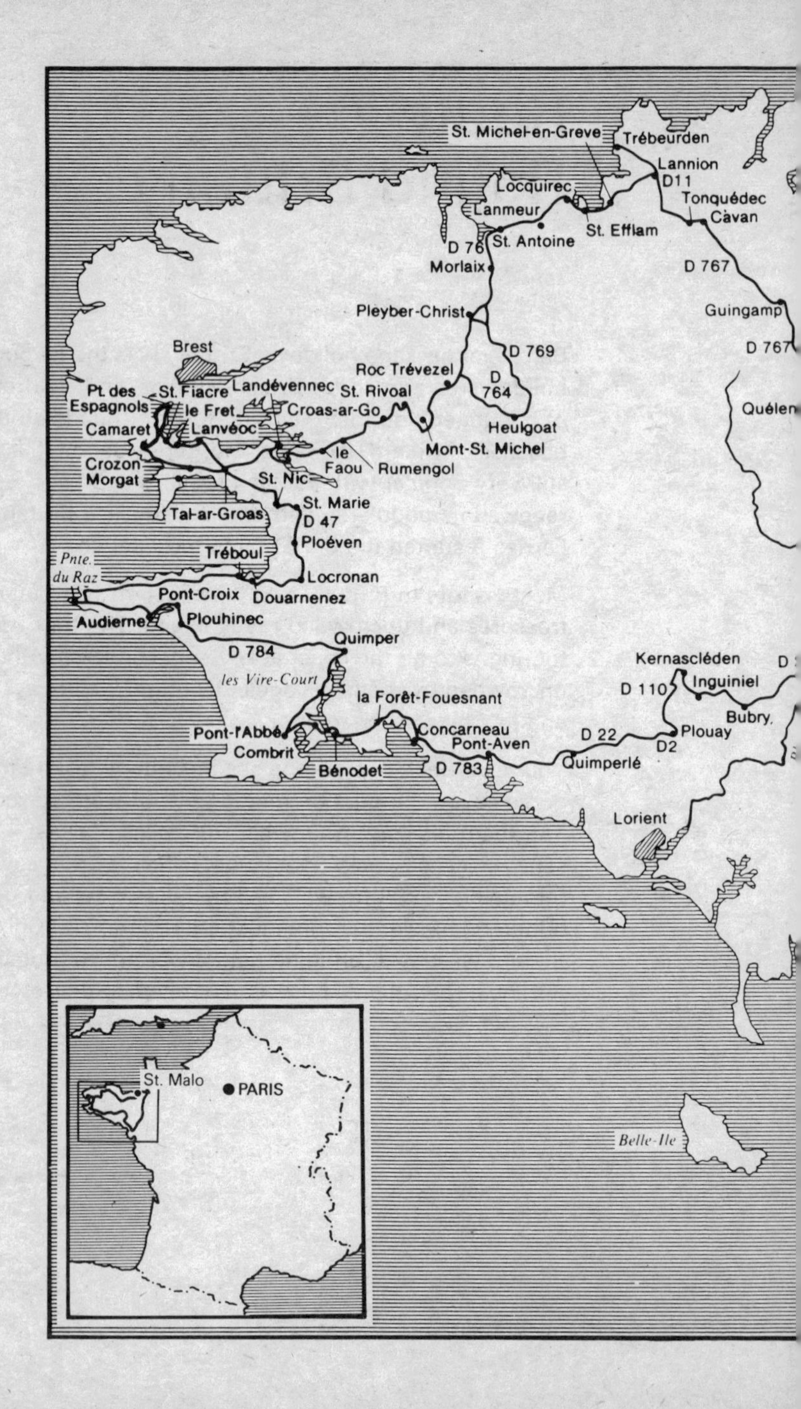

St. Michel-en-Greve
Trébeurden
Lannion
D11
Locquirec
Tonquédec
Cavan
Lanmeur
St. Efflam
D 76
St. Antoine
Morlaix
D 767
Pleyber-Christ
Guingamp
D 767
Brest
D 769
Roc Trévezel
D
764
Pt. des Espagnols
St. Fiacre
Landévennec
St. Rivoal
Quélen
le Fret
Croas-ar-Go
Heulgoat
Camaret
Lanvéoc
Mont-St. Michel
le Faou
Rumengol
Crozon
Morgat
St. Nic
St. Marie
Tal-ar-Groas
D 47
Ploéven
Pnte. du Raz
Tréboul
Locronan
Pont-Croix
Douarnenez
Audierne
Plouhinec
Quimper
D 784
Kernascléden
les Vire-Court
D 110
Inguiniel
la Forêt-Fouesnant
Bubry
Pont-l'Abbé
Concarneau
Plouay
D 22
Pont-Aven
D2
Combrit
Quimperlé
Bénodet
D 783
Lorient
St. Malo
PARIS
Belle-Ile

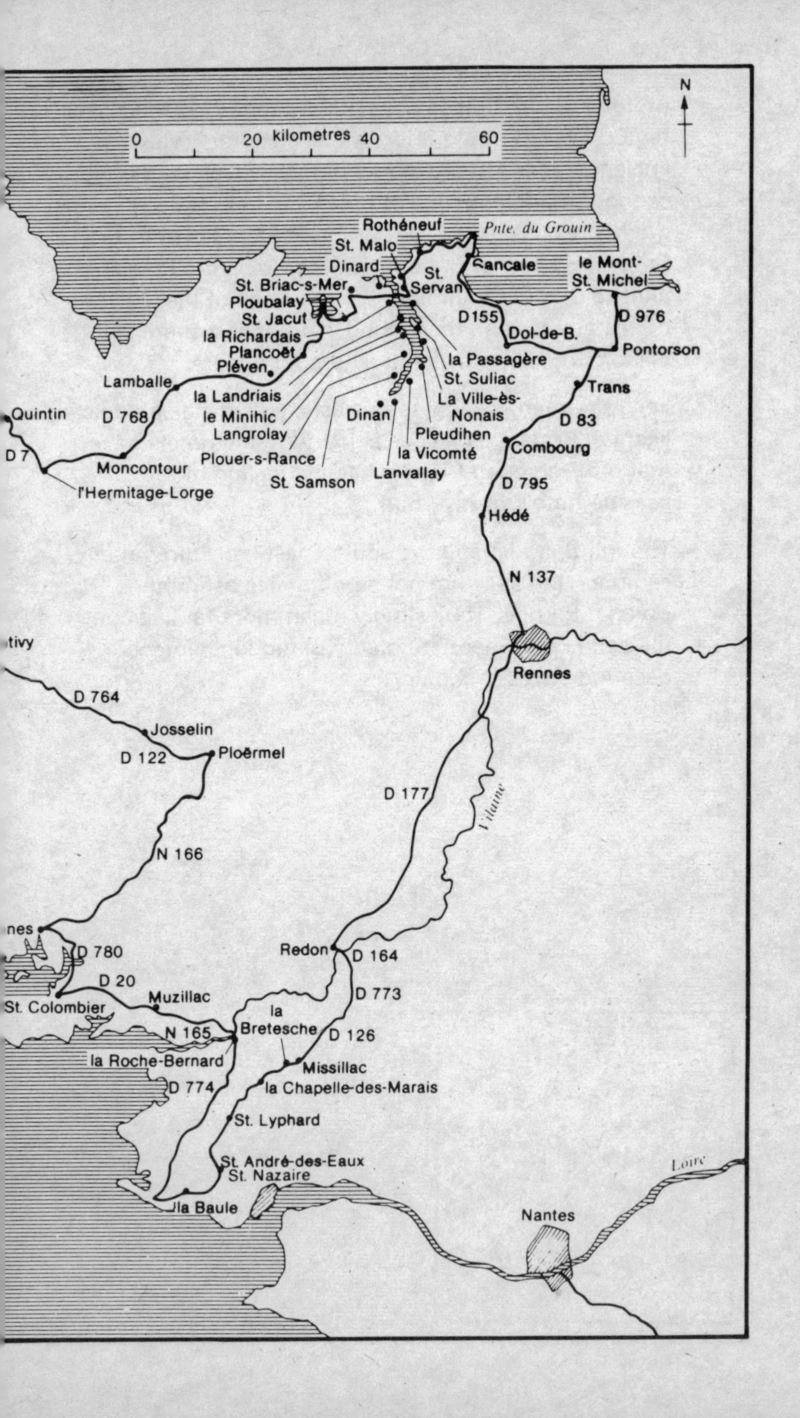
N
0
20
kilometres
40
60
Rothéneuf
Pnte. du Grouin
St. Malo
Dinard
St.
Servan
Sancale
le Mont-
St. Michel
St. Briac-s-Mer
Ploubalay
St. Jacut
la Richardais
Plancoët
Pléven
D155
Dol-de-B.
D 976
Pontorson
la Passagère
St. Suliac
La Ville-ès-
Nonais
Lamballe
la Landriais
le Minihic
Langrolay
Plouer-s-Rance
St. Samson
Dinan
Pleudihen
la Vicomté
Lanvallay
Trans
D 83
Combourg
Quintin
D 768
D 7
Moncontour
l'Hermitage-Lorge
D 795
Hédé
N 137
Rennes
tivy
D 764
Josselin
D 122
Ploërmel
D 177
Vilaine
N 166
nes
D 780
D 20
Redon
D 164
D 773
St. Colombier
Muzillac
la
Bretesche
N 165
D 126
la Roche-Bernard
Missillac
D 774
la Chapelle-des-Marais
St. Lyphard
St. André-des-Eaux
St. Nazaire
Loire
la Baule
Nantes

Bretons regard France as another country, as the Welsh regard England. And it is – a Celtic country where ancient legends and history are interwoven so that you cannot untangle them. Armorica became Brittany gradually because the old Britons fled there from the Saxon invasion of Britain. Not until 1488 did France annexe Brittany – through the marriage of the Duchess of Brittany to the French King. And people there still talk of 'Frenchmen' as if they are foreigners.

For fishermen, sailing enthusiasts, and shellfish addicts like me, Brittany is a special joy. And the hotels have that old-fashioned friendly 'family' feeling of the seaside hotels of my youth.

Though Benodet and the south coast have lured many campers, the sites are not so obtrusive as in other parts of Europe. They simply mean more families on the sands. But there are plenty of hidden, almost deserted coves in the north.

Route 7
Round Brittany

St Malo	See Route 6 (page 162)	
D301 St Servan (5km)	See Route 6 (page 162)	
N137 right by airfield on D5 to La Passagère back to N137, right on D117 to St Suliac, D7 right to La Ville-ès-Nonais, road right to join D29 to Pleudihen, La Vicomte, N176 Lanvallay, D2 under cross-river viaduct to Dinan (36km without diversions)	St Suliac – Grève, 99.58.40.35: overlooks river. Good choice; lovely fish. New owners. Good-value hideaway. Bedrooms renovated. Menus C–F. Rooms C. Shut 10 November–10 December. Pleudihen – at Mordreuc, down side road – Abri des Flots, 96.83.20.43: five-course meal with fine vegetables has gone up – to 40f in 1988! Incredibly good value meals. Overlooking river Rance. Mme Nauxel has run it for 26 years. Menus A, C. Rooms B. Brochetterie, 96.83.31.10: nice clean logis with pleasant welcome. Menu A. Rooms C–E. Shut Wednesday, Thursday; 1–25 October; part February.	If arriving late and wanting to reach hotel, cross Rance estuary by D168, then right on D266 to Dinard (9km) – see Route 1 – but tour of Rance is a 'must' and can still be done following day. La Passagère – good views over river Rance. At St Suliac, turn left at church, leave car 1km further on, walk on footpath past old mill to point of Mont Garrot (more lovely views). From La Ville-ès Nonais, short detour to Port St-Jean Bridge over river Rance with splendid valley views. Pleudihen: famous for apples 'Doux Eveques', and cider; tidal mill on side road to Mordreuc, attractive hamlet on river bank. La Vicomté (walk to point) is new snob area of Dinan; nice houses. Lanvallay – views of old Dinan, ramparts, belfries.

Dinan	See Route 6 (page 166)	
D12 St Samson-sur-Rance, Le Minihic-sur-Rance, right on to D114 for 400m, then D3 to La Landrais, back on to D114 to La Richardais, Dinard (34km) D766 St Briac (9km)	St Briac – Houle, in main street, 99.88.32.17: awkward opening and closing dates, but a nice hideout. Restaurant open only 1 March–30 September and shut Wednesdays March–mid-June! Menus A, B. Rooms A–C. Hotel shut January, February; Wednesdays March–mid-June.	Le Minihic – old fisherman's cottages; La Landrais – park car; walk 1.6km along Hures Promenade (old customs officers' walk) beside river. La Richardais: church with fine fresco in green, brown, ochre of Stations of the Cross. Stained glass by the great modern artist Max Ingrand. Allow 4–5 hours with sightseeing stops for tour round river Rance. St Briac – charming little resort; fishing; yachting harbour. Two bays with fine sand, pines, with sea views of islands. Narrow streets of old fisherman's houses. Coast views from Balcon d'Emeraude.
D5 minor road, then right on D168 Ploubalay, D168, D26 St Jacut, D62 left for short time on D786, then right on D768 Plancoët D28 Plèven (28km)	St Jacut – Vieux Moulin, 96.27.71.02: old windmill, with some rooms shaped like wedges, bathrooms in round towers. Very good sea food. Open only March–October; no lunches. Menus A–C. Rooms A–C. Plancoët – Source, 96.84.10.11: nothing to look at but fine cooking of bargain-price meals. Try shellfish, home-made terrine of pike, veal sweetbreads in wine, couscous Thursday, Friday. Menus A–D. Rooms A, B. Shut Mondays.	St Jacut – long peninsula continues into sea with islet of Hébiens; two safe beaches. Nice sea views; several crêperies (pancake cafés). Eleven beaches. (I have *not* counted). Pleyden: on edge of lonely Runadaye forest, beside long lake formed by river l'Arguenon.

Chez Crouzil, 20 les Quais, 98.84.10.24: Jean-Pierre Crouzil, here 38 years, cooks fish as well as anyone in these parts. Cancalaise oysters, too. And game in season. Straightforward fine cooking. Don't be put off by position. Menus B–G. Shut Sunday evening, Monday; November.

Plèven – Manoir du Vaumadeuc, 98.84.46.17: expensive but superb. Fifteenth-century manor of Vicomtesse du Breilde Pontbriand. Magnificent furnishings. Modern comfort. Good simple cuisine. Ingredients from own farm. Superb old wines (d'Yquem '47 3800f!). Menus D–F. Rooms E–G. Shut 5 January–20 March.

D28 Lamballe (16km)

At La Poterie (2km on D28) – Manoir des Portes, 96.31.13.61: I was there when it first opened and it was cosy, charming, friendly, with excellent regional cooking. Some readers now disappointed, claiming sloppiness, draughts, disappointing menus. Perhaps I was *too* enthusiastic! Even critics tell of excellent dishes on the carte, superb fish, friendly welcome, nice rural surroundings. Open fire; grounds with étang for fishing. Some bedrooms small. Menus C–D. Rooms E–F. Shut 31 January–25

Charming little town of whitewashed houses on hillside; big market for pigs, cattle; fine old buildings; Gothic-Romanesque church on terrace overlooking Gouessant river valley; views. Old houses in place du Martrai include 15th-century executioner's house (now Tourist Information Office and small museum). Only chapel survives of Lamballe Castle – pulled down by order of Richelieu because owner, Lord of Penthièvre, son of Henry IV, conspired against him; castle besieged in Religious Wars by 'Bras de Fer' –

Lamballe continued	February; restaurant Mondays low season. Tour d'Argent, rue Dr Lavergne, 96.31.01.37: excellent value; genuine small-town Relais with pleasant dining room 500 yards away. Logis, Relais Routiers and 2-star hotel. Simple bedrooms, renovated. Nice shellfish. Good wine list. Menus A, C, D. Rooms A–C. Restaurant shut Saturdays except in July, August.	Calvinist captain La Nouë who had metal hook in place of lost arm. He was killed at siege. Henry IV said sadly: 'Pity that such a little fortress destroyed so great a man.' Lamballe's one-way traffic system is difficult. Best known for its stud farm for Breton draught horses and old style post-horses. Has about 150 stallions; go out daily in tandem, pairs or fours, but sent away to stud-stands mid-February to mid-July; also dressage school (40 horses), riding school.
D768 Moncontour (15km)		Attractive old fortified town of granite where two valleys meet. Six fine Renaissance stained-glass windows in church; alleys and stairs lead down to ramparts. Place Penthièvre fine example of 18th-century architecture; Notre Dame du Haut (5.5km back towards Lamballe on D768; right at crossroads on D6 Collinée, right on D6A – ask for key at nearest farm) – wood statues of healer saints; go to them with good humble hearts and they will help, it is said; votive plaques marked 'Merci' show that some believers are left.
D44 Ploeuc, L'Hermitage-Lorge, D168, then soon D7 through forest of Lorge to Quintin (29km)	Quintin – Commerce, 96.74.96.67: the sort of simple little country hotel which made France famous for hospitality and good-value meals. Charming rustic restaurant, pleasant	First right off D44 on D25A at Henon is Elevage du Rocher de Bremar – famous for duck and goose-liver pâté. 3.5km south of L'Hermitage-Lorge, where D778 meets D7

	bedrooms and excellent old-style cooking at low prices. My readers love it. Most, says chef-patron François Le Gaudu, order langoustines, stuffed clams or house pâté, then coq au vin or salmon with Béarnaise sauce; they *adore* desserts – usually chocolate mousse or meringue chantilly, drink mostly Muscadet and get up from the table happy! Bargain menus, good cheap wines. Menus A–D. Rooms A–C. Shut Sunday evening, Monday lunch except 1 July–15 September; 15 December–15 January.	to Uzel, is a noticeboard: 'This is Lorges, centre of Resistance for the Département, where 55 men of the Resistance, after torture, were murdered and buried in this wood by Nazi hordes. In the night, freedom listens to us.' A stone points to a dark pinewood on a hill. Quintin: another charming old town; old houses rise in terraces from Guet river: riverside lake; very good fishing; 17th-century wing to castle; in church, a piece of the Virgin's girdle brought from Jerusalem in 13th century.
D28 Quélen, D767 Guingamp (46km)	Guingamp – Relais du Roy, place Centre, 96.43.76.62: Louis XIII appreciated the cooking at this Relais, so they called it Relais du Roy. He also appreciated the local duchesses. Fine old building furnished with taste and comfort. Impeccable service and table setting (Limoges china). Excellent cooking, outstanding fish, from mussels in cider to sole aux cèpes and lobster. Bedrooms all have bathrooms. Menus B–F. Rooms F. Shut Sunday in winter, Christmas.	Countryside on route from Quintin of tiny hamlets, chapels, streams, pools, roadside crosses; little traffic; overgrown green lanes were once roads for horses and carts. Guingamp is a town of cobbled streets, old houses and cathedral but busy through traffic.
D767 Cavan, small road left Tonquédec Castle, D31B to join D11 into Lannion (30km)	Lannion – Serpolet, 1 rue F. le Dantec, 96.46.50.23: good modern cooking (near to nouvelle) from young chef (when open!) Menus A (weekday), F. Shut Saturday lunch, Sunday evening,	Château de Tonquédec – impressive skeleton on heights overlooking valley. Built 13th century, dismantled by order of Richelieu, an even greater demolition expert than Oliver

Lannion continued

Monday 27 April–11 May; 6–21 September; 1–11 January.

At Le Yaudet (8km by D786 towards Morlaix, then D88A) – Genets d'Or, 96.35.24.17: 300 metres from bay with quiet beaches; pleasant hotel, simple bedrooms; good traditional cooking of fish, shellfish, chicken, game. Meals good value, bargain wines. Menus A, C, D. Rooms A, B. Shut Mondays low season; January, February.

Cromwell. Two courtyards with two towers, a keep with walls over 4m (13ft) thick; climb 76 steps for views of fertile plains and deep wooded valleys. (Open early spring to 30 September)

Lannion, port on river Léguer, with many old half-timbered houses, looking like a set for a musical on Old Brittany. Best of houses (15th–16th century) in place Général Leclerc and alleys leading off. Staircase of 142 steps leads to Brélévenez church, built by Knights Templar in 12th century, but view from top is rewarding. Big golf ball on heath to North is radome of telecommunications centre which links France to US.

D65
Trébeurden
(9km)

Family Hotel, 85 rue Plages, 96.23.50.31: well named; friendly, comfortable; typical old, tall, thin Breton building with balconies – in pink granite; will take one-nighters even in season, which many resort-hotels will not. Specialities: fish; shellfish; pâtisseries. Menus A, B, D. Rooms D–E. Restaurant shut 1 October–31 March. Hotel open all year.

Ti Al Lannec, allée de Mezo Guen, 96.23.57.26: I loved it from when the young Jouannys took over about 12 years ago and I still do. So do thousands more people now, so book! Many improvements since then, inside and creating a terrace

Old Breton resort, still attractive but hilly. Overlooks bay littered with islands; prevailing westerlies give splendid sailing. Several fine sand beaches; harbour; rocky peninsula Le Castel attached to mainland by thread of sand; path along it – coast views. Long beach round peninsula.

From Trebeurden to Trégastel and Perros Guirec called Rose Granite Coast; masses of rose-red rock divide the beaches, even pop up in fields and gardens.

with lovely sea views. Superb cooking of delicious fresh fish, poultry and lamb. Individual touches but basically classically simple. Very helpful family. Good value weekday lunch menu. Menus A (children), C (weekday lunch), D, F, G. Rooms F–G. Shut mid-November–mid-March. Restaurant shut Monday lunch.

D65 back to Lannion, D786 St Michel-en-Grève, St Efflam, right on D42, D64 round Corniche l'Armorique to Locquirec, D64 Lanmeur small road (C4) right to St Antoine, D76 beside estuary of Dossen (Morlaix) river to Morlaix (50km) join route here from Roscoff.

St Michel – Plage, 96.35.74.43: enclosed and open terraces overlooking beach; new dining room. Menus good value with choice. Excellent shellfish, with good choice of fresh white fish. New owner and chef (1986) but tradition maintained. Menus A, C. Rooms C, D. Open all year.

Locquirec – Port, 98.67.42.10: very Breton family hotel looking down on interesting harbour. All bedrooms have sea views, some with balconies. Menus A–C; cheap house wine. Rooms B, C. Shut September–Easter.

Morlaix – Europe, 1 rue d'Aiguillon, 98.62.11.99: a brasserie is open, the dining room moved, but thank goodness the brilliant young chef Patrick Jeffroy is back at the cooker. He went walkabout in 1984. A dedicated inventor of dishes; the menus and carte come as a constant surprise. But his basic cooking is so careful,

One of my favourite areas of Brittany. St Michel-en-Grève: charming little beach resort, end of magnificent Lieue de Grève beach 4km (2½ miles) long, 2km (1¼ miles) wide at low tide; sands firm enough for training horses; trout streams run through little valleys into sea; wooded coast road past Grand Richer (rock mass) 80m (261ft) high (steep path up – about half-hour return).

St Efflam – hermit from Ireland (AD 470); beside his chapel is domed fountain.

Plestin church, 16th century, was mined and burned by Germans in 1944; rebuilt.

Armorique Corniche – road follows eccentric coast, heavily indented.

Locquirec – super little fishing port and resort; fine views by walking round the point; delightful walled harbour; sands; old church once belonged to Knights of Malta.

Morlaix continued

too, that simple dishes are a delight. Try hot lobster wrapped in sheets of lightly smoked samon, or his escalope of salmon cooked very quickly on a very hot surface, served on a golden-brown galette de sarassin (buckwheat pancake). Excellent value. Hotel owner Jacques Feunteuna is a dedicated winesman and keeps a splendid cellar. Strong criticism of décor (*not* comfort) of bedrooms by my readers – and Gault-Millau. Menus D–G (restaurant); A–D (brasserie). Rooms B–F. Shut 18 December–18 January.

Marée Bleue, 3 rampe St Melaine, 98.63.24.21: Michel Coquart's old stone house up an alley worth hunting out for excellent traditional cooking: guinea fowl and duck as good as the fish and shellfish. Menus A–F. Shut Sunday evening (low season); Monday; 1 week November; 3 weeks February.

At St Thegonnec (12km SW Morlaix by N12, D118) – Auberge St Thegonnec, 6 place Marie, 98.79.61.18: I am proud to have been one of three judges who picked out young Alain Le Coz's little stone auberge as Brittany Ferries' Restaurant of the Year in 1984. Now he is deservedly in all French guides. He makes no claim except for simple fresh cooking of fresh ingredients in a simple village auberge. I

Morlaix – huge railway viaduct across Dossen estuary (known as Morlaix river) dominates old town. Fine old buildings, especially Grand'Rue (market). Once corsair headquarters (including Jean Bart, Duguay Trouin, Cornic). In 1522, corsair John of Coetanlem sacked Bristol; in reply, 80 English ships entered bay, sailors ransacked Morlaix while citizens were at Guingamp festival. English sailors drank too much; many were caught asleep in a wood by returning Morlaix citizens and massacred. So town's arms show a lion facing English leopard with motto: 'If they bite you, bite them'. Castle built at harbour entrance to discourage English.

St Thegonnec (12km SW Morlaix by N12, D118) – remarkable monumental Renaissance arch with elaborate Calvary to village church.

wish there were more like him. But then he is the son of Manick Le Coz of La Plage, Ste-Anne-La-Palud. Superb value. Rooms simple. Smiling welcome from young Madame Marie-Thérèse. Menus A, C. D. Rooms B, C. Shut Monday evening, Tuesday low season; 15 December–5 February.

D769 for short distance, then small road to Pleyber-Christ, small road left back to D769 through Arrée mountains into forest of Ambroise. Join D764 right, then D146 Huelgoat (33km)

At Locmaria-Berrien (after Ambroise forest, just off D764) – Truite, La Gare, 98.99.73.05: Mlle Lucie Le Guillou has been here at the cooker since 1936 and I wish her many more years. Doyen of Brittany cooks. The Michelin star has gone but not the superb trout, lobster, quail, and her delicious terrine. Superb wine cellar collected over years – probably Brittany's best. Old Breton furniture, peaceful garden. Menus C, E, G (gastronomic). Rooms A–C. Shut Sunday evening, Monday (except July, August); 1 January–1 March.

Huelgoat – Ty Douz, rue Gén-de-Gaulle, 98.99.74.78: very good value restaurant with lakeside terrace, another overlooking lake. Good cooking of simple old-style dishes. Very good moules farcies (stuffed mussels), lake trout in almonds. Wines cheap. Five menus A–C. Shut Friday except 1 July–30 September; January.

If not interested in churches stick to D769 – attractive road. Pleyber-Christ: arch dedicated to dead of World War 1 leads to Gothic-Renaissance church containing many treasures, including remarkable beams and carved chests.

Huelgoat is in unusual landscape of hills, rocks, hollows, streams and waterfalls; lovely trees – beech, oak, pine, spruce; fine fishing, including trout. See Chaos du Moulin (granite rocks in green setting); Grotte du Diable (path in loops down a hollow to river where it goes underground); trembling rock (100-ton rock sways on its base when pushed).

D764 NW to Roc Trévezel, D785 Montagne-St-Michel, D785, D30 to St Rivoal D42 Croas-ar-Go through Cranou forest to Rumengol, Le Faou (54km)

Le Faou – La Vielle Renommé, place Mairie, 98.81.90.31: quite modern but already so renowned that you must book to eat in summer despite big dining room. Serious traditional Breton cooking: local fish. Copious portions; delicious palourdes farcies (stuffed clams) and langouste Cardinale (lobster in half-shell covered in lobster and truffle sauce, browned under grill). Don't expect anything 'inventive', but do try panaché de la mer à l'aigrelette (a sort of fritter of mixed fish). Cheap Gros Plant wine; good Breton cider. Menus A (weekdays)–F. Rooms B–D. Shut Sunday evening, Monday (except July, August); 10 November–1 December; part February.

Relais de la Place, place Mairie, 98.81.91.19: recommended to me by readers unable to get into Vieille Renommé next door. 'Serious cooking. Very relaxed. Big portions. We didn't feel hungry for two days!' Menus A (weekdays)–F. Rooms A–C. Shut Saturday October–1 July; 19 September–12 October.

Westward through Arrée mountains. Road left D36 leads to St Michel reservoir lake.

Trévezel: rock escarpment about 365m (1200ft) high looks like miniature Alps. Leave car by road, walk for wide panoramic views (½ hr return). St Michel mountain: car park signposted; chapel and panorama at 380m (1250ft); peat bog at foot of hill – called locally 'Entrance to Hell' because of its winter grimness.

St Rivoal: open-air museum of old Breton houses; interesting.

Winding, hilly road through Cranou forest (oaks, beeches).

Rumengol: famous for its 'pardons' – festivals of forgiveness on Trinity Sunday; 15 August (Assumption Day). These pardons held all over Brittany; religious festivals still often followed by secular celebrations.

Le Faou is super little port. Wide market square with 16th-century covered halls.

D791 Corniche road through Térenez, round Bay du Folgoat on small roads right to Landévennec, D60 back on to D791, right at Tal-ar-Groas on D63 to Lanvéoc, D55 to Le Fret, St Fiacre D355 Espagnols Point, Camaret-sur-Mer (57km)

Landévennac – Beau Sejour, 98.27.70.65: another recommended by readers for views of rivers and boats and for meals popular with French people. I have not seen it. Menus A (weekday)–F. Rooms B, C. Shut Monday (all day in winter, evening May–September); January.

Camaret – France, 98.27.93.06 modern, in old style, on harbour quay. Very fresh fish; lobster ragoût, grilled lobster, scallops, all delicious. Viviers. Wines from 40f to 1200f (Mouton Rothschild '75). Bedrooms pleasantly furnished; some in annexe. Interesting paintings and tapestries. Menus A (lunch), B, D, F, G. Rooms D, D, F. Open 1 April–11 November. Shut Thursdays low season.

Views over Le Faou river, then whole Landévennec Peninsula and Aulne river.

Landévennec: ruins of old Benedictine Abbey and new one (1965). D60 is picturesque road. New Térenez bridge has central span 272m (893ft).

Le Fret: little port with boat service across Rade de Brest to big naval port of Brest.

Espagnols Point: in fine weather remarkable views over whole vast roadstead of Brest. Named after troops sent here in 1590 by Philip II of Spain to help Liguers – league of fanatical Catholics – fight Henry IV.

Camaret: little seaside resort and lobster port; small beach beyond natural dyke which defends port from Atlantic. After English, Spanish and Dutch attacks, military architect Vauban fortified it in 1689. Anglo-French fleet tried to make landing but troops were defeated by dragoons and Breton 'Home Guard' with pitchforks and scythes. In Camaret Bay in 1801, American engineer Fulton tried out a submarine (5-man with pointed oars, speed 2 knots – stayed down for 6 hours) Camaret has a naval museum.

D8 Crozon, D887 Morgat (15km)	Le Roof, boulevard France-Libre, 98.27.08.40: locals tell me it is the best restaurant in an area short of good ones. Inevitably specializes in fresh fish cooked fresh. Menus B–F. Shut Monday low season; October.	Morgat – sheltered resort with great sandy beach. Tunny fishing boats. Magnificent panoramic views of coast and islands from Pointe de Pen-Hir (68m high – 227ft). It is a bird sanctuary.
Back through Crozon on D887, 15km onward take D63 right marked St Nic, left at St Nic on D108 to rejoin D887 for Ménez Hom Armorique. At St Marie right on D47 to Ploéven, D63 to Plonévez-Porzay, Locronan (46km)	At Plonévez-Porzay – Manoir de Moelliën, 98.92.50.40: fine old manor of 1642 with tower, it was restored from a ruin by Marie Anne Le Corré. Once home of one of Châteaubriand's mistresses. Good value. Fine cooking of seasonal specialities. Try duck fricassé in cider, salmon rillettes, fish ragoûts. Comfortable bedrooms in stables. Menus A–F (shut Wednesdays in winter). Rooms E. Shut 12 November–20 March. At Ste-Anne-la-Palud, 3km W of Plonévez-Porzay on D61 – Plage, 98.92.50.12: well-deserved Michelin star and accolades all round France for the big hotel of Mme Manick Le Coz beside a vast beach and dunes in a big bay. Garden, heated pool and superb old-style cooking with some inventions – wonderful shellfish, 'best sole in the world' (gastronome Marc de Champerard), desserts like grandmother made. Relais et Châteaux hotel. Expensive. Menus E (weekday)–G. Rooms G. Open 9 April–15 October.	Ménez Hom (330m/1082ft) – windy moorland peak at approach to Crozon Peninsula, used for centuries to defend Brest and area. Germans dislodged by US and Free French in siege of Brest, 1944. One of best viewpoints in Brittany. On 15 August, Folklore Festival at Summit. (Hill reached by taking D83 – 1.5km – just before Chapel of St Marie or by parking by the chapel and walking 50m (55yds) to hill.) Chapel beautiful with ornamented altar-pieces. Locronan – superb little town of old granite houses; once manufactured sailcloth, now 'Ville d'Art' with artisans working in glass; weaving wool, linen and silk (see weaving mill of old India Company in place Eglise; Tour Carée workshop, rue Lann); museum of contemporary art depicting Breton scenes, furniture, costumes. Lovely old square with well.

Locronon – Prieuré, 98.91.70.89: in town, very attractive old granite house; jolly dining room; pretty flowery bedrooms; excellent shellfish; 6 good value menus; cheap wine. Menus A–E. Rooms D, E. Shut October; Monday off season.

Fer â Cheval, 1km D63 SE, 98.91.70.67: modern version of traditional Breton architecture. Bedrooms improved, own grounds in wooded countryside. Sea 6km. Rooms D, E. Restaurant in old town centre, place Eglise (98.91.70.74). Menus A–G. Open all year.

D7 Douarnenez, Tréboule (10km) D7, D784 Pointe-du-Raz, D784 Audierne, D765 Pont-Croix, local road S Plouhinec, D784 Quimper (96km)

Douarnenez – Bar Criée, Port, 98.92.43.43: I discovered this splendid cheap fish restaurant in a second-floor room 10 years ago. Readers have loved it. Real bargain, super fresh fish. Alas, I have not been for two years and letters remain unanswered. If it's still there, go! Lovely bay views. Menus (1987) A, C, E. Lunch only.

Athanor, 1 rue Henri-Barbusse, 98.92.88.97: recommended to me by visiting Parisians, especially for a Breton version of paëlla! Menu A. Shut Tuesday.

Auberge de Kervéoch, 5km on Quimper road, 98.92.07.58: M. et Mme de Brusq's daughter and husband Joël Guitton have taken over, 'refaite

Douarnenez – historic fishing port, originally sardine boats, now mostly crayfish, langoustine; watersport centre; sailing schools; surfing; beaches 2 miles away. Superb scenery round bay enclosing legendary town of Ys, submerged by sea. Isle in estuary, le Tristan, was 16th-century HQ of brigand La Fontenelle-Ligeur who terrorized Brittany. Fish still auctioned at Rosmeur harbour; tourist sea fishing and boat trips leave from here in high summer. New fishing port in new harbour. Over river bridge is Tréboul, with narrow streets round little port; pleasure boat harbour; sailing centre.

Quimber continued

entièrement l'hôtel' from improving bedrooms to changing plates, glasses, linen. But it is still a delightful, quiet old farm, hidden in trees, furnished in old dark wood, with an open fire. More elaborate menus. Imaginative cooking (try the new dessert – Roquefort en Bavarois aux Noix). Joël Guitton is on his way up. You are expected to take dinner if you book a room. Menus B–G. Rooms D. Open Easter–15 October each day, plus French school holidays.

Quimper – Tour d'Auvergne, 13 rue Reguaires, 98.95.08.70: old hotel, once social centre of Quimper, now shuts its restaurant from 1 October–30 April. Menus B–D. Rooms C–E. Shut 20 December–5 January.

Capucin Gourmand, 29 rue Reguaires, 97.26.11.12: Luc le Rhun has left but new chef still lures locals with hot oyster gratinées, excellent scallops, and turbot with leek sabayon sauce. Menus C–E. Shut Sunday evening, Monday; part August.

Tritons, allée de Locmaria, 98.90.61.78: no lunches but open until 1 a.m. serving fine old dishes such as potée Bretonne with meat and various cabbages and green vegetables, Breton duck with cider and cream sauce, braised beef or poultry (daubes). Cheap and cheap wines. Menus A–C. Shut Monday; September.

Interesting and spectacular route. Road left leads to Réserve de Cap Sizun, bird sanctuary for sea birds in wild setting (auks, gulls, crested cormorants, guillemots). Guided visits 15 March–31 August – binoculars help.

For Pointe-de-Van, park at Trouguer; path round headland little known.

Trépassés Bay (Bay of Dead because Druids were taken across for burial on Sein Island); tide race here frightening; great swell of sea rolls magnificently into this bay. Alas, like Land's End, Raz point has become a tourist trap – car parks, souvenir shops, crêperies – but the walk round the point is spectacular and rewarding; do not attempt it if you hate heights. Use a guide and wear non-slip shoes; do not leave safety rope.

Ile de Sein men are fishermen who regarded even digging fields as women's work until recently. Once they lived by luring ships on to rocks and wrecking them. In June 1940, the entire male population, even 13-year-olds, sailed to England to join the Free French.

Lane off D784 leads to fishing hamlet of Bestrée; another to St Tugen (16th-century chapel).

Audierne: pretty fishing port on estuary of Goyen river – lobsters, crayfish, tunny, June–October; beach 1.5km (1 mile) away.

Pont-Croix, built on terraces up from river Goyen; photogenic; narrow streets between old houses to bridge; chapel with fine stained glass.

Despite traffic problems, Quimper is still one of my favourite towns. It is a happy place. Odet and Steir rivers meet here. Though dominated by huge Gothic cathedral with lacy spires, it is very much a market town and stalls spill out to line streets near to covered market. Splendid old streets, riverside roads; pottery (came from Nivernais in 1690). Quimper produces crêpes dentelles, crisp, lacy biscuits rolled like casing for cannelloni.

Worth taking drive round Odet river to Benodet and return (44km). Boats on Odet to Benodet (1½ hours); tides rule sailing times.

D785, D20 Les Vire-Court, D20 to D785 Pont l'Abbé (20km)

Pont l'Abbé – Bretagne, 24 place République, 98.87.17.22: for many years we have regarded Marcel Cossec as one of the best fish chefs in Brittany and cannot understand why many French guides have failed to notice him. Perhaps because he sticks to traditional and

At Vire-Court, river winds between high, wooded cliffs; narrowest point called 'Virgin's Leap'; inevitable story of girl leaping it to avoid rape. River bends so much that a Spanish fleet was too frightened to turn the bend and just sailed away.

Pont l'Abbé continued

regional recipes, not 'modern inventive'. Delicious fish. Pretty terrace; charming bedrooms. Since 1980. Very friendly welcome from Marcel and his wife. Menus A, B, D, F, G. Rooms C–E. Shut Mondays low season; 15–30 October; 15–30 January.

At Lesconil, little fishing port 9km from Pont l'Abbé by D102 – Plage, 98.87.80.05: views of harbour; excellent choice of menus and dishes. Fine locally landed fish. Menus A–G (shut Monday except July, August). Rooms B—D. Open Easter–14 October.

At Léchiagat (Le Guilvinec) another fishing port 6km W of Lesconil – Port, 95.58.10.10: on quayside; owned by same couple as Plage at Lesconil (M et Mme Gaby Struillon). Seven menus. Second cheapest (80f in 1987) remarkable value. Most expensive superb – if you can eat your way through it! Menus A–G. Rooms, B, C. Open all year.

Pont l'Abbé – 'capital' of Bigouden, country area where many women still wear the tall white coiffe on their heads at festivals. Bigouden museum in 14th-century castle, with costumes and furniture. Open 1 June–15 September.

Kerazan Manor (3km on D2), castle left to French Institute by Joseph Astor who left money, too, to endow courses at the castle in embroidery and needlework for young Breton women. Fine collection of paintings and drawings from 15th century to today.

D785, D44 Bénodet (11km)

Armoric, 3 rue Penfoul, 98.57.04.03: alas my old favourite for good value meals no longer serves meals – only b-and-b – and wine. Of 40 bedrooms, 12 have direct garden access to help handicapped or people of 'troisième age' (nice French phrase for oldies like me over 60). Rooms (all with WC,

Bridge (610m/2000ft long) over Odet opens up resort of Bénodet to west. Charming place, with fine beach, but taken over by campers in summer these days, so crowded; good yacht harbour; casino, lively high season. Boat trips to Quimper up river Odet (½ hr); also to Loctudy (pretty seaport – ½

most baths) B–D. Open only mid-May–mid-September.

Minaret, Corniche de l'Estriatre, 98.57.03.13: old Moroccan house with minaret and fine Moorish garden. Superb views over attractive Odet estuary. Fine dining room with view. Varying reports of meals but once well known for fish. Expected to take dinner if you stay June–September. Menus A (weekdays)–E. Restaurant shut 1 October–31 March.

Poste, place Poste, 97.57.01.09: cheerful modern hotel in centre; comfortable bedrooms with bath, WC. Menus A (weekdays)–B. Rooms D, E. Shut January. B-and-b annexe hotel down road: Ker Vennaik, ave Plage, 98.57.15.40: very comfortable. You can eat at Poste. Open 1 March–1 November.

Ferme du Letty, 2km SE Bénodet by D44, 98.57.01.27: an enigma. I knew it as an attractive crêperie in an old stone farmhouse where I took my children. Now run by a local couple and my spy – a local gastronome – thinks it is a splendid place for the freshest fish and luscious desserts. And Michelin gives it a star. Gault-Millau ignores it. Champérard is almost vicious, even about the décor

hr) and Glénen Isles (famous sailing school; some isles uninhabited – kept as bird sanctuaries – 1¾ hrs).

Bénodet continued

('glacial'). He does like one dessert – millefeuille aux framboises. I hesitate to go and add my opinion to the confusion! Menus E–G. Shut Thursday lunch and Wednesday; 5–28 October.

Domaine de Kéréven, Clohars-Fouesnant, 2km N Bénodet, 98.57.02.46: old family manor in big estate. Very comfortable, well run. Menu B. Rooms (all with bathrooms) D, E. Shut October–Easter.

D44 Fouesnant, La Forêt-Fousenant, little road right through Kersicot to Concarneau (15km)

At Beg Meil (6km S Fouesnant on D45) Thalamot, I seem to have known it for ever; the grandchildren run it now and (between ourselves) have tidied it up, improved the friendly service, added four rooms with bath, WC. Super local fish – red mullet, scallops, St Pierre (John Dory), shellfish. Menus A, C, E, F. Rooms (prices seasonal) B–F; half-board terms. Open mid-April to beginning October.

Fouesnant – Armorique, rue Cornouaille, 98.56.00.19: delightful old Breton inn with super dining room, flowery courtyard, modern bedrooms in garden annexe. Bourgeoise cuisine, copious helpings, old Breton dishes. Known for its cider; shellfish. Menus A–F. Rooms B–C. Open 1 April–October. Shut Mondays low season.

Beg Meil, 6km right on D45: my old hideout with nice beach backed by pines now gets terribly crowded mid-summer and summer weekends, with parked cars spoiling it a bit and car queues to reach it.

Interesting little port, lobster boats large sand beach with dunes.

Fouesnant – very pleasant little town among fruit orchards; produces best cider in Brittany.

La Forêt-Fouesnant – separate village, was hidden and quiet until Port-la-Forêt, huge port for yachtsmen and pleasure craft, opened in 1972 – but separate from village – across estuary.

La Forêt-Fousenant – Baie, 98.56.97.35: our old favourite remains as popular as ever with families. Menus range from a bargain cheap meal to a super gourmand meal with lobster. Menus A, C, E. Rooms B–D. Open all year.

Auberge St Laurent, 2km on route to Concarneau, 98.56.98.07: good restaurant in old Breton cottage, near sea, log fires, garden. Lobster from vivier. Cheap wines. Menus A, C, G. Shut Monday.

Du Port, 98.56.97.13: cheap, simple, very good value. Menus A, C. D. Rooms A, B. Restaurant open all year: hotel shut 1 November–Easter.

Manoir du Stang (1km N of Forêt-Fouesnant on D783, private road), 98.56.97.37: true haven of peace and discretion in enchanting gardens 800m from the Atlantic 'a vol d'oiseau'. In the Hubert family for 200 years. Menu F; half-board for 2 people (1987) 840–1040f, includes dinner, room, breakfast, oranges pressées. Open 2 May–25 September.

Concarneau – Douane, 71 ave Alain-Le-Lay, 98.97.30.27: my old favourite restaurant has gone upmarket at night, but still serves a good-value lunch menu. Happy atmosphere. Well-chosen wines. Near fish sheds and fish is truly fresh and

Concarneau – Ville Close (14th-century walled town) surrounded by modern fishing harbour. Ville Close is totally surrounded by thick ramparts; despite many souvenir shops, crêperies and restaurants, still looks 'original' and impresses me

Concarneau continued

excellent. Menu (lunch only) B; carte. Shut Sunday evening; part February.

Coquille, 1 rue Moros, 98.97.08.52: in new port; 'rustic Breton' restaurant with wall paintings by the patronne. Outside tables, terrace with view of busy harbour. Good value. Mostly fish. Try Saint-Pierre (John Dory) with peppers. Menus A, D, F. Shut Sunday evening except July, August; 11–25 May; 20 December–15 January.

Ocean, plage Sables Blancs, 98.56.97.35: the Henaffs from the Baie, Foret-Fouesnant, were due to open this new hotel-restaurant in April 1988. Good hotel at reasonable prices sorely needed in Concarneau. Rooms E. Menu prices undecided.

after 20 visits; fishing museum in former arsenal (open Easter–30 September); shellwork display centre shows artistic designs made of shells. Worth seeing inner harbour, where fishing boats unload (Concarneau is third biggest fishing port in France and has tunny fleet), and outer harbour with brightly coloured pleasure boats.

D783 Pont-Aven, Quimperlé (28km)

Pont Aven – Moulin Rosmadec, 98.06.00.22: Pont Aven once had more mills than houses. This 15th-century mill, now a comfortable gourmand restaurant, is in lovely riverside position in a rose garden. Charming beamed dining room. Deservedly, Pierre Sébilleau has long been a favourite in Britanny, but a few readers suggest that he is flirting with modern sauces unsuccessfully. His grilled lobster and langoustines are excellent, his sole suprême

Pleasant resort where river Aven opens into tidal estuary. Made famous by Gauguin and his school of lesser artists in 1890s; they preached: 'Paint what you see, not what is there.' Artists not very popular with locals; Gauguin had punch-ups with fishermen in Concarneau and broke a leg. None of his paintings in local museum, though sometimes he appears in temporary exhibitions. He moved to little port of Le Pouldu, at mouth of river Laita (14km from Quimperlé on D49)

almost supreme. Menus C–F. Four expensive, attractive rooms added F–G. Shut Wednesdays; February; part October.

Taupinière, 4km on route de Concarneau, 98.06.03.12: little Pont-Aven (3295 inhabitants) is very lucky to have two great restaurants with Michelin stars. Guy Guilloux is the newer star and openly experimental and inventive in his cooking, though his famous dish is big langoustines grilled on an open fire. Expensive, too. Try oysters poached with paprika. Excellent ham. Very interesting if you have the francs. Menus F–G. Shut Monday evening, Tuesday; 20 September–20 October.

At Port-Manech, 12km S of Pont-Aven (little resort among pines, with sands, fishing harbour) – Port, 98.06.82.17: menus A–C. Rooms B–D. Open Easter–30 September.

At Raguénè Plage, 12km SE of Port-Aven – Chez Pierre, 98.06.81.06: started as a café in 1977 by Xavier Etuillou's grandfather. Now hotel with modern annexe, charming garden. Super shellfish, excellent cooking. Menus C–F. Rooms B–E. Shut end September–10 April.

where there is a statue to Gauguin next to chapel.

Quimperlé – beautiful old town where rivers Ellé and Isole join to form Lafta. Superb old houses, many with projecting upper storeys. Curious church of Ste Croix based on Church of Holy Sepulchre in Jerusalem. But 12th-century belfry collapsed on to it in 1862; rebuilt with separate belfry.

Quimperlé continued	Quimperlé – Auberge du Toulfoën, La Plaine, route Pouldou, 98.96.00.29: country inn, near riding stables. Pleasant. Known for crêpes, seafood. Cheap wine. Menus weekdays A–C; Sundays D–F. Rooms B–D. Shut Mondays; 25 September–31 October.	
D22, D2 Plouay, D769, D110 through Valley of Scorff, skirting forest of Pont Calleck to Kernascléden (32km) minor road south to Inguiniel, Bubry, D2 Pontivy, D764 Josselin (32km)	Bubry – Moulin de Coët Diquel, 97.51.70.70: modern, in Breton traditional style; warm, solid furnishing; heated pool, terrace on to étang (small lake); fishing; all bedrooms different; family run. Menus A–E. Rooms D–E. Shut 1 December–14 March. Pontivy – Villeneuve, route de Vannes, 97.39.83.10: logis with casserole for good regional cooking. Menus A–D. Rooms B–C. Josselin – Château, 97.22.20.11: alongside river, opposite castle walls; old favourite of mine, now popular, too crowded high season. Fine view of castle from dining room. Bedrooms improved. Reasonable prices for good quality. Menus A–E. Rooms B–D. Shut Christmas, February. Commerce, 9 rue Glatinier, 97.22.22.08: another with views over canal and chateau. Attractive dining room with log fire in season. Oysters raw, or hot, stuffed with herbs or cooked with almonds. Good terrine of	Lovely run. On D110, ¼km (½ mile) past Chapel of Ste Anne-des-Bois, steep road takes you in 200m (¼ mile) to lake and children's home, once Pont-Calleck castle. Pleasant Kernascléden church, finished 1453, was officially built 30 years before Chapel of St Fiacre at Le Faouet (15km away), but every local child knows they were built simultaneously, by the same workers, who were carried with their tools each night from one to the other by angels – ultimate in 'moonlighting'. Beautiful building – slender tower, rose-carvings, delicate tracery. Bubry has a big 'pardon' religious festival for St Hélèn (4th Sunday in July). Green, pretty area. Pontivy has two towns – one of old houses and moated castle with 20m (64ft) ramparts (closed November, December; Monday, Tuesday except June–September); and planned 'new' military town built by Napoleon. Pontivy is on river Blavet;

	lotte with shellfish sauce. Excellent value. One very cheap menu. Menus A–F. Rooms C–D. Shut Wednesday; March.	Napoleon had trouble with our Royal Navy, especially moving ships from Nantes to Brest, decided to build canal between them. Pontivy was half-way, so he made it military centre. Blavet was canalized to improve communication with sea. Josselin is a charming little town in photogenic setting on the river Oust, near where it joins the Nantes–Brest canal which joins the river Blavet at Pontivy. Its riverside castle is like an illustration for a fairy-tale. Mostly built by Oliver de Clisson, who sided first with England, then with France (he became Constable of France), was called 'The Butcher' (his motto was 'I do as I please'). He married a widow of the great de Rohan family of Josselin, who still own the castle. Castle open daily 1 June–2 September; Sundays, 19 March–31 May.
D122 Ploërmel, N166 Vannes (46km)	Vannes – Marée Bleue, place Bir-Makeim, 97.47.24.29: good value restaurant just outside old walls. Cheap lunch remarkable value. Locals pack it. Menus A, C, F. Rooms A, B. Shut Sunday evening in winter; 19 December–6 January. Marébaudière, rue A. Briand, 97.47.34.29: hotel – same owners as Marée Bleue above; use that restaurant; all rooms with bath, or shower, WC, D–E. Shut 19 December–6 January.	Little D122 runs alongside canal to Ploërmel (old houses; Duc Lake, 2.5km N, has beach, watersport centre). Road through moorlands of Lanvaux passes 1km from Fortresse de Largoët (11 towers) half-ruined castle where Henry Tudor was imprisoned when he fled after Wars of Roses; he became Henry VII of England.

Vannes continued

Lys, 51 rue Maréchal-Leclerc, 97.47.29.30: alas, I have not returned to young Fernand Corfmat's restaurant since its early days when meals were some of the best bargains in Brittany. Varying reports, but he is praised by those who like 'modern inventive' cooking; menus still reasonable though carte prices have shot up. Don't be put off by dreary street. Menus B (weekdays)–F. Shut Sunday evenings in winter, Mondays; 12 November–12 December.

The Roof (at Conleau, 4.5km SW), 97.63.47.47: modern, outside terrace and dining room overlooking gulf boats and island. Very popular – book. Very good food. Menus A, C, E. Rooms C–D. Shut Mondays in winter; mid-January–mid-February.

At Toulbroche, before Baden, 10km SW Vannes on D101 – Gravinis, 97.57.00.01: excellent fish according to market and season; good desserts. Modern. Garden. Menus more ambitious, prices higher. Gourmet menu superb for lobster lovers. Menus B, E, G. Rooms A–B (singles); C–F (doubles). Seasonal prices. Restaurant shut Monday; Sunday (in winter); 4 January–4 February.

At Larmor-Baden (5km S of Baden on D316 – 16km SW Vannes) – Isles, 97.57.03.31:

Vannes – old market centre in Gulf of Morbihan, turning industrial. Old walled town grouped round cathedral is delightful.

Cathedral was built between 13th and 19th centuries and looks like it. Much mixture of styles. Medieval Parliament building (near cathedral) converted to interesting covered market, with craftsmen working in metal, leather; artists; crêperies. Oyster museum above tourist office (29 rue Thiers); Vannes is pretty town but so tourist-minded, it could become a 'museum' in old area.

Fine boat trips from Vannes into Gulf of Morbihan to Arz Island (3km/2 miles long), Moines Isle (6km/4 miles long) – quiet seaside resort where the women's beauty has aroused poets, and woods have such names as Wood of Love, Wood of Sighs, Wood of Regrets. Trips 2 hrs to whole day from Vannes.

little hotel with terrace washed by sea at high tide. Much used by locals. Good wine list. Menus C, D. Rooms (sea views) D, E. Shut Thursdays.

N165, right on D780 along coast of Gulf of Morbihan, St Colombier, D20 Muzillac, N165 La Roche-Bernard (54km)

Muzillac – Auberge Pen-Mur, 97.41.67.58: prices have risen but cheaper menus still great value. Menus A–F. Rooms A–E.

La Roche-Bernard – Deux Magots, place Bouffay, 99.90.60.75: very popular auberge in house built in 1700. Pleasant bedrooms. Careful traditional simple cooking producing fine results. Try scallops flambées; superb moules marinières. Copious portions. Wonderful value in cheaper menus. Menus A, B, C, E. Rooms D, E. Shut Monday; Sunday evening low season; 15 December–15 January.

Auberge Bretonne, place Duguesclin, 99.90.60.28: (*not* Hotel Bretonne): if all 'modern' style chefs were as good as Jacques Thorel and offered such value menus, half the world would be converts. He combines lovely fresh regional ingredients, regional cooking and modern to make superb meals. Four menus, no carte. Bedrooms often booked months ahead. Bistro-style changed to posher restaurant. His smiling wife Solange offers a choice of 800

On Gulf of Morbihan lived 1st century BC the Veneti – powerful tribe of Gaul with fine fleet. Julius Caesar had to conquer them to hold Armor – Brittany. He built galleys at mouth of Loire. Gauls had 220 large sailing ships. Brutus, Caesar's Lieutenant, met them with flat galleys, rowed by oars. Alas for Gaul, the sea was calm and windless. Brutus had sickles tied to ropes which Romans threw into rigging of Gallic ships; masts and sails tumbled; Roman soldiers boarded the ships and killed crew.

La Roche-Bernard – tiny town on tributary of Vilaine river near coast, overlooking river; in 17th century its shipyards were famous; now port for pleasure boats on Brittany's inland waterways. I took a cruiser from her to Dinan some years ago. Now you can hire one from a British company. But still a likeable little port, with a beautiful modern suspension bridge. In the Revolution, the Mayor was shot down by the King's soldiers for refusing to shout: 'Long live the King'. He kept shouting: 'Long live the Republic'. The Tree of

La Roche-Bernard continued	different wines (15,000 bottles). Menus D–G. Rooms C–E. Shut Thursday; Friday until 5 p.m.; 15 November–15 December.	Liberty was set on fire and he was thrown in it, still alive. I feel that he won.
D774 La Baule (28km) through the Brière Nature Park, D127 St André-des-Eaux, D47 St Lyphard, D51 La Chapelle-des-Marais, D50, D2 La Bretesche, Missillac (31km)	Wide choice of hotels and restaurants of all sizes, types and prices; some take only 'pensioners' – half-board for whole week in season. But ask, there are more vacancies these days. Espadon, 2 ave Plage, 40.60.05.63: magnificent fifth-floor position with super beach and sea views, night and day. Simple, good cooking of superbly fresh fish. Try cassoulettes de belons aux épinards (oysters with spinach); very good fricassé of lobster; lamb from nearby salt marshes. Menus C–G. Shut 3–31 January. Palmeraie, 7 allée des Cormorans, 40.60.24.41: charming Logis surrounded by flowers and palms, with vine-covered terrace. Entirely renovated; all rooms with WC, bath or shower; many with balconies; but small. Meals cheap, limited choice. Must book. Menus B–C. Rooms (prices seasonal) D–E. Open 25 March–1 October. Chalet Suisse, ave de Gaulle, 40.60.23.41: restaurant popular with regular visitors; good fish. Menus A–G. Shut Monday evening, Tuesday evening, all Wednesday (except July, August); October.	Elegant resort, rarely fully closed; lively spring/autumn; crowded mid-summer; but splendid 5km (3 miles) of fine sand, is never crammed. Protected by 1000 acres of maritime pines. Nice promenade; smart villas and gardens; night life; casino; yacht harbour; international show-jumping; good riding stables; many festivals. *Chic* atmosphere; colourful scene. I like it very much; some call beach 'most beautiful in Europe'. Brière Regional Nature Park; strange marsh and peat bog of 99,000 acres, caused when sea flooded forests 5000 years ago; drained by pumps and canals since, but areas still flooded. Rich in wildfowl and fish; grazing in summer; small channels ablaze with yellow iris mid-May to late July. Boat trips from villages. La Chappelle-des-Marais has in its town hall a fossilized tree trunk 7m (23ft) long. Guérande, between drained marshes and Marais Solents, once a bay where Julius Caesar's galleys under Brutus defeated sailing ships of the Veneti; now salt marshes because sea retreated. Town's medieval walls are intact; 15th-century,

Tennis Hotel, 1 ave Lyon, 40.60.24.04: little bed-and-breakfast hotel in pines 150m from the beach; shut in 1978; reopened now after total renovation; bar, garden. Rooms B, C. Open all year.

Missillac – Golf de la Bretesche, 40.88.30.05: hotel comfortably converted from the Bretesche castle stables and farm, with its own tower; delightful country-house hotel with golf course laid out originally for a French woman champion. Good riding centre. Heated pool (1 June–30 September). Rooms E. Meals for half-board or full board. Shut February.

flanked by 8 towers, 4 fortified gateways; moats, filled in to make boulevard.

Missillac – 14th-century Bretesche Castle, beside a little lake, is delightful – fairy-tale turrets, ramparts shielding lawns; beautiful background of water, woods and the greens, fairways and bunkers of golf course of nearby hotel. Castle built by de Montfort family; Kings of France stayed to hunt in the Bretesche forest alongside. Damaged in Revolution; sold with big estate for £400. Visits except Mondays and also Thursday morning in season.

D126, D773 D164 Redon (30km) D177 Rennes (64km) N137 Hédé (22km) D795 Combourg (14km) D796, D83 Trans, D90, N176 Pontorson (28km)

Rennes, Hédé, Comboug – see route 6

Pontorson – Bretagne, rue Couesnon, 33.60.10.55: a delight; 14th-century house with exposed wood frame, carefully renovated; beautifully finished, sympathetically furnished within. Menus A–C. Rooms A–C. Shut Monday; 15 November–7 February.

Chalet, place Gare, 33.60.00.16: cheap and excellent value. Fish, salt-marsh lamb, other ingredients from the region. Cheapest menu 43.50f (1987). Menus A, B. Rooms A, B. Shut Mondays (low season); January.

Pontorson – you are in Normandy. Church founded by William the Conqueror in thanks for his army having been saved from Couesnon quicksands towards Le Mont-St-Michel. True Bretons believe they are now in foreign parts.

Pontorson continued

Montgomery, 13 rue Couesnon, 33.60.00.09: Logis in a fine 16th-century house where the Counts of Montgomery lived. One of them accidentally killed Henry II of France in a jousting match. Beautiful old furniture and panelling. Pretty garden. All bedrooms with bath and WC. Regional cooking, superb local lamb. Excellent wine-list. Local cider. Menus A–C. Rooms D. Open Palm Sunday–end October.

D976 Le Mont-St Michel (9km)

Guesclin, 33.60.14.10: famous Logis run by M. Nicolle, hotelier known all over France; shellfish, of course – local people once lived by selling cockles and the bay was full of oysters until disease wiped them out last century; try lamb. Sheep thrive round here on salt-washed turf (pré-salé). Menus A–F. Rooms C. Shut Wednesday low season; mid-October–mid-March.

Mouton Blanc, 33.60.14.08: historic monument; serves historic and filling St Michel omelette as first course or sweet as dessert. Menus A–F. Rooms A–D. Shut mid-November–mid-February.

La Digue, 33.60.14.02: modern, very comfortable hotel on edge of town; old-style furnishings; panoramic views of abbey and bay from dining room; shellfish; mussels in cream, pré-salé lamb; good house pâtisseries.

What new to say about 'La Première Site de France', the 'wonder of the Western World'? It *is* wonderful, this abbey on a hillock, protected by quicksands. Not surprising, since it was the Archangel Michael himself who, in the 8th century, told the Bishop of Avranches that he wanted a chapel built to him on the mound – and tapped the cleric's head with his finger to stress the point. But you need to be reasonably fit to climb the 90 steps, once guarded by a fortified bridge, leading to the terrace – or in summer to push your way uphill from the car park through seething thousands, past souvenir shops, crêperies and restaurants, to reach the abbey. Only 6000 are allowed in at a time, so you might have to wait. But the throng of pilgrims has been as great for centuries. In the 100 Years' War, the English, who held the

Menus A–E. Rooms C–E. Shut 11–24 November; 1 January–15 March; restaurant shut 20 October–25 March.

At Brée en Tanis, 9km SE of Mont St Michel, Sillon de Bretagne, on N175, 33.60.13.04: pleasant Logis where chef Bernard Jacquet cooks true regional dishes. Menu A–C. Rooms A–C. Shut 15 January–15 February; Tuesday low season.

approach area, sold safe-conduct passes and tourists bought souvenirs of effigies of St Michael and lead caskets to fill with sand from the beach. Many drowned in quicksands. From the Revolution until the State started to restore it in 1874, it was a prison; prisoners made straw hats in the church. Church restored for worship in 1922.

Biggest crowds are often outside Hôtel de la Mère Poulard, watching them make omelettes in a long-handled copper pan over an open fire – so successfully that Mother Poulard's little café now has a Michelin star and high-priced menus.

Prices mostly sky high in this place.

D976 return to Pontorson, N176 Dol-de-Bretagne (28km)

Dol – Bon Accueil, 23 bis rue Rennes, 99.48.06.14: happy, friendly little restaurant with remarkable cheap menus. Beubry family get many British customers and think them 'marvellous, with remarkable courtesy and amiability'. Menus A; carte. Very cheap wines.

Bretagne, 17 place Châteaubriand, 99.48.02.03: very good value cheap menus of traditional dishes (blanquette de veau, boeuf Bourguignon, moules marinières, grilled sardines). Good choice of menus. Terrace for fine weather

Rich agricultural land reclaimed from sea and marsh. Near Mont-St-Michel, Dutch name 'Polders' used; rest called Marais of Dol (marshland); was forest until 8th century, then sea poured in.

At Dol we are back in Brittany. Fine old town on a 20m (64ft) cliff. Bishopric of Dol founded around AD 530 by one of Brittany's 7847 saints – St Samson, a Welshman from monastery of Llantwit in Glamorgan and adept at killing dragons, witches and wizards, by telling them to drop dead. No

Dol de Bretagne continued

meals. In same family since 1922. Menus A, B, C. Rooms A–C. Wines reasonable. Shut October. Restaurant shut Saturday in winter.

Bresche-Arthur, 36 boulevard Deminiac, 99.48.01.44: hundreds of readers have praised it over 10 years – 2 complaints! Friendly Christian Faveau speaks English. Excellent cooking – try poulet Vallée d'Auge, house duck foie gras, salmon escalope, bar aux algues (bass in a seaweed cooked like spinach – much better than it sounds), home-smoked fish, fresh shellfish from underground tank, hot goats' cheese from Beaufort monastery. Busy in season. Bedrooms improved. Restaurant staff now wear Breton costume. Menus A–D. Rooms (all with WC, bath or shower, TV) D. Shut November.

Roches-Douves, 80 route de Dinan, 99.48.10.40: restaurant recommended to me by modern cuisine enthusiasts for imaginative cooking. I have not tried it. Cheapish menu 'excellent but not for hungry people'. Sounds very nouvelle! Small, attractive. Menu B, plus carte. Shut Sunday evenings, Mondays.

longer a bishopric, but Dol's 13th-century cathedral is called St Samson's, with stained glass showing its history. Old houses in Grande-Rue-des-Stuarts. Big Saturday market.

Champ-Dolent Menhir (2km – D795 for ½km (600 yd), turn left into tarred road – leave car, walk): menirs were stones set up in prehistoric times at springs, near dolmens or in lines, probably as religious monuments in sun and moon worship; dolmens were burial chambers; the one here stands 9m (30ft) high. Mont Dol (3km NE) – granite mound 65m (208ft) high; remains of prehistoric animals (mammoth, rhinoceros, elephant, reindeer) and flint tools unearthed from its slopes. Road round it; also narrow steep road with hairpin bend to top.

Tower (open Easter to All Saints' Day). Signal tower (1802), once part of semaphore chain for passing messages (Brest to Paris); now part of chapel. The Devil had a fight with St Michael on Mont Dol; now courting couples wrestle.

D155 to coast, follow it to D76 right to Cancale (23km) D201 round Pointe du Grouin to Rothéneuf, St Malo (23km)

Cancale – Phare, at port, 99.89.60.24: all local fish, and a good filling fish soup in generous portions. Seven bedrooms. Menus A, B, C, F. Rooms B, C. Shut Wednesdays; December, January.

Continental, at port, 99.89.60.16: good for lobster; try homard à l'armoricaine (with that super tangy sauce – pricey, of course). Rooms vary greatly. Menus C, E (restaurant shut Monday). Rooms A–E.

Bricourt, 1 rue du Guesclin, 99.89.64.76: those who say that there's no good cooking in Brittany should be made to eat in this 18th-century house built by a St Malo corsair. At 32 Oliver Roellinger, former engineering chemist, is one of the best creative chefs in France. He cooks so delicately and arranges the food so attractively that you could mistake a classic old dish for nouvelle cuisine. No good suggesting dishes because he keeps changing them, but lobster and lamb from Mont St Michel salt marsh (pré-salé) are always good bets and if on the card do try duck in perry (pear cider). Heavenly desserts. Pretty garden with pond and rare ducks. Menu B (weekdays only), carte expensive; rooms G. Shut Tuesdays, Wednesdays.

Le Vivier-sur-Mer – oyster beds laid down quite recently, not yet a rival to Cancale.

Cancale – lobsters, clams, mussels, most fish; but above all – oysters, bred at sea, farmed in ponds down on the muddy sands; sold in thousands to wholesalers, in boxes to retailers, in dozens to travellers from quayside stalls, and in fiercely competitive restaurants beside quay. Not a pretty place, but one of the few from which I could not drive away because I was the worse for food – not wine! Take Muscadet or Gros Plant wines with your crustaceans.

Cancale continued

Hotel Pointe de Grouin (4km N), 99.89.60.55: delightful; wonderful sea views; elegant dining room; one of our favourites in Brittany. Yves Simon cooks very well. Menus C–G. Rooms B–D. Open 1 April–30 September.

Route 8 Round the Loire Valley, Loir and Cher

The Loire is the longest river in France. The bit we regard as 'the Loire', usually from Nantes to Nevers, especially from Angers to near Orléans, is the most beautiful, surrounded by lovely châteaux and delightful towns, and very popular. The difficulty is to see these delightful places without being caught up with a mass of people in between. One trick is to follow the less popular bank of the river, as we have done from Angers to Tours. You could also skip Orléans, by taking small roads from Cléry to Sully.

Those beautiful Loire châteaux were mostly built for love, not war. The best are Montgeoffroi, Chenonceau and Azay-le-Rideau, little towns of Beaugency and Sancerre (a delight with a bonus of its splendid wine), and take the route suggested from Nevers to Aubigny and back to the Loire on tiny roads through tiny places to get a taste of the countryside away from tourists.

N
Le Mans
Sarthe
la Possonnière
le Gué-du-Loir
Couture-s-Loir
Troo
Poncé-s-le-Loir
Château-du-Loir
Marçon
Vendôme
Nogent
la Chartre-s-le-Loir
les Roches-l'Evê
Montoire-s-le-Loir
St. Aubin
St. Jacques-des-Guérets
Marcilly-s-Maulne
Baugé
Beaufort-en-Vallée
Château-la-Vallière
Candé-s-Beuvron
Angers
Montgeoffroy
Noyant
D 766
Chaumont-s-Loire
St. Mathurin
D58
Linières-Bouton
Noizay
Vouvray
Nazelles-Négron
Mazé
Brion
Mouliherne
Rochecorbon
D27
St. Rémy-la-Varenne
les Ponts-de-Cé
Savonnières
Villandry
D81
D55
Amboise
Gennes
Cunault
Tours
D 88
Civray
Langeais
Brissac-Quincé
D 751
Druye
Chenonceaux
Saumur
Loire
Bois-Tireau
Rome
Rigny-Ussé
D 134
D 145
D 751
Saché
Fontevraud-l'Abbaye
Villaines-les-Rochers
Couziers
Chinon
Azay-le-Rideau
Chavigny Castle
Lerné
Indre
Creuse
Vienne
Poitiers

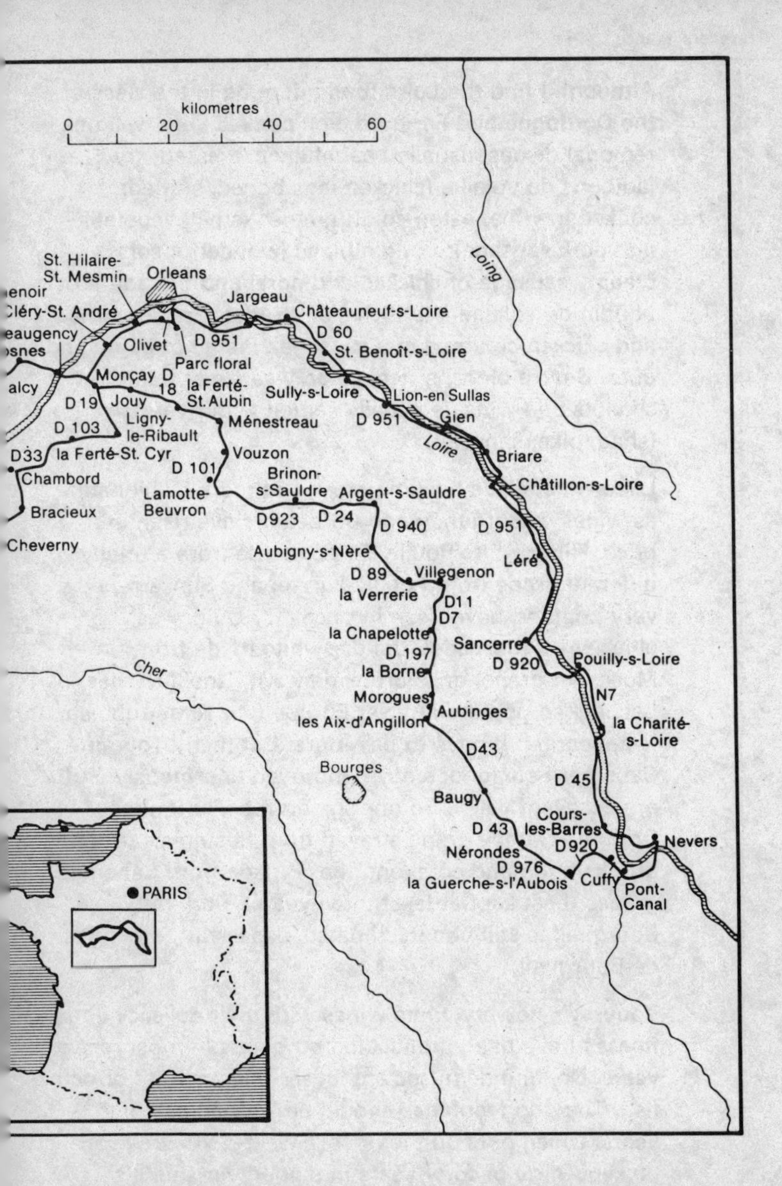

kilometres
0
20
40
60
Loing
St. Hilaire-
St. Mesmin
Orleans
Cléry-St. André
Jargeau
Châteauneuf-s-Loire
D 60
Olivet
D 951
St. Benoît-s-Loire
Parc floral
Monçay
D
18
la Ferté-
St. Aubin
Sully-s-Loire
Lion-en Sullas
D 19
Jouy
Ligny-
le-Ribault
Ménestreau
D 951
Gien
D 103
Loire
Briare
D33
la Ferté-St. Cyr
Vouzon
D 101
Chambord
Brinon-
s-Sauldre
Châtillon-s-Loire
Lamotte-
Beuvron
Argent-s-Sauldre
Bracieux
D923
D 24
D 940
D 951
Cheverny
Aubigny-s-Nère
Léré
D 89
Villegenon
la Verrerie
D11
D7
la Chapelotte
Sancerre
D 197
D 920
Pouilly-s-Loire
Cher
la Borne
N7
Morogues
Aubinges
les Aix-d'Angillon
la Charité-
s-Loire
D43
Bourges
D 45
Baugy
Cours-
les-Barres
D 43
Nevers
Nérondes
D 920
D 976
la Guerche-s-l'Aubois
Cuffy
Pont-
Canal
PARIS

Although I find the Loire food not quite in the class of the Dordogne and Périgord, you can eat very well on regional dishes, usually beautifully presented; try jambons de volaille (chicken legs boned, stuffed, cooked in wine, eaten cold): gogues (small vegetable and pork sausage); boudin blanc (wonderful soft creamy sausage of chicken and pork) and the gourmet boudin de volaille à la Richelieu (truffles, mushrooms and chicken creamed in a sausage). Plenty of game and duck. Beurre blanc, a rich, creamy sauce of butter, shallots and wine, is usually served with river fish (shad, pike, sandre).

Loire wines have become more and more fashionable as wines of Burgundy and Bordeaux have risen in price. Flinty white Pouilly-Fumé (made from a totally different grape from Pouilly-Fuissé) and Sancerre, now very popular, have risen in price. Try Quincy as alternative. Muscadet, the dry white made from Muscadet grape, once drunk only with shellfish, has become so popular all over Europe that some rubbish is appearing. It pays to pay more. But many Touraine Cabernet-Sauvignons have improved enormously and are excellent value. So are Chinon reds, both those from the Gamay grape strayed from Beaujolais (often drunk young and cold) and those made from Cabernet grapes (best kept at least three years). Dark red Bourgueil is still underestimated, especially St Nicolas-de-Bourgueil.

Vouvray's flowery white wines with their delicacy and finesse have been prolific and gorgeous in most recent years. Dry and demi-sec are lovely as an aperitif or with fish. The good vintages should be kept at least five years, which puts up the price! Sweeter Vouvray can be kept thirty or forty years in a good vintage. It's nectar after ten years.

Route 8 Round the Loire Valley, Loir and Cher

Angers

De France, Restaurant Les Plantagenets, place Gare, 41.88.49.42: grand old hotel of sort too many towns have knocked down. Instead, completely modernized with sound-proofing and double-glazing for bedrooms. But good solid wood furniture. Run by Bouyer family since built in 1890. Down-to-earth menu prices; good choice on carte. Good Loire wines. Le Pub snack bar. Menus A–D. Rooms F. Shut Christmas–6 January.

Le Quéré, 9 place Ralliement, 41.87.64.94: Paul Le Quéré is one of the best modern chefs in Loire area and his restaurant a shrine for disciples of nouvelle cuisine. He cooks with incredible lightness (mille-feuilles aux fruits, for example) and makes most delicate sauces. Try farm chicken stuffed with foie gras, lobster in puff pastry with sauce of

Former capital of Anjou, on banks of river Maine, 8km before it joins the Loire. Centre for Anjou wines, liqueurs, fruit, vegetables. Once belonged to England under Henry II. King John lost it. Old city (13th-century castle, 12th-century cathedral) plus modern city (electronics, farm machinery factories); many parks; old ramparts now tree-lined boulevards. City of tapestries – Apocalypse tapestry, displayed in special gallery in castle, is longest woven in France. Originally 164m (540ft) long, it was thrown into the street during the Revolution and citizens cut bits off for carpets, horse blankets and cart covers! In 1843 the Bishop rescued two-thirds of it. About 100m (320ft) on show; woven from 1373–80 for Louis I in Paris. More tapestries in castle's Logis Royal (15th-century Flemish, of the Passion) and

Angers continued	Chaumes wine. An inventive chef, too. His wife Martine, quarter-finalist in Best Sommeliers of France contest, hunts out little-known Anjou wines – especially sweet. Menus D–G. Shut Friday evening, Saturday; 1–15 July. Saint-Jacques, rue Saint-Jacques, 41.48.51.05: good value; regional dishes and wine; pike or sandre (perch-pike with more delicate flavour) from local rivers in beurre blanc (butter whipped with stock of shallot and Muscadet wine); chicken in Cabernet red wine of Anjou (in coq au vin dishes it makes a great difference which wine is used – I don't like coq au battery acid!). Menus A, C, D. Rooms A, C. In narrow street with traffic.	Logis du Gouverneur (lives of saints). But other great work is in St John's old hospital – 78m (258ft) masterpiece of 10 tapestries 'Chant du Monde' (Song of the World). Its black background exploding in intense colours, purity of line, scintillating design by Jean Lurçat, greatest of modern tapestry artists, who died in 1966 when planning another seven hangings for this series. Those shown took nine years to weave. They were Lurçat's Humanist reply to religious despair of Apocalypse. He wrote a commentary himself; on sale (in English translation) at the museum. Curnonsky (real name Maurice Edmund) 'Prince of Gastronomes', born here 1272 (Tournedos Curnonsky sauteed with marrow bone, tomatoes).
N160 Les Ponts-de-Cé, D748 Brissac-Quincé, D55, D56 St Rémy-la-Varenne	Gennes – see route 1 (page 42) Les Rosiers – see route 1 (page 42)	Loire divides into three arms at les Ponts de Cé; bridge crosses all three. Isles between have octagonal tower from castle, scene of bloody battle in 1793, and a church. Brissac castle is most impressive from outside and within; in lovely park with river Aubance running through.

D132 beside river to Gennes (39km)

Bridge over Loire at Gennes leads to Les Rosiers.

Second Duke of Coseé-Brissac, made Marshal of France for handing over Paris to Henry IV, started it between 1610 and 1620 (perfect example of its time). He had to leave 2 towers of medieval castle – he could not blow them up! Damaged in Revolution; restored from mid-19th century. Present Duke lives there. Intricate painted ceilings, rich tapestries, fine period furniture. (Open daily except Tuesday.)

Moulin de Bablut (restored windmill) alongside vineyards on D748, open for wine tastings. Red wine from Gamay grape is strong, full of flavour.

St Rémy-la-Varenne; nice village among trees; 10th-century church.

Boumois Castle (7km on D952 – also 8 km from Saumur (below) by bridge over Loire, left on D952): fairy-tale castle from road; Gothic primness from rear; round towers with conical 'hats'; 15th–16th century. Here lived Aristide-Aubert Dupetit-Thouars, French admiral who died fighting Nelson at Aboukir in 1798 (see Chinon Route 1, page 44). In grounds are huge dovecotes with 1800 nesting holes. Only the Lord could keep doves; used for shooting

Gennes continued		practice and food and allowed to feed, protected, on peasants' land – one reason why downtrodden peasants joined the Revolution.
D751 Cunault, Chenehutte-les-Tuffeaux, Saumur (15km)	Saumur – See route 1 (page 41)	Saumur – See route 1 (page 41)
D145 through forest to Fontevraud-l'Abbaye small road (V3) Couziers, left, then quickly right to reach D117, left on D117 to Chavigny Castle, Lerné, La Devinière, left on D759, right on D751, left on D749 over river Vienne to Chinon (31km)	Fontevraud – see route 1 (page 43) Montsoreau – see route 1 (page 43) Chinon – see route 1 (page 44)	Fontevraud Abbey – see route 1 (page 43) Château de Monsoreau – see route 1 (page 43) Chinon – see route 1 (page 44)
D751 through Chinon forest for 9km, then sharp left on D134 le Teillay and little white roads to Rigny, Ussé (14km)		See Ussé castle in morning mist or fading evening light and you will know instantly why Charles Perrault chose it as setting for the *Sleeping Beauty*. Backed by the oak and pine forest of Chinon where kings from Chinon castle hunted wild boar, it stands with terraced gardens on a ridge above the Indre river, a stone's throw from the Loire. A medley in white

		stone of towers, pointed rooftops, tall chimneys spanning styles from 15th–17th centuries. Best seen from bridge 200 yards away. Charming Gothic chapel of 1520 in grounds with superb Italian wood sculptures (Virgin by della Robbia). Guided tours of castle but inside is not so interesting.
local road (C12) across Indre river to Ile St Martin, right on D16 to bridge leading over Loire to Langeais, right on D57 to Azay-le-Rideau (9km)	Langeais – Hosten et Restaurant Langeais, 2 rue Gambetta, 47.96.82.12: a lorry ran into its salon, Jean-Jacques has taken over from father Jean Hosten and dishes are somewhat modernized. Still a very good restaurant but pricey with no set menus. Carte G. Rooms D–E. Shut Monday evening, Tuesday; 10 June–10 July; 10 January–10 February. Duchess-Anne, 10 rue Tours, 47.96.82.03: rather sombre-looking old Logis but good value old-style bourgeois meals. Menus B–G. Rooms B–D, Shut February; Sunday evening, Monday low season. Azay-le-Rideau – Grand Monarque, 47.45.40.08: owned by Jacquet family since 1900. Looks a little worse for wear inside but keeps its tradition for hospitality and excellent value meals. Traditional regional cooking. Menus B, C, F. Rooms B–E. Shut mid-November–mid-February.	Langeais château (across Loire) unaltered since built in five years from 1465 for Louis XI as defence against Bretons. Charles VIII and Anne of Brittany married here. Their room hung with fine tapestries. Busy, noisy town with traffic; interesting little shops. Big Sunday market. Azay-le-Rideau château is not quite so lovely as Chenonceau but second best. Renaissance gem of grace and strength, white walls and blue-grey slate reflected in ornamental lake and river Indre, from whose bed the castle rises on one side. Built 1518–27 by Gilles Berthelot, Treasurer-General of France – related to Catherine Briconnet who built Chenonceau and Jacques de Semblencay, the King's Treasurer. Semblencay was accused by King Francis I of corruption and beheaded; Berthelot fled to Italy, his books were examined and he was found guilty of fiddling the nation's accounts. The

Azay-le-Rideau continued	Aigle d'Or, ave A. Riché, 47.45.24.58: new restaurant recommended to me locally, not yet tried. Chef came from Château d'Artigny. Menus A–F. Shut Wednesday; Sunday evening low season; February.	King grabbed his château as he had done Chenonceau. Interior is Renaissance showpiece with fine furniture – (closed Sunday).
across Indre river, then on D57 to Villaine-les-Rochers, NE on D217, right on D17 to Saché; across Indre river on small road (C7) to Rome, Bois-Tireau, Druye, left on D121 then right past La Racaudière signposted to Villandry, D7 to Savonnières (27km)	Saché – Auberge au XIIe Siècle, 47.26.86.58: at foot of Saché château; Jean-Louis Niqueux, one of best chefs in region, also came from Château d'Artigny. Keeps balance between classical and modern dishes. Pricey. Nice matelote au Chinon; I had unusually tender pigeon. Menu E, plus carte. Shut Tuesday; February. Savonnières – Cèdres, route Villandry, 47.53.00.28: attractive Relais du Silence in nice garden with swimming pool among trees. Rooms E–F. Restaurant Cèdres alongside under separate management (47.53.37.58): pricey. Menus C (weekdays), F, G. Good choice of Loire wines. Shut Sunday evening, Monday low season; February. At Joué-les-Tours (5km SW of Savonnières on D86) – Château de Beaulieu, 1 rue Epend, 47.53.20.26: beautiful 18th-century manor in superb grounds. 'Maître Cuisinier de France' Jean-Pierre Lozays's classic cooking appeals more to me than to Christian Millau. Gault-Millau accuses him of	Villaine-les-Rochers – famous for wickerwork baskets; green rushes and black and yellow osiers cut in winter, soaked in water until May. Village priest found craft dying, so formed cooperative in 1849. Still going – prototype of French peasant coops of which there are tens of thousands. To see basket-makers at work apply at La Vannerie in village. On Azay road is troglodyte village; local people once lived there; believed to be gypsies who brought traditional art of wickerwork with them. Caves still used for work. Also a ferronnerie (iron foundry) making beautiful items in iron. Saché has château where French writer Balzac wrote much of his best work, and went to escape his creditors. Museum. Villandry on Cher just before it joins Loire. Imposing classical Renaissance château entered by bridge across moat into arcaded courtyard. Part open to public contains Spanish paintings, 13th-century Moorish

'certain banalities' and being 'ultra traditional'. But I *love* sauce Périgueux and prefer tournedos Rossini to magret of duck with passion fruit. Pleasant ordinary menus, plus 'gastronomique' and 'dégustation'. Menus D, F, G. Rooms E–G. Open all year.

ceiling. Garden is a masterpiece: top level is water garden; second is garden of love depicted by shapes of hedges and by flowers. The bottom vegetable garden is divided into patterns by flower beds and vegetables known in France in the 16th century.

Savonniéres – natural bathing beach on Cher river.

D288 North of Savonniéres, right on D88 alongside river Loire to Tours (16km)

Restaurant La Ruche, 105 rue Colbert, 47.66.69.83: charming little bistro; menu A; carte; only serves fresh produce according to season. Shut Sunday, Monday lunch.

La Renaissance, 64 rue Colbert, 47.66.63.25: Jacques Barthés and his wife, here since 1963, offer all my classic favourites like coq au vin, steak au poivre, escalope, entrecôte Marchand-de-Vin. Solid old France in old Cathedral quarter. Louis XIII dining room with old beams. Splendid value for meals and wines. Menus A–C. Shut Monday; Sunday evening in winter.

Barrier, 101 ave Tranchée, 47.54.20.39: what to say about one of the world's greatest chefs except that although, like me, he gets no younger, my readers swear that his meals get better every time they go! Who else could make roast local pigeon, mousseline of salmon

Tours – has become very industrial, filling four-mile gap between Loire and Cher. Old centre still most attractive; cathedral started in 13th century, finished in 16th, is classic Gothic building incorporating all styles; rich flamboyant decoration makes it awe-inspiring; alas, limestone crumbling and remedy not found; superb stained-glass windows 13th–16th century. Many museums, from Gemmail (rue de Murier) on stained glass to Wine Museum (16 rue Nationale). Museum in 17th-century Archbishop's palace includes Rembrandt's 'Flight into Egypt'.

Good daily market in Les Halles (food and veg.); famous flower market Wednesday, Saturday.

University city since mediaeval days, so it stays young and lively.

Tours continued

with beurre blanc, cock in old Cabernet wine or apple tart into masterpieces? Certain tax problems caused the restaurant to shut temporarily but he is back – with classic cooking, expensive menus worth every centime and reasonably priced wines. Menus F, G. Shut Sunday evening, Monday; part February.

La Gourmandine, 49 rue B. Palissy, 47.05.13.75: Patrick Terriew spent some years with Nikko de Paris and in Osaka, Japan, and admires Japanese cooking (or should I say *non*-cooking?), but has not gone over the top. Pigeon with Chinon sauce, sandre (Loire river fish) with cider butter and rustique terrine de colvert (wild duck) hardly hint of the orient. Nor does his regional menu. Very good cooking at reasonable prices. Menus C–E; excellent wines of Loire and Bordeaux. Shut Sunday, Monday lunch; mid-July–mid-August; Christmas eve–14 January.

Univers Hotel, Restaurant Touraine, 5 boulevard Heurteloup, 47.05.37.12: Conan Doyle and Rudyard Kipling, Napoleon and Winston Churchill, Hemingway, Stanley Baldwin and John D. Rockefeller stayed here. For 130 years the Grand Hotel of Tours, modernized plumbing but the same solid wood, satin

drapes and calm. Chef Gérard Clément was long with Barrier – so the same dependable traditional French cooking. Menu D, carte. Rooms E–G. Restaurant shut Saturdays.

Rosny, 19 rue Blaise-Pascal, 47.05.23.54: useful little hotel taken over by Pommiers of La Lanterne 4km away (see Rochecorbon). Rooms D. Shut Christmas, New Year.

---

cross Loire on to N152 Rochecorbon; left soon on Route Vallée Coquette (GR3) to Vouvray, D46 to Vernou, D1 Noizay, Bardouillère Nazelles-Negron, right into Amboise (28km)

Rochecorbon (3km from Tours) – Les Fontaines, 6 quai de Loire, 47.52.52.86: Napoleon III period manor in a park with ancient trees. Furnished in same period style. No restaurant. Rooms C–E. Open all year.

Lanterne, on N152, 48 quai de Loire, 47.52.50.02: superb value; old regional dishes. 18th-century Relais du Poste below tower known as La Lanterne. Summer garden service. No rooms. Menus A–C. Shut early January–end February.

Vouvray – Grand Vatel, 47.52.70.32: Rabelaisian murals encourage you to enjoy generous portions of tasty dishes. Menus C–F. Rooms C–E. Shut Mondays; part December, part March.

Vernou – Hostellerie des Perce-Neige, 13 rue Anatole-France, 47.52.10.04: pleasant old bourgeois family house in lovely gardens where sipping wine is a delight.

Rochecorbon – just off N152; troglodyte (cave) dwellings built into cliff face.

Vallée Coquette – you pass Vouvray wine caves dug into chalk hillside. When more space is needed for a heavy vintage, owners simply dig deeper into hillside!

Typical are caves at La Caillerie of Daniel Jarry, where you can taste and buy (9 a.m.–7 p.m.). He produces superb dry and demi-sec white wines with fruity smell, flowery taste which will keep 10 years or more – but can be drunk young. Vouvray wines should be delicate. Sweet Vouvray can be kept 30–40 years. Superb with strawberries, raspberries. Sparkling wine is produced, too. Vouvray Wine Cooperative has shop on corner of N152–D47.

Vernou continued

Very good cooking. Try trout, sandre from Loire. Wines from modest to very expensive grands vins. Bedrooms vary. Menus C–F. Rooms C–E. Shut Sunday evening, Monday low season; 31 January–1 March.

D31 Amboise (23km)

Château de Pray, (2.5km by D751 NE): 47.57.23.67: lovely 13th-century château with turrets; delicious gardens, grounds with terrace overlooking Loire. A favourite of ours and most readers but a few have disliked conventional cooking and a few rooms below standard. Menus D–F. Rooms F. Shut 1 January–10 February.

Mail Saint Thomas, place Richelieu, 47.57.22.52: François Le Coz, one of the Loire's best young chefs, has moved from his old Mail by the river to a Renaissance manor house in a beautiful garden. Try his guinea fowl supreme and foie confit au Vouvray. Some inventive dishes. Remarkable choice of Touraine wines back to last century. Menus F–G. Shut January; Tuesdays.

Auberge du Mail, 32 quai Gén. de Gaulle, 47.57.60.39: alas, I have not visited Le Mail since François Le Coz left, but I hear that bedrooms have been renovated. French guides approve of old-style cooking. Menus C–F. Rooms

See it from north bank or the bridge. Château largely demolished after Revolution, but what is left impressive and interesting. Charles VII stole it from Counts of Amboise, Louis XI gave it to his queen. Their son, later Charles VIII, brought back from Italy in 1495 Italian artists and craftsmen who changed French artistic styles. In 1498 Charles cracked his head on a low lintel and died. Louis XII continued the work. Francis I turned it into centre of court junketing, with magnificent festivals, balls, masquerades, tournaments, even fights between wild animals. He brought Leonardo da Vinci here and the great artist finished his life at the nearby manor house.

Catherine de Medici, widowed queen, brought her boy-king son, Francis II and his girl wife, Mary, later Queen of Scots, here when Protestants were rising up after St Bartholomew's Day massacre.

A foolish Protestant arranged for others to meet him at Amboise to start a revolt in

D. Shut Friday low season; 15 November–15 December.

Bone Etape, route Chaumont (2½km by D751 NE), 47.57.08.09: the Brinon family's 'rustic' modern restaurant with pretty garden still pleases readers for its cheaper menu, its freshwater fish from Loire and good old coq au vin. Reasonably priced Touraine wines. Menus B–F. No rooms. Shut Tuesdays.

La Brèche, rue Jules-Ferry, 47.57.00.79: near station; popular locally for cheapish meals with bourgeois cooking – rillette, good terrine, salmon, ray, nice cheeses including Tomme goat's cheese. Garden tables. Menus A–C. Rooms A–D. Shut Saturday evening, Sunday in winter; 1 December–10 January.

1560. Betrayed to powerful Duke of Guise, they were tortured, broken and hanged from castle balconies, still writhing in agony for days. Royals and Court would come out after dinner to watch them. But the royal family were destroyed too – the boy king, Francis II died within months, his brother Charles IX, after a bloodstained reign, died in terror and remorse. Duke of Guise and Henry II both murdered and Mary Stuart was beheaded.

In Clos Lucé (15th century) are da Vinci's bedroom, copies of his drawings, and models of machines he invented. Hôtel de Ville has fascinating museum of the Post, including letters, envelopes and stamps.

D81 through Amboise Forest to Civray, left on D40 Chenonceaux (10km) N76 along Cher river bank to Montrichard (8km)

Chenonceaux – Bon Laboureur et Château, 47.29.90.02: Antoine Jeudi copes as excellently as ever with feeding tourists from the whole world visiting the gorgeous château. Fine old-fashioned French regional dishes so well cooked that even the 'modern' priests of Gault-Millau guide cannot forbear to cheer. Fresh local products – vegetables for which Loire is famed, river fish, salmon, duck, chicken, rabbit, steak, superb vegetable soups. Excellent Loire wines. Charming rooms

Château de Chenonceau is the most beautiful castle I have ever seen; more, it is the most beautiful *house*, for it was designed by a woman, Katherine Briconnet, between 1513 and 1521 to be lived in; not by a man to withstand attack or seige. Another woman, sexy Diane du Poitiers, mistress of Henry II (who kept her in funds by levying a large tax on church bells), added a lovely garden and bridge between the château and Cher river banks. When Henry was killed accidently in a jousting

Chenonceaux continued

now all have baths. Swimming pool due in 1988. Menus E–G. Rooms E–F. Shut 1 December–1 March. (French oddity – castle's name has no 'x' at end, village does!)

Renaudière, 47.23.90.04: cheaper alternative to Bon Laboureur. Pleasant garden; good food. Excellent value. Menus A–D. Rooms B–D. Shut 15 November–1 March; Sunday evening, Monday lunch.

Gâteau Breton, 47.23.90.14: very cheap menus with remarkable value, 4 courses for 38f in 1987! Menus A–B. Shut 15 November–15 February; Tuesdays.

Montrichard – Bellevue, quai du Cher, 54.32.06.17: modernized hotel with views of Cher river. The commendable Ginette Dauret left in 1987. Still offers comfortable rooms, old-style cooking (brochet beurre blanc, coq au vin, rognons à l'ancienne, tarte tatin) and good choice of Loire wines. Menus A–F. Rooms E. Open all year.

Tête Noire, rue du Tours, 54.32.05.55: very well kept by Coutant family. Annexe across road overlooks river Cher; bedrooms well modernized. Traditional cooking. Menus B–G. Rooms C, D. Shut Fridays in winter; 3 January–5 February.

match, his wife, Catherine de Medici, took Chenonceau from Diane and banished her to the draughty pile of Château Chaumont, which she soon left. Catherine had the splendid two-storey gallery built on the bridge, and laid out the superb park. She held incredible parties, with mermaids, nymphs, satyrs and cavaliers welcoming guests from moat. The stories of intrigue, love affairs and politics of Chenonceaux could not possibly be told in this space. See it for yourself and read a book on it – very rewarding. Open daily. 'Son et Lumière' performances in summer (mid-June–mid-September, start 10 p.m. but check this); also has wax museum with scenes from its history.

At Monthou-sur-Cher (9km from Montrichard by N76, left on D21) – Château du Gué Péan, one of the greatest Renaissance châteaux in France; white, blue roof; round courtyard with pool; superb round towers at each corner. Magnificent Louis XV and XVI furnishings; monumental white fireplace; paintings by Fragonard, Gérard, David. Wonderful library with autograph collection of famous people.

Montrichard – Old houses and streets (rue Nationale) more attractive than ruined castle. Church of Ste-Crois, with lovely Romanesque

At Chissay, 4 km W on N76 – Château de Chissay, 54.32.32.01: one of the Savry family's excellently run hotels. Superb turreted castle of 13th–16th century with royal connections. Expensive luxury. Menus E–F. Rooms G. Shut January–March.

door, is where poor Jeanne de France (aged 12, hunchbacked, crippled, and twisted face) was married by Louis XI to Louis of Orleans, heir to the throne. When he became Louis XII he discarded her by a disgraceful legal trick to marry Anne of Brittany, widow of Charles VIII. He wanted to keep Brittany.

Another church at Nanteuil (330 yards W of Montrichard) has statue of the Virgin where pilgrims come on Whit Monday. Its power is to cure fear! In swamps near by lived in the Dark Ages a monster who fed on cattle and children. A young monk waded in alone carrying only a veil from the Virgin's statue and led the monster to the church using the veil as bait. People still come to pray for courage. Wine kept to mature in quarries upstream.

D28 Vallières-les-Grandes, D27 Chaumont-sur-Loire (18km)

At Rilly-sur-Loire (4km W of Chaumont on D751) – Voyageurs, 54.20.98.85: pleasant auberge. Bistro-style dining room; good value traditional meals. Some bedrooms now have bathrooms. Menus A–C. Rooms B–C. Shut Wednesday in winter: 24 December–30 January.

Château de Chaumont looks fearsome beside most elegant Loire châteaux; fine views over valley. Guides say Catherine de Medici lived here when Henry II, her husband, was killed accidentally in a joust and she became Regent, and one room is said to have been given to the astrologer in whom she believed, Ruggieri. But evidence is slight. More likely she bought it to swap for Chenonceau with her

Chaumont-sur-Loire continued		husband's mistress Diane de Poitiers, who didn't like it and left it immediately. Madame de Staël, the great writer, lived here during her banishment from Paris by Napoleon – and didn't like it. The stables are most elegant – lined with velvet.
D751 Candé-sur-Beuvron, D173, D751 Blois (18km)	Candé-sur-Beuvron – Lion d'Or, 54.44.04.66: pleasant rustic inn with traditional cooking; some interesting dishes (trout rillettes with smoked salmon: sweetbreads braised in Madeira wine). Cheap, good value. Meals A–D. Rooms A–C. Shut Tuesdays; December. Caillière, 36 route Montils, 54.44.03.08: most attractive hostelry made from old cottages with charming terrace, but French guides and gastronomes disagree about Jacky Guindon's cooking, which is very 'nouvelle' – one accuses him of outdated 'nouvelle cuisine of ten years ago'. The Michelin star has gone, but Gault-Millau still give him a high 15 marks. Alas, I have not been there for two years. Wide range of menus C–G. Rooms D–E. Shut Wednesday; 15 January–1 March. Blois – Hostellerie de la Loire, 8 boulevard Maréchel Lattre de Tassigny, 54.74.26.60: pleasant old-style hostelry overlooking the Loire and the 1724 bridge. New patron Daniel Renoult previously	Blois – centre of big farming area – strawberries and bulbs to vegetables and wine. Château played big part in French history. In 16th century Louis XII and his wife, Anne of Brittany, made it centre of Court life (like Versailles later). States General (Parliament) met here twice, once to suppress Protestant Church (1576); in 1688 Henri de Guise, head of violent Catholic 'League' and most powerful man in land, called States General here with intention of deposing Henry III and making Guise King. Henry guessed the plot, murdered Guise in the château. Henry was murdered eight months later. In 1662 Louis XIII banished his brother, Gaston d'Orleans, a perpetual conspirator, to Blois, gave him money to rebuild the château to keep him quiet. Gaston hired great architect Mansart. 'Son et lumière' most nights 26 March–19 September (not Thursday except in July, August) – show in French, followed by one in English (starts 10 p.m. to 11.15 p.m. midsummer). No booking. Tickets at entrance.

	well known as chef at Train Bleu, Lyon station. Fine old-fashioned dishes from vegetable soup to profiteroles, Loire salmon, game from Sologne. Menus D–E. Rooms B–D. Shut Sunday low season; 15 December–15 January. Grand Cerf, 40 ave Wilson, 54.78.02.16: wide range of menus. Regional cooking and wines. Menus A–F. Rooms A–C. Shut Friday low season; February.	Château Beauregard (just off D765 on way to Cheverny): delightful; one of prettiest in Loire. Built 1550 as 'hunting lodge' for extravagant Francis I. Remarkable gallery with 363 portraits of important people, and Delft-tiled floor showing army of Louis XIII. Still lived in.
D765 Cour-Cheverny D102 Bracieux, D112 Chambord (33km)	Cour-Cheverny – St Hubert, 54.79.96.60: famous for game from Sologne in season. Cheap Cheverny wines. Old-style cooking in friendly old-style hotel. Menus B, C, F. Rooms C. Shut Wednesday; December. Taverne Berrichone, 54.79.96.49: ordinary bistro; simple; good value; locals use it. Menus A–C, snacks. Rooms A. Bracieux – Bernard Robin, 1 ave Chambord, 54.46.41.22: Bernard Robin is one of the greatest modern chefs, producing beautiful light dishes, such as mousse of asparagus tips, young rabbit in jelly and herbs, carp from Sologne, game (October–end December), sandre (river fish) with remarkable tomato butter. The French adore his cooking. Splendid range of Loire wines. Old coaching Relais. Menus E–G. Shut	Château de Cheverny – one of nicest; white, 'fat and friendly'; still has its 17th-century furnishings and lavish decoration. Some rooms almost overpowering. Fine park, with long drive; 18th-century Orangerie converted for receptions. Château built 1634; previous château now part of outbuildings; present owner, Marquis of Vibraye, descendant of Huraults family who built it. Open to public. I prefer it to Blois or Chambord – not so stark nor like museum. Château Chambord must be one of the most uncomfortably ostentatious houses ever built. Its park surrounded by walls 20 miles long, 365 chimneys; 440 rooms separated by 80 staircases; Francis I ('always hunting stags or women') built it as a hunting lodge. Possibly he needed the

Chambord continued

Tuesday evening, Wednesday; 20 December–1 February.

Chambord – Hotel St Michel, 54.20.31.31: superb position with rooms and charming terrace facing castle; front row seat for castle's 'son et lumière'! Excellent cooking of local specialities, especially civet of venison, salmon, rabbit with prunes, lamb, pheasant. Good Loire wines. A favourite of ours. Rooms modernized. Menus C–F. Rooms E. Shut 15 November–18 December.

rooms – whole Court always travelled with him; 12,000 horses carried them, their servants, furniture, crockery, baggage. Francis loved show and was determined to outshine Henry VIII of England and Charles V of Spain. But he stayed at Chambord a total of 40 days. Now château belongs to the State, is open most days except Tuesdays, but most of park is a National Hunting Reserve for a privileged few, such as members of the Government and friends.

Castle 'son et lumière' shows in evenings 1 May–30 September.

D33, D103 La Ferté-St Cyr, D103, D61 Ligny-le-Ribault, D19 past Monçay, les Gachetières to D951 Cléry-St André, St Hilaire-St Mesmin, right on D14 Olivet, D14 Parc Floral, Orléans (62km)

La Ferté – Commerce, 54.87.90.14: very old rustic creeper-clad Logis on roadside. Game (including venison) in season. Menus A–C. Rooms B, C.

Saint Cyr Hotel, 54.81.90.51: Modern, family run, homely atmosphere; open fire; very nice bedrooms (all with bath, some WC); small dining room; traditional cooking. Menus B–E; Loire wines. Rooms B–C. Shut Sunday evening, Monday in winter; 15 January–1 March.

Cléry-St-Andre – Hotel Notre Dame, 38.45.70.22: typical corner logis in small town; used by local people; friendly. Menus A–F. Rooms A–C. Shut Wednesday.

La Ferté-St Cyr – centre for fishing in étangs (small lakes) and streams, and woodland walks. Pheasants are reared round here.

Beaugency (straight on at crossroads of D19 and D951 – 5 km): beautiful old town across the Loire; see this route on return journey. Return route crosses this outward route near Monçay.

At Cléry-St-André, left on D18 across Loire river is Meung-sur-Loire, attractive small town; walks under lime trees along river Mauves, tributary of Loire, rich in fish. Château was English headquarters of General Talbot and Earl of Salisbury in final days of 100 Years' War. Talbot lost to Joan of Arc; Salisbury had

St-Hilaire-St-Mesmin – L'Escale du Port-Arthur, 205 rue de l'Eglise, 38.80.30.36: very quiet on banks of Loiret near where it joins Loire. Superb position overlooking river; comfortable bedrooms mostly with bath or shower and river views; pleasant dining room; try tasty feuilleté of scallops; salmon in grain-mustard sauce (super); chicken in crayfish sauce; hot salad of crottin (smelly goats' milk cheese with unpleasant name – goats' dung – and gorgeous taste). Menus C–F. Rooms B–D.

Olivet – Le Rivage, 635 rue La Reine Blanche, 38.66.02.93: my favourite of long ago has been renovated; superb terrace alongside Loiret river. Excellent traditional cooking by young chef; not cheap but still good value. Superb wine list. Menus C–F. Rooms C–D. Shut 15–28 February.

Orléans – Jean, 64 rue Porte-St-Jean, near Joan's statue in place Martroi, 38.53.63.32: good value meals. Menus A–D. Shut Sunday, August.

Les Antiquaires (the old Auberge Saint-Jacques) 2, rue au Lin, 38.53.52.35: Michel Pipet (ex-Maxim's) strikes a happy blend of traditional and light modern. Perfect, careful cooking of everything from lobster and salmon of the Loire to entrecôte Rossini and fish in

his head blown off at Siege of Orléans. Bishops of Orléans mostly held it 1200–1789. Beautifully furnished. Terrible dungeon well where prisoners were kept.

François Villon was held here – great 15th-century poet who was also a tramp and a burglar. Open Easter–November.

Olivet – would pick quiet little St Hilaire or Olivet on Loiret river for staying overnight rather than modern Orléans. Olivet in charming setting on river banks, where Orléans people have always gone for fishing, boating, picnics; river banks lined with fine old houses and watermills; riverside paths, cafés, restaurants; like a modernized scene from Renoir. Market gardens; fields of flowers, nurseries.

New town of Orléans with new university campus has been built south of Floral Park. Park covers 86 acres – superb from April to November. Old trees, fountains, modern sculptures surrounded by massed blooms – tulips, iris, dahlias, chrysanthemums, 200,000 rose bushes. Still attractive in winter, when it is open only afternoons. In centre is remarkable 'source' of Loiret. True source at St Benoit, but river re-emerges here, with water bubbling out at 1400 cu. ft a minute, temperature

Orléans continued

vermouth sauce, lovely desserts. Excellent wine list includes the local Orléans gris – rare these days. Good value. Menus C–E. Shut first 3 weeks of August; Easter; Sunday, Monday.

La Crémaillère, 34 rue N-D-de Recouvrance, 38.53.49.17: very expensive, superb. Simple, near perfect cooking of best fresh ingredients especially fish. Menus F–G. Shut Sunday evening, Monday; August.

12–15°C (54–59°F), which helps flower cultivation. Also, flamingoes, many ducks and other web-footed friends winter here. Little train runs through park. Restaurant, rather like eating in greenhouse (rubber plants and tree décor).

Orléans – nice modern city, rebuilt after wartime destruction but little left for Joan of Arc fans. Statue of her in place Martroi by Foyatier (1855) with bas-reliefs on pedestal in Renaissance-style by Vital-Dubray. When Joan arrived with her troops in 1429, French defenders were tired and dispirited, English attackers down to 2000 tired men, the rest had been withdrawn. She breathed new spirit into the French; English thought she was a witch. Her courage and morale saved Orléans. In cathedral at top of splendid modern shopping stree, rue Jeanne d'Arc, is statue of Cardinal Touchet (died 1926) whose life's work was to propagate the cult of the Maid and get her made a saint by the Pope; succeeded in 1920; made patron saint of France. Statue of her in town hall by Princess Marie of Orléans, daughter of King Louis-Philippe.

D951 Jargeau over Loire on to D60 to Châteauneuf-sur-Loire, St Benoît-sur-Loire (17km)	Châteauneuf – La Capitainerie, Grande rue, 38.58.42.16: Most pleasant inn with charming terrace alongside park. Seasonal dishes. Menu E. Rooms C, D. Shut February; restaurant shut Monday. 	Châteauneuf – likeable market town; lovely riverside walks; waterfowl; wild park with rare trees, shrubs, red squirrels; wild rhododendrons in June; huge magnolias; big carp in moat. Domed rotunda of old castle now town hall. Castle rebuilt in 17th century as miniature Versailles. Little left except park. Church of St Benoît (St Benedict) one of finest Romanesque buildings in Europe (started 1026 – mostly 11th century). Benedictine abbey here in 7th century. Abbot stole remains of St Benoît from Monte Casino monastery in Italy in a raid! Under Charlemagne became one of Europe's leading educational centres, with 20,000 pupils. Renowned for Gregorian Chant.
D60 Sully-sur-Loire: small white road over Loire beside river to Lion-en-Sullas, D951 to Gien; over bridge to D952 to Briare; D952, N7, D50 to Châtillon-sur-Loire, D951 Léré, D751, D955 Sancerre (67km)	Sully – Esplanade, place Pilier, 38.35.20.83: opposite château; pleasant garden, terrace and pretty glassed-in terrace. Specializes in fish from Loire and sea. Menus B–E. Rooms B, C. Grand Sully, 10 boulevard Champ-de-Foire, 38.36.27.56: old country hotel completely restored. Regional dishes. Menus D–F. Rooms E. Shut 15–30 December.	Sully rebuilt after war damage but very pleasant; river spanned by long, graceful suspension bridge, Dark and forbidding fortress château with broad, deep moats, beside river; towers and sentry walks; but inside walls is pretty Renaissance pavilion. At the Château, after victories, Joan of Arc presuaded the Dauphin to go to Reims to be crowned King of France. After failing to take Paris, she returned to Sully and was kept waiting a month. Finally she rode away to be captured and burned.

Sancerre continued

Pont de Sologne, rue Porte de Sologne, 38.36.26.34: in huge old dining room they serve traditional dishes on two menus, both good value. Known for fish. Menus A, D. Rooms B–D. Shut January.

Gien – Beau Site Hotel, Poularde restaurant, 13 quai Nice, 38.67.36.05: on river front. Good range of menus. Traditional regional dishes – veal kidneys; civet de marcassin (young wild boar); tarte tatin (apple). Menus A–F. Rooms D, E. Shut 1–7 September; 1–15 January.

Rivage, 1 quai Nice, 38.67.20.53: much praised meals with inventive bias (sweetbreads of lamb in cider-vinegar and honey). Try snails in Sancerre wine. Good patisseries. Big dining room beside river Loire. Menus B–G. Rooms A–D. Shut early February–early March.

Sancerre – Auberge Alphonse Mellot, pl de la Halle, 36.54.20.53: 'Auberge Dégustation' – inn for wine-tasting; Mellot family own vineyard (La Chatellee) and cellars, and sell most Sancerre wines. 'Menu-Dégustation' – terrine, ham omelette, crottin de Chavignol goat's milk cheese (see page 241). Collection of old wine-making equipment.

Voltaire found refuge here with the Duke of Sully when he had to flee the Court for making epigrams too biting and true. The Duke, a liberal who loved new ideas, built him a theatre; he wrote comedies and tragedies to be performed in it.

Gien – a town of flowers and a pottery factory, 160 years old. Church dedicated to Joan of Arc was destroyed (1940); modern church in pink brick (specially baked in wood-fired kilns) and black. Coloured windows by Max Ingrand, great modern stained-glass artist; pottery capitals to pillars show episodes from Joan's life. In rue Lejardinier are some medieval houses. In 1429 through Golden Lion Gate, now gone, 7 riders (one a 'young boy') rode weary and sodden. Joan was on her way to save France. Château (1484) contains International Hunting Museum (superb tapestries and paintings, fine Desportes collection).

Sancerre – delightful, walled town on steep hill with narrow, steep roads and pretty little houses, capped by terrace with lime tree shade and views over the Loire you will never forget. A huge curved viaduct below takes a road to by-pass St Satur, a very old village.

Tour, 31 place Halle, 48.54.00.81: probably the best restaurant in these parts. Daniel Fournier cooks classical dishes excellently. Menus C–F. Shut Monday low season; 5–20 January; 1–15 December.

St-Thibault-St-Satur-Etoile, quai de Loire, 48.54.12.15: lovely position overlooking Loire: elegant restaurant; good local cooking. Grills over wood fire; good Loire eels; coq au vin. Menus B, C, F. Rooms (mostly simple) A–D. Shut Wednesday out of season; 15 November–1 March.

Auberge, St Thibault, 48.54.13.79: built 1610; country furnishing; restaurant leads to flower-garden; meals good value; pleasant bedrooms; try trout in Sancerre wine; chicken in Sancerre; ficelle Auberge (stuffed pancake); pâté d'amandes (almond paste – local speciality). Menu A–C. Rooms A, B. Shut Tuesday in winter; 12 November–8 December.

In 1534, Protestant Sancerre withstood for seven months a Catholic siege; people ate powdered slates and leather. Finally gave in but remained Protestant. 16th-century Protestant church and old Catholic church. Sancerre known for its dry white wine made from Sauvignon grapes (delicious as aperitif with fish, fowl or just for drinking); also makes red and rosé with Pineau d'Aunis grapes (very old-fashioned).

Chavignol – 3km before Sancerre on D955, on to D183 at Fontenoy; wine-growers' village making Chavignol Sancerre; also 'crottin de Chavignol' (goats' droppings of Chavignol) splendid strong goats' milk cheese.

In Sancerre is rue Macdonald. In 1746 a band of Scots fled with Prince Charles after defeat at Culloden; settled at Sancerre. One was a schoolmaster from Uist; his house is no.3 rue Macdonald. His son Etienne went away to military academy, became one of Napoleon's Marshals and Duke of Taranto.

St Thibault-sur-Loire (D955 before reaching Sancerre, D4 – 5km): on Loire banks: Fête on 16 August with river races and fun is famous in France. Large island upstream where goats are grazed; ferried across each morning on huge punt-raft: provide

Sancerre continued		goats' milk cheese. Lively village; fisherman's chapel to St Roch, protector from pestilence, and of fishermen.
D920, then over Loire on D59 Pouilly-sur-Loire (24km)	Relais Fleurie, Restaurant Coq Hardi, ave Tuilerie, 86.39.12.99: our old favourite; attractive old hostelry, flower gardens, river view from terrace – splendid place to taste Pouilly Fumé wines. As well as being an excellent cook. Jean-Claude Astruc is a local wine expert. Duck, chicken in local wine, river fish (sandre, salmon – try salmon à l'orange). Wine co-operative opposite; superb Fernand Blondelet 100 yards away. Taste and buy at either. Menus (excellent value) B–F. Rooms C. Shut Wednesday evening, Thursday in winter; 15 January–15 February. Vieille Auberge, 86.39.17.98: good value meals sensible wine list. Menus A–E. Shut Tuesday evening, Wednesday in winter; 15–28 February. Espérance, 17 rue René-Couard, 86.39.10.68: reliable conformist cooking has earned Jacques Raveau a Michelin star. Try duck in red Sancerre wine. Pricey. Pleasant atmosphere. Excellent choice of wines. Menus E–G. Rooms D. Shut 1–20 December; 5–31 January; Monday, Sunday evening except mid-summer.	Château de la Grange (on D920): built in reign of Henry IV; curious, many-sided dome. Home of Pouilly-Fumé, the flinty dry white wine (not to be confused with Pouilly-Fuissé from Burgundy). Made from Sauvignon grapes, its recent popularity has made it rather dear. The litre-lappers' cheaper substitute, Pouilly-sur-Loire wine is made from Chasselas, grown originally for Kings at Fontainebleau, but not so fruity as Fumé. Do not judge this town from what you see on N7; go down to the Loire and savour its river views (and wines) from Relais Fleurie (see restaurants).

N7 La Charité-sur-Loire (13km) over river Loire to D45, left to Cours-les-Barres, D12, then left over N7, Loire D40 to Nevers (20km)

La Charité – Bonne Foi, 91 rue Camille-Barrière, 86.70.15.77: my discovery delights my readers and now pleases Gault-Millau. At 30 Didier Guyot is an accomplished imaginative chef. Good value. Menus B–F. Shut Sunday evening, Monday.

Grand Monarque, 33 quai Clemenceau, 86.70.21.73: good cheap, 'menu terroir' of local products, plus others using best products of market. Old worn-out hostelry rescued and modernized. Menus B–G. Shut Wednesday in winter; February.

Nevers – Auberge Porte du Croux, 17 rue Porte-du-Croux, 86.57.12.71: very nice, pretty, quiet; terrace overlooking gardens with tower and ancient city wall. Charming welcome. Fish direct from Atlantic coast or from the Loire. Fine old-style desserts. Very good value. Menus C–F. Rooms B–C. Shut most August; Friday evenings, Sunday.

La Folie, route des Saulaies (4km on D504), 86.57.05.31: Logis; swimming pool; good value. Menus A–C. Rooms B, C. Shut 20 December–10 January; restaurant shut Friday; Sunday evening.

La Charité built in ampitheatre down to Loire: lovely river scene with handsome 16th-century stone bridge. Name came from 11th-century monks who gave best alms to pilgrims on long route to Compostella. Joan of Arc failed to take it from Burgundians – beginning of her end. Fine view of town from bridge. Local wines of Charité worth tasting.

Nevers – where Loire joins river Nièvre; famous for fine china. On hill, dominated by cathedral and ducal palace. Italians introduced china-making in 16th century. Turreted Porte du Croux (14th-century tower gate) is superb. Collection of Nevers china in museum (shut Tuesday). At Convent of St Gildard, boulevard Victor Hugo, in chapel, is a macabre display – body of St Bernadette in glass cask (the girl who saw visions at Lourdes and became a nun here in 1867). Certified 'uncorrupted', but darkened and wax-covered. New church dedicated to her looks solid as a Nazi West Wall bunker, but interesting inside. Old Nevers lives alongside new tower-blocks and supermarkets.

Nevers continued

Molière, 25 rue Molière, 86.57.29.96: modern, useful overnight; no restaurant. Rooms B, C. Shut Sunday in winter; 20 December–20 January.

Château Rocherie at Varennes Vauzelles (4km N on D7), 86.38.07.21: charming hideout from N7 in big park; big rooms do vary. Pierre Reparet (ex-Troisgros) is an enthusiastic chef with experience. Menus B–F. Shut Sunday evening, Tuesday in winter; 1–15 November; 1–15 January.

At Magny-Cours (12km S on N7, route Moulins) – Renaissance, 86.58.10.40: attractive creeper-clad hostellerie, very comfortable. Jean-Claude Dray cooks superbly, mostly regional traditional dishes (whole roast veal kidney in shallot confit; Charolais beef fillet in cream and morilles sauce) but some modern. Inevitably very pricey. Menus G. Rooms D–F. Shut Sunday evenings, Monday; February; 1–7 July.

---

south on N7 3.5km, then right D976 Pont Canal; soon, little road right D45 N to Cuffy, left on D50E through Bois des Ribaudières to D920, turn left to St Guerche-sur-

Nérondes – Lion d'Or, 48.74.87.81: simple, useful Logis with low price meals. Menus A–C. Rooms A, B. Shut Sunday; 15 December–15 January; 3 weeks September.

Just before Pont Canal at Guetin, Canal Latéral crosses river Allier by aqueduct; barges mount a stairway of three locks, descend a similar flight.

Morogues – Château de Maupas; private house of Marquis de Maupas; much restored 15th-century château amid formal French

l'Aubois, D976 right to Nérondes, 2 km past Nérondes right to D43 Baugy, les Aix d'Anguillon, at far end of village take D185 (*not* D46) to Aubinges, Morogues (67km)		gardens; beautifully furnished; mementoes of amusing and liberated Duchess of Berry, a Neopolitan princess who married French duke of royal blood, and who started fashion for sea-bathing at Dieppe, and for climbing the Pyrenees, horrifying French society.
D46 La Borne, D197 through Bois d'Henrichemont to la Chapelotte, D7, D11 Villegenon, D89 La Verrerie, Aubigny-sur-Nére (42km)	Aubigny – Chaumiére, 1 place Paul-Lasnier, 48.58.04.01: rows and rows of copper pans in Daniel Brunneval's kitchen and tables laden with salmon, trout, lobster, huge joints, pretty desserts show how seriously he takes cooking. Traditional dishes of the Berry beautifully cooked – tourte à l'oeuf, duck in honey, served with rare local Châteaumeillant red wine. A rewarding stop. Menus A, B, G. Rooms A–C. Charmilles Restaurant, Central Hotel, 6 rue Château, 48.58.17.18: Logis casserole for good regional cooking. Menus A–C. Rooms B–C. Shut Sunday evening, Monday lunch except July, August; 15 January–15 February. Fontaine, 27 rue Gen-de-Gaulle, 48.58.02.59: Aubigny is blessed with little auberges with bargain meals. Excellent value. Menus B, C.	La Borne – small village in woods; pottery produced for 300 years from local clay; craft being replaced. La Verrerie – summer château of Scottish Stuarts. Earl of Darnley, who married Mary, Queen of Scots, settled here when fighting English. Louis XIV took back Aubigny when last Stuart male heir died, gave it to Louise de Keroualle (Duchess of Portsmouth and mistress to another Stuart – Charles II). Her descendants are Dukes of Richmond; sold château in 1834. Marquis of Vogué bought it – descendants still own it. Stands reflected in lake – a Renaissance 'fairy' castle. Elegant and beautiful; fine furniture, tapestries; superb little chapel; 16th-century wall paintings. (Open February–mid-November except Tuesday.)

Aubigny continued		Aubigny is superb village. Stuart château is now the town hall. This was given to Duchess of Portsmouth, too.
D940 Argent-sur-Sauldre, D24, D923 Brinon-sur-Sauldre, Lamotte-Beuvron (35km)	Argent – Relais de la Poste, 48.73.60.25: just off main road; pleasant; known for good cooking. Menus B–D. Rooms B–D. Shut Monday, 5 January–5 February. Lamotte-Beuvron – Hostellerie de la Cloche, ave République, 54.88.02.20: friendly, cosy, run by family with young, enthusiastic team; on noisy N20, but back is quiet; good value; old regional recipes and original dishes by careful, enthusiastic chef. Game in season; river fish; home-made terrines. Menus A–E. Rooms A–B. Shut Tuesdays low season.	Argent – makes lingerie and hoisting machinery; 15th-century château with terrace overlooking Sauldre river. Pleasant route through forests, farms of Sologne (swamps area drained by Napoleon III, now fertile) and small lakes; misses busy N20 except when crossing it.
D101 Vouzon, D129, D108 Ménestreau, D17 La Ferté–St Aubin, D18 Jouy, D103 to near Monçay, D19 over Loire Beaugency (54km)	La Ferté – Perron, rue Général Leclerc, 38.76.53.36: old-style hunting inn; beams, brick, open fire; local dishes – wild boar, ham, carp, other game, river fish. Menus B–F. Rooms B–D. Shut 15–30 January. Ferme de la Lande, route Marcilly-en-Villette (2½km NE), 38.76.64.37: French friends say this is the best cooking in area but I have not yet tried it. Lovely old Sologne house. Patrice Garden is a distinguished chef. Menus C (weekday), E (weekends). Shut Mondays.	Menestreau – among small woodland lakes; village of flowers. La Ferté-St Aubin – Ferté means small fortress. River Cosson flows through castle moats, lined by elegant 17th-century balustrades, large park. Ar Monçay outward route crosses this one. Beaugency – lovely old town, excellent for a rest while exploring châteaux; quieter, more charming than Blois. But beware – the Devil still lives in Tour du Diable, next

Beaugency – Ecu de Bretagne, place Martroi, 38.44.67.60: auberge with flowered surrounds; name existed as inn since Joan of Arc. Mostly traditional and regional dishes – try crayfish omelette; original dishes include honey-roast rabbit (delicious); terrine of sole in red wine; pike cutlets in nuts; game fondu. Menus B–F. Good-sized rooms A–D. Shut February.

door to old abbey which became a hotel. The splendid Loire bridge (440m/1444ft long, 22 arches) made Beaugency a war target through history – as a river crossing. French themselves blew up part in 1940 to delay Nazis. Replaced perfectly; central arches are original. English took town four times in 100 Years' War.

Beach for river swimming; good fishing. 15th-century castle with interesting museum of historic dress, coiffe head-dresses, furniture.

D917 Josnes, then left D70A Talcy, D70 Mauvoy, right on D50 Marchenoir, D917 Oucques, Vendôme (54km)

Oucques – Commerce, 54.23.20.41: typical, small town hotel with excellent cooking. Try canard bigarde (bitter orange sauce); terrine with chopped avocados and langoustine tails; good chicken in cream and leek sauce, trout in leek purée. Menu A–F. Rooms B. Shut Sunday evening, Monday; 20 December–31 January.

Vendôme – Vendôme Hotel, Cloche Rouge Restaurant, 15 faubourg Chartrain, 54.77.02.88: hotel renovated recently, rooms now modern, well-equipped. Locals like the traditional cooking. Menus A (weekday lunch), B–D. Shut 20 December–5 January.

Daumier, 17 place République, 54.77.10.15: very good value menus;

Château de Talcy: Renaissance; built 1520 by Italian cousin of Catherine de Medici; Ronsard the poet, wrote love sonnets to owner's daughter Cassandre; granddaughter Diana inspired love poems from Agrippa d'Aubigné.

Small wonder that a descendant was Alfred de Musset, one of France's greatest poets. Defence-keeps added later give outside a fortress look, but inside a lovely arcaded gallery, and rooms are exquisitely furnished. I could live here – especially as the 400-year-old winepress still works, giving 10 barrels of juice at one pressing.

Vendôme – has atmosphere; old abbey church of St Trinity is higgledy-piggledy

Vendôme continued

strong on fish. Menus B, C, F. Shut Sunday evening, Monday; January.

mixture of architecture from 11th to 16th century. River Loir (without an 'e') divides here into several arms, spanned by many bridges. Inevitable attractive hilltop castle; too much urban building at bottom of hill. Honoré de Balzac went to school at Oratorian's College in 1807. Always in trouble for rebellion, he spent much time in the punishment cell, reading in peace. Now it is a lycée – I hope with rebellious students who read what they want and become magnificent writers.

D5 Le Gué-de-Loire, Bonaventure, D24 Les Roches L'Eveque, D917 Montoire (19km)

Cheval Rouge, place Foch, 54.85.07.05: Robert Velasco, owner and renowned chef, is 'Maître-Cuisinier de France'. Try his cooking and you will know why. Full use of local ingredients in season – especially salmon. Little shaded terrace; many Loire-area wines with nice Bourguiel. Menu C–G. Rooms A–C. Shut Tuesday evening, Wednesday; February–mid-March.

Villiers – clings to hillside above vineyards, looking across to Château Rochambeau; church has 16th-century murals of St Christopher, patron saint of travellers. Also 15th-century choir stalls.

Le Gué-du-Loir – at meeting of Loir and Boulon rivers; lush meadows. Renaissance Bonaventure Manor, now in ruins, belonged to a Bourbon – father of Henry IV and ancestor of poet Alfred Musset.

Les Roches l'Evêque – troglodyte houses, some with wistaria round entrance. Near by is troglodyte chapel.

At Montoire, on 24 October 1940, Marshal Pétain, 1914–18 war hero, embittered old man, met Hitler and sold out France for a 'peace' which was not. Such a nice place for a 'sell-out'! Ruined castle; Chapelle-St-Gilles has famous murals, some 12th-century.

Lavardin, up river, is tiny photogenic hamlet; fine old buildings, truly romantic castle ruins. Climb ladder of keep to sentry walks for magnificent view. Called 'the most French of French villages'.

D917 Troo, across river Loir to St Jacques-des-Guérets, D8 (for 3km) right on D10 to La Possonière, D57 Couture-sur-le-Loir, D305 La Chartre-sur-le-Loir (28km)

La Chartre – France, place République, 43.44.40.16: Aston Martin and Lagonda teams used to stay here for Le Mans 24-hour race in Stirling Moss's day. Very French-looking, with pavement tables, umbrellas, tubs of flowers; old-style comfort inside; lovely gardens with terrace, flower beds; excellent value meals; traditional cooking. Menus A–F. Rooms B–C. Shut 15 November–15 December.

Troo – odd town on steep slope, still with troglodyte houses cut into hillside (Rue Haute); town built in tiers, linked by narrow alleys, passageways, stairways. Underground is labyrinth of galleries used as refuge in old wars. Remains of 11th-century fortifications.

St Jacques-des-Guérets – church with mural paintings from 12th century.

La Possonière – manor birthplace of poet Pierre de Ronsard (1524); visits only with written permission of owner.

At Poncé-sur-le-Loir (3½km past Couture-sur-Loir, across Loir on D57, left 1km on D305); attractive château (open daily; afternoon only on Sunday); remarkable Renaissance staircase with superb sculptured ceilings (well worth seeing); huge dovecote with 1800 holes; museum of local crafts;

La Chartre-sur-le-Loir continued		church has murals of crusades; craftsmen in outbuildings (iron-forging; glass-blowing; Grès de Loir pottery; weaving; carpentry). La Chartre-sur-le-Loir – a fair sweet white wine produced here.
D305 Marçon on to join N138 right to Château-du-Loir (16km) D10 over Loir at Nogent, St Aubin, D38 Château-la-Vallière, D766 Marcilly-sur-Maulne, Noyant, D767 Linières-Bouton, right on D62 Mouliherne, D58 NW through forest of Chandelais to Baugé (67km)	Château-du-Loir – Grand' place Hôtel de Ville, 43.44.00.17: fine old 'grand' hotel, renovated, in attractive flowery square. Readers recommended it to me. Chef Christophe Constantin, with 5 years experience in London restaurants, cooks in modern manner with modern decorations. Try duck with peaches, sandre, pike mousseline. Menus A–F. Rooms B–D. Noyant – Lion d'Or, 2 place La Lune, 41.89.50.34: cheap, very good value hostellerie. Good fish. Menus A–C. Rooms A, B. Shut 15–30 November. Baugé – Boule d'Or, 4 rue Cygne, 41.89.82.12: good fresh river fish (including salmon); local duck. Menus A–E. Rooms A–C. Shut Sunday evening, Monday; mid-January–mid-February.	Château du Lude – 17km from Château-la-Valière NW on D959, D306: mediaeval fortress transformed into charming home in Renaissance. Lovely gardens, terrace. Visits 1 April–30 September. Magnificent 'son et lumière' June–September played by 350 local people in costume. Fireworks. Baugé – interesting and delightful little town in very heart of Anjou, among forests, heaths; market town; old part has lovely big houses. Château much restored (now town hall, fine museum of old weapons); open to public 1 June–15 September, a favourite residence of Good King René. In 15th century, Duke of Anjou inherited the Kingdom of Sicily, but could not take the crown. Anjou was annexed by France in 1484. René retired to Provence. St Joseph Hospital, founded 1643, has remarkable historical dispensary.

D60 left on D211 to Brion, D7 Beaufort-en-Vallée, N147, D74 Montgeoffroy, 2km further on D74 to Mazé, D55 to St Mathurin, D952 by river Loire into Angers (43km)

Beaufort-en-Vallée – fine views from hilltop, with castle ruins. Surrounded by rich plains.

Château Montgeoffroy – a masterpiece; probably most interesting château in France. Built, decorated and furnished in 1772 for Marshal of Contades by greatest craftsmen of the time, it remains totally unchanged and unmodernized. You can see exactly how noblemen of late 18th century lived. Open Easter–All Saints' Day. Don't miss this château!

Route 9
Round Dordogne, Lot and Quercy

The wonderland that we call the Dordogne but which is really Périgord, parts of Limousin and Quercy, is the tourist discovery of the last twenty years. But it is still almost empty much of the year, and even in July and August whole areas of it are still and silent. It has so many hideaway villages, valleys, wooded hillsides and tiny roads that you could hide armies there. I sat by a roadside in summer for a whole morning, a mile from where tourists were arriving in hundreds to see a famous château, and only one person passed me. As for the Lot, though Cahors attracts many people (and deserves to, for its medieval bridge alone), this more rugged, rockier country has not pulled in sightseers in the same way as the Dordogne, though the river Lot is most attractive and you will find the route alongside it from Cahors a revelation.

It is easier to see the highlights of the Dordogne and still find some privacy between than it is in the Loire valley, which is so near Paris. Dordogne and Lot châteaux were for defence – the front line in big wars. Even a sketchy knowledge of history makes the whole tour much more interesting: especially the story of the 100 Years' War between England and France, of the Plantagenet kings of England and Aquitaine, such as Henry II and Richard the Lionheart, and their very bold, and often very bad, barons. The river Dordogne was often the front line, with the English, who once ruled Guyenne (Périgord, Quercy Rouerge) to the south, the French to the north. South and north, I have taken you through areas which few Frenchmen know.

The truffle, the walnut, the goose, the duck, superb river fish, with fresh vegetables, are used here to make some of the best dishes in the world. Making a sauce Périgueux, with white wine scented with shallots and truffles, mixed with the juice of the meat or poultry it is to accompany, is a great art. Bleue de Causses (or de Quercy) is a blue-veined cheese matured in caves naturally, like Roquefort, but made from skimmed cow's milk, not ewe's milk.

Bergerac red and delightful fruity, aromatic white wines have improved vastly. Pécharmant of Dordogne is a full-bodied red. Traditional Cahors red is deep, strong, fruity, to be kept for some years, but a modern lighter red now being produced for early drinking.

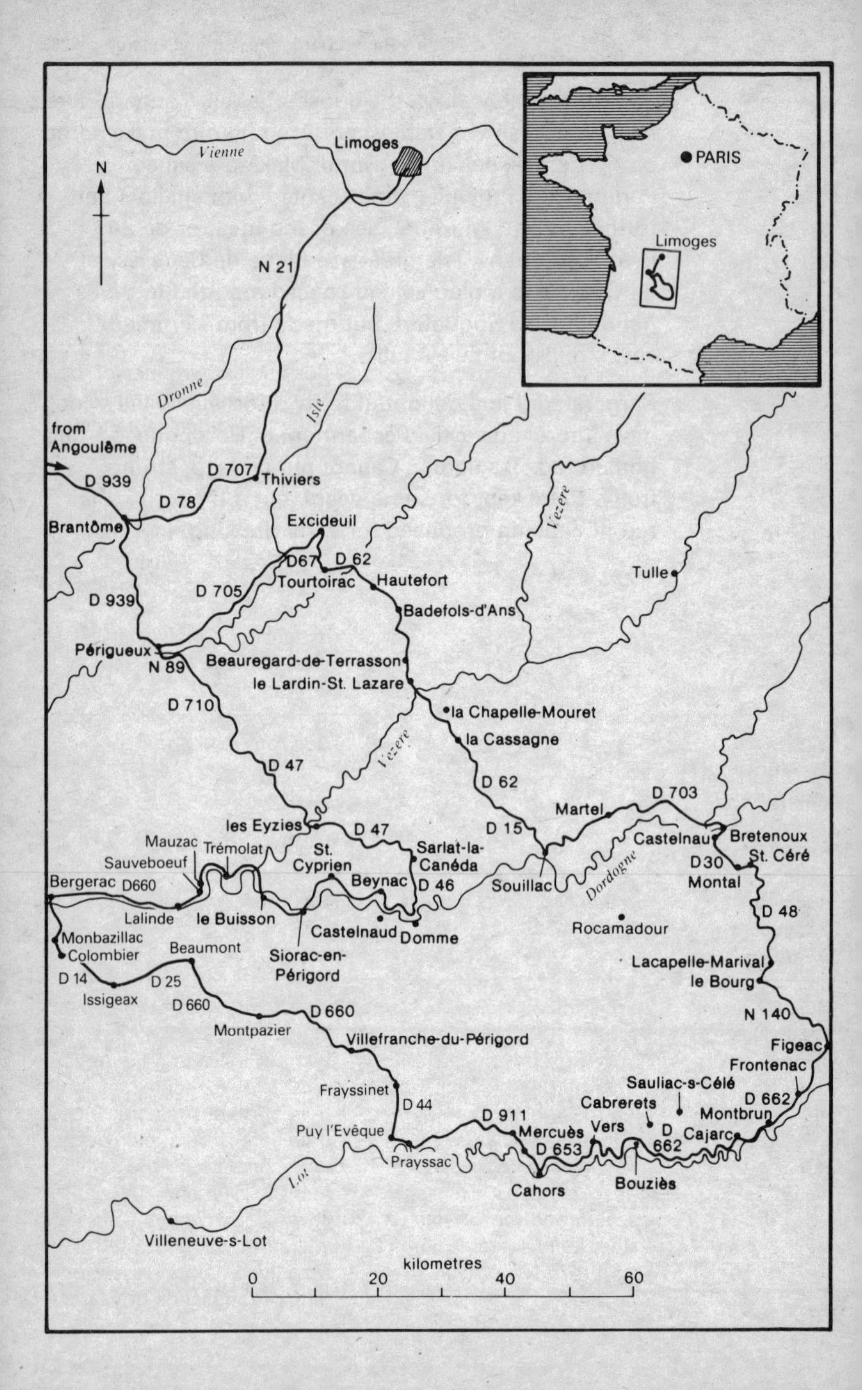

PARIS
Limoges
Vienne
N
N 21
Dronne
Isle
from
Angoulême
D 939
D 707
Thiviers
D 78
Brantôme
Excideuil
D67
D 62
Tourtoirac
Hautefort
D 705
D 939
Badefols-d'Ans
Vezere
Tulle
Périgueux
N 89
Beauregard-de-Terrasson
le Lardin-St. Lazare
D 710
la Chapelle-Mouret
la Cassagne
Vezere
D 47
D 62
D 703
Martel
les Eyzies
D 47
D 15
Castelnau
Bretenoux
Mauzac
Trémolat
St.
Cyprien
Sarlat-la-
Canéda
St. Céré
Sauveboeuf
D 30
Montal
Bergerac
D660
Beynac
D 46
Souillac
Dordogne
Lalinde
le Buisson
D 48
Castelnaud
Domme
Rocamadour
Monbazillac
Colombier
Beaumont
Siorac-en-
Périgord
Lacapelle-Marival
D 14
D 25
le Bourg
Issigeax
D 660
D 660
N 140
Montpazier
Villefranche-du-Périgord
Figeac
Frontenac
Frayssinet
Sauliac-s-Célé
D 44
Cabrerets
D 662
D 911
Montbrun
Puy l'Evêque
Mercuès
Vers
D
Cajarc
D 653
662
Prayssac
Lot
Cahors
Bouziès
Villeneuve-s-Lot
kilometres
0
20
40
60

Route 9
Round Dordogne, Lot and Quercy

Thiviers (join here from Limoges)		Busy little town; market for foie gras, poultry, truffles (little black magical fungus – grows underground beneath oaks; snuffed out by trained pigs or dogs); Périgord is main source; brings out delicate flavour in other ingredients – pâté, terrine, etc.; now incredibly expensive. Small goats' cheese made here. Sold at famous fairs.
D707, D78 Brantôme (26km) (join here from Angoulême)	See route 1 (page 47)	See route 1 (page 47)
D939 Périgueux (27km)	See route 1 (page 49)	See route 1 (page 49)
N89, D710, D47 Les Eyzies (43km)	Centre, place Mairie, 53.06.97.13: attractive old house in shady square with pretty garden by river Vézère. Gérard Brun cooks in pure Périgourdine style, with confit, cèpes, local duck, goose, chickens, Excellent cooking and remarkable value. Menus A–G. Rooms C, D. Shut 10 November–20 March.	Prehistoric man, who came south to these caves for warmth in second Ice Age would get a shock if he saw tens of thousands of travellers in cars and coaches who come so far to see his humble cave home. Even if cavemen leave you cold, you will surely be interested. Men lived here in caves for tens of thousands of years,

Les Eyzies continued

France, Auberge du Musée, 53.06.97.23: comfortable, traditional old hotel. Menus include excellent Périgourdine gastronomic. Pretty summer terrace. Menus A–G. Rooms A–D. Shut 2 November–March.

Centenaire, 56.06.97.18: Roland Mazère is one of the best chefs in France. He tries to revive Périgourdine cooking while inventing modern dishes – and largely succeeds. His various versions of foie gras, pot-au-feu of mixed meats and his pâtisseries are superb. Pricey, of course. Mouth-watering wine list (rated one of best 25 in France by l'Académie des Vins) ranges from Haut-Brion at 2200 francs to reasonably priced excellent Cahors from Jean Jouffreau and Bergerac Pécharmant from the Comtesse de St-Exupéry's Château de Tiregand. Comfortable modern bedrooms, pool, 'body-building' gymnasium (Roland Mazère is an amateur sportsman – tennis, golf). Menus F, G. Rooms E–G. Shut 3 November–1 April.

At Tamniès, left from D47 after 3km on to D48 for 9km – Laborderie, 53.29.68.59: centre of hilltop hamlet; best bedrooms with views in annexe. Cooking very regional; good value. New swimming pool. Menus A–F. Rooms B–E. Shut 15 November–4 April.

leaving behind bones, tools, weapons, pottery, jewellery; they left the caves for sunny slopes when world grew warmer. Archaeologists started to uncover flints, carved bones and ivory, skeletons coloured with ochre. Font-de-Gaume cave has prehistoric wall paintings of horses, bison, mammoths, reindeer; visitors have come since 18th century and left their graffiti. Grand Roc Cave (good view from stairs up to it) unusual show of stalactites, stalagmites, other formations. Cro-Magnon Cave discovered when railway was laid (1868); 3 skeletons of great importance to historians. See Museum of Prehistory in 11th-century castle of barons of Beynac, beneath overhanging rocks; books and pamphlets available (shut Tuesdays).

D47 Sarlat (21km)

Saint-Albert (hotel-restaurant), 11 rue E. Faure, Montaigne (hotel), place Pasteur, 53.59.01.09: happy memories over years of many evenings eating, drinking and laughing with local people in Saint-Albert. Modernized nowadays; winner 1987 of coveted Italian 'Oscar Européen du Tourisme', so it draws more tourists; but locals still use it. Posher bedrooms in Hotel Montaigne opposite. But same informal friendly atmosphere, willing service from Michel Garrigou and family. Lovely Périgourdine dishes. Arrive hungry! Well chosen wine list includes 16 Cahors back to 1961 from Jean Jouffreau (Château Cayrou and Gamot), Court les Mûts Bergerac. Menus B–F. Rooms B–E. Shut Sunday evenings, Monday in winter.

Rossignol, boulevard Henri Arlet, 53.59.03.20: Jacques Rossignol offers all the great regional dishes – confit of goose and duck, neck of goose, stuffed trout, plus classic bourgeois dishes. Good value. Menus A, C, D. Cheap wines (Bergerac). Shut Monday; part November, part March.

Charming town where 2 rivers meet. Attractive route. I loved Sarlat when it was a half-forgotten, crumbling town with medieval and Renaissance houses; tourists were few, little happened there. That was before 1966 when Société d'Economie Mixte started rehabilitating mansions, cleaning lovely honey-coloured stone, putting plumbing into grateful citizens' houses. Now, in summer especially, you must climb steep narrow side roads and alleys to miss tourist crowds. But still delightful, with big market where, in last weeks of July, first of August, classical drama arrives with players from Comédie Française. Also goose market in Place des Oies Saturday morning. Alas, geese are mostly in tins or pots! In 100 Years' War, an English garrison town for 10 years from 1360; in 1970, 350 coins found bearing effigy of Black Prince.

A local lad who became Pope made town a bishopric in 1316; remained so until 1790.

D46 to Vitrac (near Domme), D703 Le Roque Gageac, Beynac, St-Cyprien (31km)

At Caudon-de-Vitrac (3km E of Vitrac) – La Ferme, 53.28.33.35: many years since, when this farm was made into a restaurant, they offered huge meals with all

Caudon-de-Vitrac continued

the wine you could drink, for a few francs. Probably because of my capacity for wine, or because 'groups' go there, you now pay for wine. Still big meals, farm cooking, superb value. Beside Dordogne river. Menus A-D. Shut Monday; October.

Domme – Esplanade, 53.28.31.41: pretty bedrooms, superb views over Dordogne 150m (492ft) below to Sarlat. Excellent classic cuisine by René Gillard (braised duck liver, stuffed lamb, beef Rossini, veal kidneys bordelais). Menus C–G. Rooms C–F. Shut Monday low season; 4 November–10 December; February.

Domme – across river bridge on rocky crag overlooking lovely Dordogne valley countryside; with 14th-century medieval buildings. From Belvedere de la Barre one of the best panoramic views in Dordogne – caves where local people hid in 100 Years' War and Wars of Religion, open to visitors (Palm Sunday to 31 October).

La Roque-Gageac – Belle Etoile, 53.29.51.44: perfect vine-shaded terrace for meals on hot days. Menu A–F. Rooms B–C. Open 12 April–15 October.

La Roque-Gageac: another castle (Malartie) with superb riverside site under cliffs; village streets just alleys; Tarde Manor with round turret was home of 16th-century humanist, Canon Tarde.

Excellent river beach.

Beynac – Bonnet, 53.29.50.01: I stayed here first in the '50s to walk, eat, drink, sleep and to fish in Dordogne river across the road. Hardly a car passed. Still quiet, right below cliff where castle is perched. Walk down towpath of river and you are alone. Terrace overlooking river. Old-style logis, run by Mlle Renée Bonnet in tradition of her family. Little altered except better plumbing; friendly, good food, restful. I love it. So

Beynac castle has splendid views over Dordogne. In 12th century Richard Lionheart's front line against French. De Montfort partly dismantled it in 1214 but rebuilt soon after. Now being restored by department of Beaux Arts. Well worth seeing (open 1 March–5 November).

do readers: 'Nicest stop on all our holiday', they write. Menus C–E. Rooms C, D. Shut 15 October–1 April.

St Cyprien – L'Abbaye, 53.29.20.48: modern hotel; good. Menus C–G. Rooms D–G. Shut 15 October–15 March.

Gabarres (poled flat-bottom barges) once took wine and barrel wood down Dordogne to Bordeaux. Some years ago I helped pole one (with auxiliary engine) down river. Now you can take a shorter trip from Beynac (25f; June–October). A super way to see the river.

Over river bridge just before Beynac, then right, are ruins of Castelnaud – built by French as defence against English at Beynac. Impressive 12th-century ruins tower over valley. Changed hands between French and English, and also centre of cunning family feuding in 16th century when Anne de Caumont, whose father had been poisoned, became France's richest heiress; kidnapped and forcibly married at 7; widowed at 12; kidnapped and married to a boy of 9; marriage annulled; kidnapped again at 18 and married to Comte de St Pol, of royal blood. She left him; her son killed in battle as page to Louis XIII, she took to a convent, was disinherited! Alexandre Dumas could not have made a better plot! Castelnaud being restored.

St Cyprien clings to hillside above river; massive 12th- to 14th-century church; ruined Château de Fages (Renaissance – interior restoration of painted walls, ceilings in progress).

over bridge D48, D50 to Siorac-en-Perigord (8km)	Siorac – Scholly, place Poste, 53.28.60.02: classic French cooking with super rich sauces in hotel-restaurant away from traffic with delightful shady terrace; peace, excellent food; Dordogne river for swimming, fishing, boating. Menus C–G; fine wine cellar. Good rooms E–F. Open all year. L'Escale, 53.28.60.23: modern hotel in old style right on banks of river; terrace overlooks water; quiet, peaceful; very reasonable prices for ambience, position and quality. Menus A–C all Périgordian specialities; also try local crayfish in rich, sharp Armoricaine sauce. Improved rooms B–C. Shut 11 November–1 April.	Siorac – massive 17th-century château, town hall is one wing. Belvés (4km S of Siorac on D710) – delightful little town on hilltop encircled by boulevard on ancient ramparts. Château, old houses, bell towers. Covered market where Saturday market held (famous for walnuts). Views over Nauze Valley. 14th-century church was a priory.
D25 Le Buisson (7km) over bridge on D51 to Limeuil (5km) D31 west to Trémolat (17km)	Limeuil – Les Terrasses (Hotel Beauregard), route de Trémolat, 53.22.03.15: good cooking by Daniel Darnet (ex-Joe Rostangat, Antibes) in country restaurant above Dordogne river. 'Casserole' logis. Menus B–G. Rooms B–D. Shut 1 October–mid-May; dinner only, except Sundays. Isabeau de Limeuil, rue du Port, 53.22.93.55: Jean-Michel Chinour is an inventive chef and great showman, so each meal becomes a theatrical performance. Alas, he was changing menus when I had	South of Le Buisson to Cadouin and beyond are little roads off the tourist tracks with hamlets living the old life of Dordogne. Limeuil – beauty spot where river Vézère joins the Dordogne with lovely Pont Coude (elbow bridge) spanning both rivers. Limeuil set on steep hill with many mediaeval houses. Trémolat – village so French that Claude Chabrol chose it as setting for film *Le Boucher*. Strange decaying fortified church. Nearby on Dordogne river is a watersports centre

a nice meal there recently, so I have no prices. But the food is always interesting. Also a snack bar.

Near Le Bugue (6km N of Limeuil by D31) – Auberge du Noyer, Le Reclaud de Bouny Bas, (5km W along D703 from Bugue), 53.07.11.73: lovely 18th-century farmhouse superbly renovated by English couple – Jenny and Paul Dyer. Charming furnishings. Quiet garden with woodland; swimming pool. Traditional cooking. Menus A, C, D. Rooms D, E. Shut 15 November–15 March.

Trémolat – Vieux Logis, 53.22.80.06: pretty old logis in lovely garden, cosy rooms with antique furniture, charming ambience and welcome, log fires, delicious meals in a delightful galleried dining room; fine wine list, immaculate service. One of our favourite inns in the world. Madame Giraudel-Destord and her son Bernard have performed a miracle in turning a country logis into a little heaven. Now the great Jean Dive has redecorated five rooms in 'Victorian' style. We have never had a bad dish – from peasant omelette to foie gras and confit of duck. Young chef worked for Boyer at Reims, Roux Brothers in London. Better book! Menus C–G. Rooms G. Open every day of the year.

with yachting, canoeing, rowing (regattas held in summer).

small white road D31 round Cingle de Trémolat to Mauzac (8km) Sauveboeuf (3km) D703 Lalinde (4km)	La Panoramic, Cingle de Trémolat, 53.22.80.42: superb views from terrace. New owner Colette Perrin has brightened hotel. Meals good value; mixed regional and modern cooking. Menus B–D. Rooms B–D. Shut mid-November–mid-March. Mauzac – La Métairie (3km N at Millac), 53.22.50.47: lovely old stone farmhouse converted; swimming pool; attractive garden; pretty bedrooms. Regional cooking with modern touches; lunch grill by pool. Menus C–G. Rooms G. Shut Tuesdays; 2 January–1 May. At Calès (over river) – Moulin Neuf, 53.22.50.14: simple relais with bargain-cheap menu. Lalinde – Château Hotel, rue Verdun, 53.61.01.82: formidable little fortress of 13th century, with pointed turrets, turned into a comfortable, quiet family hotel, terrace overhanging the Dordogne river with nice views, for summer eating. Town centre. Guy Genson makes his own confits. Menus C–F. Rooms D–F. Shut Fridays (except July, August); 15 November–1 March.	'Cingle' means serpent and this is the Dordogne's most spectacular twist. Superb view from Belvedere Rocamadour (also from Panoramic hotel). River swings through a half-circle of high white cliffs, joined by bridges of golden stone. Windsurfing at Mauzac. Lalinde – built as fortress town by ford across Dordogne by Edward III of England in 1270. Still has 3 castles – one ruined. Burned down by retreating Germans in 1945 as reprisal for French Resistance attacks. 3km across river is Couze-et-St-Front – busy little town; nice Romanesque church now a warehouse. Some troglodyte houses; mushrooms grown here.
D703, D660 Bergerac (22km)	At Mouleydier, 12km along D660 – Beau Rivage, 53.23.20.21: good cheap weekday menu. Menus A, E. Rooms A–C. Shut Sunday evening, Monday except	Bergerac – biggest town in Dordogne. Known for wine since Middle Ages. Lost out to Bordeaux but wines getting much better again. Produced fruity dry white,

summer; part October, February.

Bergerac – Le Cyrano, 2 boulevard Montaigne, 53.57.02.76: in a typical provincial hotel with glass-enclosed pavement terrace Jean-Paul Turon surprises you with cooking best described as 'Nouvelle Périgourdine'. But some fine old dishes like mussels stuffed with salmon and veal kidneys in Bergerac wine. Try fruits au sabayon de Monbazillac. Good value. Excellent local wines. Menus C–D. Rooms C. Shut Sunday evening (except mid-summer); Monday 2–26 December, 26 June–11 July.

Hotel Bordeaux, Restaurant Le Terroir, 38 place Gambetta, 53.57.12.83: run by the Maury family since 1855, bedrooms and their bathrooms improved recently; swimming pool. Classical cooking. Try sole with cèpes. Menus A, B, D, G. Rooms D. Shut 20 December–20 January.

Chez Germaine, 80 boulevard Chanzy, 53.57.22.17: typical little bar-restaurant offering bargain menu with huge portions – soup, charcuterie, meat, several vegetables, cheese, dessert, with wine (49f in 1987); on Périgueux road just before railway crossing.

very fruity and aromatic Sauvignon, a vivacious rosé, red wines made from similar grapes to Bordeaux but lighter. Red Pécharmant is kept 3 years in cask, another 3–10 years in bottle – beautiful balanced wine for meat, game or cheese.

Some of old town survives around the market. Wine museum. Statue in Place Myrpe of Cyrano de Bergerac, 17th-century writer and duellist romanticized by Edmond Rostand in a play of that name.

On Lalinde-Bergerac road N660, just after Creysse, a lane under railway bridge leads to Château de Tiregand, enormous 17th-century home of Comte et Comtesse de St-Exupéry. No visits but wine-tasting and sales of Pécharmant.

At St Julien-de-Crempse, 12km N by N21, D107 – Manoir Le Grand Vignoble, 53.24.23.18: beautiful Louis XIV manor in park, with pool, stables; on ruins of English bastide. Sixty horses and ponies; tennis; huge park with deer, bisons, yak, cows, donkeys and camels. Cooking a pleasant blend of regional, classic with good meat and modern. Children welcome. Good regional wines. Menus D–E. Rooms F–G. Shut 22 December–7 February: Sunday evening, Tuesday lunch in winter.

N21 for 7km, then white road marked to Monbazillac (8km) little white road to Colombier, down hill to N21, cross over it on to D14 to Issigeac (8km) D25 Beaumont (15km)

Monbazillac – La Diligence, route Eymet D933, 53.58.30.48: modernized old inn with magnificent terrace views over vineyards. Périgourdine dishes. Plans for expansion. Good value. Menus A–E. Rooms C–D. Shut Tuesday evening, Wednesday except July, August.

Closerie St. Jacques, le Bourg, 53.58.37.77: large old house made into luxury-bistro. Carte very pricey but excellent value second menu (D). (We had duck, oysters, top rumpsteak, cheese, dessert, sorbet for 125f – 1987). Menus B (weekday lunch), D, F, G. Shut Monday, Tuesday; mid-November–1 March.

At Saussignac, (take D14 W off D933, then D4 S; 11km) – Hotel à Saussignac,

Monbazillac – Château built 1550. Protestant stronghold in Wars of Religion. Beautiful; round towers, superb entrance; huge views from terrace. Delightful tapestries; wine museum in 16th-century cellars. Visits. Half-hour tour then tasting of sweet Monbazillac (12f). Also restaurant and wine shop. At Colombier is Château de la Jaubertie, a gorgeous 16th-century villa which Henry IV of France, who loved women, wine and good living, gave to his mistress Gabrielle d'Estrée. No visits but tastings in the cave of the best wines in Bergerac – made by Nicholas Ryman, former London stationer, and son Hugh, trained in Bordeaux, Burgundy, California and South Australia. Issigeac – charming, vast Bishop's palace (Château des Eveques)

53.27.92.08: centre and meeting place of wine village. Opposite 17th-century château. Modern, comfortable. Nice bar. Taken over by Dèscard Thierry, brilliant young chef from La Corniche, Rolleboise, and wife, Bernadette (ex-Corniche). Menus excellent value for excellent cooking. Court les Mûts wines of Pierre-Jean Sardoux, expert from Bordeaux Wine Institute. Menus A–C. Rooms B–D. Shut Sunday evening in winter.

Beaumont – Voyageurs 'Chez Popaul', 53.22.30.11: all renovated in winter 1987. Known for its enormous help-yourself hors d'oeuvres table of 45 items and its pricey gastronomic menu. Menus A–G. Rooms C. Shut Monday; January, February, October, November.

flanked by square towers. Built 1669. Beaumont – bastide built in 1271 for Edward I of England. One tower, gates, part of market square and fortified church remain.

D660 Monpazier (16km) Villefranche-du-Perigord (20km)

Monpazier – France, rue St Jacques, 53.61.60.06: little old country inn in 13th-century house once annexe of Château de Biron; shabby but nice atmosphere. Cheap menu excellent value; gastronomic Périgourdine menu, too. Menus A–E. Rooms A, B.

Villefranche-Commerce, 53.29.90.11: charming honey-coloured stone building with outside arcade making terrace, views across countryside; open fire in dining room; bar used by

Monpazier – fortified town built by Edward I of England in 1285; lovely old squares with alleys between old buildings; arcaded central square is delightful. Scene of peasant revolt in 1594 with 8000 teeming through countryside plundering castles. Away from tourist routes.

Markets in central square include cèpes and truffle sales.

Château Biron (8km SW along D2, D53) – vast castle and beautiful village and

Villefranche-du-Perigord (20km) continued	locals; family atmosphere; good value meals; six menus A–F; bargain wines, unclassified Cahors. Rooms C–D. Shut 15 December–1 March.	church. Mediaeval castle has dungeons, battlements, big kitchen, church with effigies of great owners, impressive door with big bolts and chains and spellbinding views. Villefranche – almost at meeting of Dordogne area, Lot and Lot-et-Garonne. Winding route, lined with trees (walnuts, silver birch, firs). Another bastide (fortified town) – 13th-century; ancient vast market hall; surrounding forests of oaks, pines, chestnuts; truffle-hunting country; peaceful; clear, clean streams.
D660 Frayssinet (10km) right on D673, immediately left on D44 to Puy l'Évêque (10km). D911 Prayssac, Mercuès, Cahors (29km)	Puy l'Évêque – Bellevue, on D911, 65.21.30.70: old-style inn used by locals. Glad I found it. Truly *belle vue* of Lot river from terrace and dining room. Path to river. Pool perched high above it. Meals good value. Bedrooms simple, comfortable. Bargain wines. Meals A–E. Rooms B, C. Shut 15 November–15 March; Sunday evening, Monday low season. At Duravel (4km W of Puy l'Eveque by D911) – Auberge du Baran, 65.24.60.34: village inn taken over in 1985 by Roger and Letitia Washbourne from Bath. Fine views of Lot valley from dining room and terrace. Traditional French cooking! Very good value. Cahors wines well chosen, cheap. Menus A (lunch), B, C. Rooms D. Shut Wednesday; January–March.	Puy l'Évêque – Main Cahors wine-producing area (see also Route 1, page 57). On steep hill above Lot river with modern bridge. Superb river views from D911 top road terrace. Wine tasting and buying at Château du Cayron (just before bridge at Puy l'Évêque take small road left D28 – château marked on yellow Michelin 79). 12th–15th century château in lovely grounds. Jouffreau family property (vignerons over 300 years). Great wine. Also at Puy l'Évêque – Clos Triguedina on D911 just W – Baldès family wines beautifully balanced. At Prayssac, 2km S on D67 to Lot river – Clos de Gamot, where Jean Jouffreau himself makes wine from 100 year old vines which are 'gras' (rich in alcohol and taste, full-

Chateau de Mercuès – see Route 1 (page 57).

Cahors hotels and restaurants see Route 1 (page 56)

bodied, fleshy). Also superb collection of old wine stocks with barrels. Cahors – see Route 1 (page 56).

D653 Vers D662 alongside river Lot to Bouziès (29km)

At Laroque des Arcs – Beau Rivage – see Route 1 (page 56)

Vers – Hôtel des Châlets, 65.31.41.53: attractive; in strange position between roads; pretty tiny waterfall just below; local ingredients, good trout. Menu A–C. Rooms A–D. Shut 11 November–1 March.

St Cirq-LaPopie – Sombral, 65.31.26.08: beautifully restored old house; popular around whole Cahors area. Splendid value. Menus A, D, F. Rooms D. Shut 15 November–15 March; Tuesday evening, Wednesday low season.

Cabrerets – Auberge de la Sagne, 65.31.26.62: charming old inn; quiet spot, gardens recently enlarged; lovely flower beds; improvements without altering character. Very good value; outstanding pâtés, confits; cassoulet. Menus A, C. Rooms B, C. Shut 1 October–1 May.

La Pescalerie, 65.31.22.55: *truly* idyllic. We adore it. Gorgeous old country house in stone, built 12th–17th century. Beautiful garden to river Célé. Flowered terrace

Route follows Lot river; good views, particularly just before Vers; past fields of sunflowers, sweetcorn.

Bouziès – high cliff riddled with caves; some were home to prehistoric families; biggest fortified at entrance, with a castellated wall, by English in 100 Years' War; called 'Château des Anglais'.

Two ways to go for explorers from Bouziès: (a) St Cirq-LaPopie by D40 (5km) on south of Lot river: village perched on rock above river; beautiful old houses; narrow streets; artisan shops; remains of 13th-century château: magnificent view as D40 winds through rocky hills; also from village, one of those called 'most beautiful village in France'. Fortified 15th-century church, with tower castle; museum contains Ming period Chinese treasures.

b) from just past Bouziès at Conduché, take D41 to Cabrerets (5km) – caves Pech-Merle have good prehistoric wall drawings, of mammoths, bison, deer, horses, human hands, female bodies; also bones of cave bears. Two 14-year-old boys rediscovered caves in 1922; had been used

Bouziès continued

for aperitifs. Exquisite old furniture, genuine 18th-century kitchen still used. Interesting, comfortable bedrooms with beams, antique furniture, original paintings. Run by 2 surgeons. One still works at Cahors hospital. Dr Hélène runs the hotel, helps the chef, cooks superb jams and croissants served with big jug of coffee for breakfast. Try stuffed goose neck, sliced like a sausage, trout from the river 'au bleu', super farm cheeses; fruit tarts. Dr Roger runs the cellar, is an expert on Cahors wines, with superb choice. French description of hotel is perfect – 'la quietitude'. Menus F. Rooms F, G. Shut 1 November–31 March.

Des Grottes, 65.31.27.02: on river banks; quiet; swimming pool; real Périgourdine cooking; good value menus; à la carte dishes include goose confit, truffled omelette, beef fillet in Périgueux sauces, cheap wines. Menus A–C. Rooms B–C. Shut 1 November–15 May.

as hiding-place in Revolution; open Palm Sunday–30 September, October (weekdays only); museum all year. Cabrerets is in dip at meeting of Célé and Sagné rivers in fairly wild country. Romantic-looking ruins of Devil's Castle (Château du Diable) cling to chilling Rochecourbe cliff; an English eyrie from 100 Years' War from which they could rule countryside.

Pescalerie Fountain sprouts from rock wall beside road – underground river surfacing; ivy-covered mill alongside. After Cabrerets road crosses face of high stone cliffs; tunnel through them, then they overhang river Célé's right bank.

Sauliac (6km further on D41): hamlet clinging to fearsome cliff of odd coloured rocks, with openings to fortified caves used as war refuges; the fit climbed ropes, others hoisted in baskets.

Return by D41 to Conduché to pick up route on D662.

---

from Bouziès, D662 Cajarc, Montbrun, Frontenac, Figeac (49km)

At Larnagal (turn left – signposted – for 4km on hilly, rough road) – Mas de Cariteau, 65.31.28.77 (summer), 1.47.31.91.10 (all year): whole hamlet restored, converted into hotel. Bedrooms spread around village. Children's park with horses, ponies, goats,

Away from main tourist routes. Quiet, sometimes deserted countryside, especially on side roads. Road follows river through rocky cliffs to Montbrun: village rises in tiers on jutting rock by steep cliffs; looks down on Lot. Ruined castle above. Road climbs steeply

swimming pool. Quercy specialities. New chef expected 1988; prices not confirmed. Previously very reasonable (C, D). Rooms C–E. Shut 1 October–1 May.

Cajarc – Du Pont, 65.40.67.84: simple, cheap; one very cheap menu. Menus A–C. Rooms A, B. Shut Saturday low season; 25 December–2 January.

Montbrun – Ferme de Montbrun, 65.40.67.71: rustic restaurant, beams. Recommended by readers. Menu C; carte. Rooms D. Shut 1 October–Easter; Wednesday low season.

Figeac – Des Carmes, 65.34.20.78: outstanding cooking in modern hotel, comfortable. Quercy dishes with individual touches; superb duck confit 'grandmère' with sweet-sour onions; scrambled eggs (brouillard) with truffles (delicious); stuffed rabbit in Cahors wine. Superb old Cahors. Menus C–F. Rooms E. Swimming pool, garden. Shut Saturday, Sunday in winter; 15 December–15 January.

At La Madeleine (7km on D922) – Belle Rive, 65.67.62.14: outstanding value; very good cooking in very cheap menus. Dining room overlooks river Lot. Menus A–D. Rooms B, C. Shut Saturday except July, August; 11 November–27 March.

after Frontenac – lovely views on right across Lot valley and of Faycelles, hillside village.

Figeac – along bank of Célé; Auvergne begins here; Needles, 12th-century obelisks, 15m (50ft) tall, marked boundaries of Benedictine abbey land. You could not pursue an enemy within boundaries. Old houses, half-timbered, with decorated boundaries, beside 'oustal dé lo Mounéds' (the Mint), fine old building. Old houses round place Sully; in alleys such as Trou de la Belle, vagrants and thieves lived until 1945; oldest street, rue Emile Zola, now has artisan shops again, as in ancient times.

N140 Le Bourg, D940 Lacapelle-Marival (21km)	Cardaillac – Chez Marcel, 65.40.11.16: charming old inn; bigger dining room added with antique chimney and furniture. Meals very good value indeed. Fine old dishes – country soup; cépes and truffle omelettes; delicious Causse lamb; tarte Tatin (apple). Wines cheap. Simple rooms. Menus A–D. Rooms A. Shut Monday; part October. Lacapelle-Marival – Terrassé, opposite château, 65.40.80.07: pretty garden; fishing pond providing for the kitchen. Classic regional dishes. Good value. Good Cahors and old Burgundy wines. Menus A–F. Shut mid-December–1 April.	7km from Figeac on N140, turn right on D18 for 2km to Cardaillac – old part around fort on rocky spur above town. 12th-century tower; lovely views from top of spiral staircase. Charming village. Lacapelle-Marival castle (13th-century) with round watch-towers, church, old gateway to town and covered market on stone piles make photogenic scene. Watch-towers 'stuck on' to four corners of huge square keep. Built by Cardaillac family, married into Plantagenets, Kings of England.
D48 St Céré D673 Montal (30km)	See Route 1 (page 52)	
D30, D14 Castelnau, Bretenoux (10km)	See Route 1 (page 52)	
D703 Vayrac, Martel, Souillac (38km)	Martel – Le Turenne, Restaurant La Quercy, ave Jean-Lavayssière, 65.37.30.30: attractive stone inn; bedrooms spacious, comfortable. Campastié family have cooked father to son since 1856. Old-style confit, truffled omelette and pâtés, truffles 'sous la cendre' – wrapped in bacon and foil and cooked in hot ash. Superb truffle soufflé. Menus	Martel – in AD 732, the Saracens (followers of Mahomet – in this case mostly Moors) were stopped at Poitiers by Charles Martel Otherwise Europe might be Muslim today! Later Martel struck again, won decisively, and built a church on the spot. It grew into a town. In 12th century, Henry II of England, a Plantagenet, and his wife, Eleanor of Aquitaine,

A–E. Rooms B–D. Shut 1 December–end February.

At Gluges (mediaeval village on Dordogne river; D23 from Martel. D43 left – 5km) – Falaises, 65.37.33.59: attractive old turreted house with pretty shaded terrace under vines. Bedrooms and plumbing improved. Inexpensive menus good value. Good classical country cooking (noisette of lamb, chicken saute, stuffed goose neck, duck confit, guinea fowl, trout). Menus B–F. Rooms C, D. Shut 1 December–1 March.

Souillac – Auberge du Puits, place du Puits, 65.37.80.32: rustic country inn. Excellent value, traditional regional meals in attractive restaurant (magret and confit of duck, tripe Quercynoise, salmon). Used by locals. Very cheap house wine to Château Margaux. Menus A–F. Rooms B, C. Shut December, November.

Vieille Auberge, place Minuterie, 65.32.79.43: a quandary! Some readers most impolite about Robert Veril's hotel and cooking. Yet French people and leading French gastronomes, including Marc de Champérard, love it (praising cooking, service, courtesy). So do French guide books. My last meal excellent – classical cooking with a light touch. Super farandole of

fell out; he accused her of sleeping with a troubadour; shut her in a tower. Their 4 sons rose against Henry. To pay his soldiers, the eldest, called the Young King Henry, pillaged abbeys, took precious stones from St Adour's body at Rocamadour and stole Sword of Roland. He returned to Martel with a fever, was found by Henry II's messenger lying in agony on a bed of cinders in penitence. Maison Fabri, old mansion with round tower, said to be where he died. 18th-century covered market. Attractive medieval streets and buildings.

Souillac – attractive market town; lively, very crowded midsummer; Dordogne river meets Borrèze here; lovely, lonely country to north.

Grew round abbey in 13th century; abbey disappeared during Revolution. Lovely 12th-century abbey church with Byzantine look. Belfry from other parish church now attached to town hall.

Our way, you enter under huge viaduct.

Souillac continued

mixed fish with shrimp butter and fillet of beef. Good choice of Cahors wines. Very popular so service can be patchy. Rooms in modern annexe (some with kitchenette); pool, garden. Menus B-F. Rooms B, C. Shut 25 November–15 March.

Ambassadeurs, av Gén-de-Gaulle, 65.32.78.36: true Périgourdine cooking with cèpes, foie gras, truffles, confit, duck, tripe; gained Trophé des Logis de Quercy 1986 for faultless regional cooking. Modern or period bedrooms (some in annexe opposite). Menus A, B, E. Wines reasonable. Rooms C. Shut Friday evening, Saturday except mid-summer; part October.

At Lacave, 4km SE by D43 – Hostellerie du Pont de l'Ouysse, 65.37.87.04: charming auberge below a huge castle perched on a cliff. Quercy cooking 'renovated' by talented chef Daniel Chambon. Freshwater crayfish in several guises, kidneys in juniper berries (genièvre), tender pigeon in pastry with cèpes; excellent desserts. Summer meals on terrace above the river. Bedrooms modernized all with bathrooms. Pleasant atmosphere. Menus D–F. Rooms D, E. Shut Monday except mid-summer; 10 November–1 March.

D15 left fork at Bourzoies on to D165 becomes D62 after 1km; through Borrèze, right on D60 Paulin, left on D62 to La Cassagne, La Chapelle-Mouret, Le Lardin-St Lazare (38km)

Little roads go deep into countryside of tiny hamlets, farms, orchards, hills, valleys, woods and small streams. You see few people except in distant fields; can get lost on little roads, ending in a farmyard.

Borrèze is sleepy village with a bar-restaurant. D62 starts climbing. At D60 junction, Salignac–Eyvignes château can be seen (entrance 2km to left – open in season except Tuesday). Medieval fortress, from 12th century, ramparts around it. Still belongs to family from which came the great Fénélon, 17th-century writer, soldier, archbishop. Covered market in Salignac square.

12th-century church in La Cassagne, and Maurice Delpech's distillery producing fruit and walnut liqueurs and famous walnut apéritif.

Le Lardin – rather dull town in lovely valley of Vézéré; paper mills sometimes smell like cauliflower cooking! Deals in walnuts and truffles from nearby farms.

Over N89 on to D62 to Beauregard-de-Terrasson, Badefols-d'Ans, Hautefort (19km) D62, D5 Tourtoirac, D67 Excideuil, D705, N21 Périgueux (50km)

Badefols – Les Tilleuls, 53.51.50.08: pretty, real old village inn opposite castle. Bar and restaurant used by locals. Attractive garden with vine, trees, tables. Incredibly good value. Six courses in menu costing 42f in 1987: House wine cost 18f. Carte and better wines are bargains, too. Menu A. Simple rooms A, B. Shut Saturday low season.

Commerce, 53.51.50.07: new owner and chef. Attractive village inn; regional specialities. One very cheap menu. Menus A–C. Rooms A. Open all year.

Tourtoirac – Voyageurs, 53.50.42.29: shaded quiet garden by river Auvézère. Much praised by readers. Madame Levignac has introduced more imagination into menus but still offers Périgourdine specialities and good value cheap menu. Menus A–C. Rooms B, C. Open all year.

Poste, 53.50.42.05: beside river; remarkable cheap menu. Rooms available. Menu A.

Fin Chapon, place Château, Excideuil, 53.62.42.38: dates from 1750 and known locally for good confits, foie gras and that splendid sauce Périgueux with tournedos. Menus A–E. Rooms B–C. Shut December, January; Sunday evening and Monday low season.

Road rises overlooking valleys of vines and poplars, passing Peyraux Château (lived in; cannot enter; but lovely views from entrance court).

Badefols-d'Ans: pretty; good views; 12th-century domed church; 14th- to 15th-century château, burned 1945; restored.

Hautefort: 17th-century château, more like a 'love' château of Loire than 'fighting' château of Périgord. Original castle of 12th century belonged to Born family; Bertrand de Born, troubadour, wrote songs of love and war. His brother, helped by Richard Lionheart, tried to take castle, so he enlisted Richard's brother 'Young King Henry', heir to English throne, to defend it. In 1186 his brother destroyed it when he was away. Bertrand became a monk. New 17th-century château. Restored; burned out 1968; restored again by Baroness de Bastard who lives there. (Open to public.) Lovely views.

Excideuil – interesting medieval town with old buildings and ramparts; ruins of historic castle which changed hands frequently between warring lords, English and French; then Protestants and Catholics. Talleyrand family let it deteriorate, moved furniture, even chimneys to their house in Chalais.

At Sorges, 9km N of D705–N21 junction – Auberge La Truffe, 53.05.02.05: very pleasant inn with garden for summer eating. Lives up to its name with outstanding Périgourdine dishes (stuffed goose neck, poule au pot), anguille (little eels) in red wine; and visits on weekends to goose farms and truffle trails. Neat, clean bedrooms. Menus A–F. Rooms B, C. Shut Mondays.

At junction of D705, N21 at Sorges – museum of the truffle, culinary fungus called Black Diamond; press-button film on how they hunt for them with pigs and dogs; how they grow beneath oak trees under earth. Open afternoons, mornings July–August. Guided 'truffle trail' walk – 3km; 1 hr. Shop selling them – very expensive, but what a souvenir of Périgord to slice into your omelette!

Index

Names of hotels and restaurants appear in *italics*

Arthur Eperon
Eperon's French Wine Tour £6.95

EXPLORE THE VINEYARDS OF FRANCE THE EPERON WAY

France is a wine drinker's paradise. From the noble vintages of Bordeaux and Burgundy and the exquisite pleasures of Champagne, to the unexpected delights of *vin de pays*, the wines of France remain the most sought after and the yardstick by which all others are measured.

Now, with all his customary authority and enthusiasm, Arthur Eperon takes you on a connoisseur's tour of French vineyards. The book is divided into sixteen areas. Each section contains a map showing the notable wine villages, an introduction which includes the address of the local wine committee or information bureau, advice on what to eat and where to stay, a suggested route for visitors to follow, a detailed description of the wines of the region, and, most importantly, precise information on where you can taste and buy them.

Arthur Eperon's personal recommendations for places to explore and new wines to discover, taste and buy – either en route to a holiday destination or as a complete holiday in itself – reflect his great love for France and his unrivalled, intimate knowledge of her wines, the result of innumerable visits over the last forty years.

Arthur Eperon
Eperon's Guide to the Greek Islands £4.99

Eperon's Guide covers 55 islands in the Aegean and Ionian seas: from the splendours of Corfu and Crete to the secret treasures of Naxos and Lefkas. Arthur Eperon's long love-affair with the islands yields a wealth of information on the hidden delights that most tourists miss.

Where to go, where to stay, where to eat, what to drink, how to travel round the islands, where to find the treasures of the ancient world, and how to get the best value for your *drachmas* – all are contained in this charming and authoritative guide.

Photography by Fanny Dubes
A PAN ORIGINAL